The Devil's Ashpit

and other

Tales of Ascension Island

Dan Kovalchik

Copyright © 2014 Dan Kovalchik

All rights reserved.

ISBN: 1499652763
ISBN-13: 978-1499652765

DEDICATION

To the memory of David Lee Cramer, Emiline Jensen Dabbs, and Michael "Newpence" Benjamin.

CONTENTS

	Acknowledgments	i
1	Starlifter	1
2	Beginnings	14
3	The Rock	18
4	Island Boy	34
5	The Southern Cross	52
6	The Base	63
7	The Ascension Diver	73
8	That's Entertainment	93
9	Repatriates	119
10	Wake-Up Call	135
11	Back In The Trenches	144
12	Things That Go Bump	171
13	That's Entertainment, Too	188
14	Movin' On	208
15	Escape	222
16	Epilog	230
	About The Author	232
	Bibliography	233

ACKNOWLEDGMENTS

I will be thanking Bendix overseas manager Ben Gallup all the days of my life for introducing women to the USNS *Vanguard* and for paving the way for the first married couple to work together at the Devil's Ashpit Tracking Station. Thanks also to Melissa Blizzard, Daryl Dabbs, Linda Elser Brown, Macy Guppy, Pat Harris, Donald Joshua, Pam Gates, Sam Milburn, Pati Peskett, and Cheryl Tingler for helping me to travel back in time.

A special thank you goes to Macy Guppy for proofreading and coaxing a better book out of me. I made the final edits, though, so any errors in the finished product are solely the responsibility of the author.

Chapter 1

Starlifter

The pain came so suddenly that my first thought was that I'd taken a blow to the head. My second thought was that the little bastards in the row behind me had violently escalated their War On The Passenger In 18F. But even through the fog, I reasoned that Donald Dont and Steven Stopit (the only names I had heard their mother call them) had been quiet for the last hour and more importantly, this "blow to the head" hadn't knocked me sideways. One second I was fine and in the next, my entire right hemisphere throbbed.

I managed to find a bright side; the pilot had just announced our descent to Melbourne International Airport. My all-day Hawaii-to-Florida flight was coming to an end. I just needed to control my impulses for a few more minutes and abandon the shock-and-awe campaign I'd been formulating against my Row 19 antagonists. In another hour I'd be relaxing in my hotel room.

But what in the world was going on in my head? Sure, I was weary from the flight and my six-foot frame was stiff and aching due to the confines of my economy seat, but fit, healthy, 26-year olds don't get headaches like this one outside of a hockey rink.

I had no clue. Instead, I winced my way through the landing, through the baggage pickup, through the car rental process, and through the half-hour drive north to Cocoa Beach. There, I winced my way into my hotel room and dialed an old shipmate's number. During my layover in Los Angeles that morning, I had called him and told him to plan on taking me to the TGIF beach bar parties that evening.

"Bob. It's me. Change of plans. I can't go out," I said, and apologized for breaking the date. I tried to explain how much my head hurt.

"Nonsense!" he countered, "A little Scotch will fix that."

It was a compelling argument.

Yes, my head was pounding so much that each word, either uttered or heard, hit another high mark on the pain scale. On the other hand, it was Cocoa Beach on a Friday night. My previous experiences there led me to believe that there was a city ordinance that decreed all residents must plant themselves on the nearest bar stool and inject cash into the local economy.

Soon, Bob and I were sucking Scotch at the Mousetrap, a bar/restaurant that looked like it had been constructed out of Space Race memorabilia collected from nearby Cape Canaveral and the Kennedy Space Center. The first double shot of Johnny Walker Red Label disappeared rather quickly. By the time the second appeared, I could already feel my headache dissipating. Thank goodness for Dr. Bob! I started to fill him in on the three month cruise he had missed.

"Never mind that," he interrupted, "What's this I hear about Ascension?"

I nodded. "Plane leaves on Wednesday."

"No, I mean *why* Ascension?"

"You know Gloria's there, right?"

"Well, tell her to come back here," he said. "I can help you get jobs with Harris." Harris Corporation in Melbourne was a major employer in Brevard County.

"Naw, thanks. I appreciate the offer, really," I said, "But I think Gloria and I are going to like it there."

"But it's...it's the 'Rock!'" he protested, reminding me of the island's reputation. Then his eyebrows went up. "Wait...I'm getting *déjà vu*. Remember that bar in King's Cross?"

"Of course," I answered. Bob was referring to a bar in Sydney, Australia. "But all I remember was Sheila after Sheila blowing you off. And not in a good way."

"Hah. Hah. Bite me."

But I knew that Bob was remembering the heart-to-heart we shared between drinks and Bob's attempts to engage Sheilas. We had compared our histories and discussed our hopes, dreams, and aspirations. Bob had grown up on Rockaway Beach in New York, with the ocean at his doorstep. I grew up in a surprisingly thickly-wooded area thirty-some miles northeast of Pittsburgh. There were few luxuries in the house and the closest beach, while only a six-hour drive, may as well have been on the Sea of Tranquility; a visit was absolutely out of the question. As a result, I didn't see the ocean until I was 22 years old. Certainly, the inaccessibility of the compound that covers 70% of the earth made it all the more desirable to see firsthand.

My fascination with oceans quite naturally extended to the islands they guarded and went back as far as I could remember, with books, movies, and television fueling the fire. Many in my generation can point to the Disney

The Devil's Ashpit

portrayal of Neverland as having provided the first spark. Peter Pan's home was a jewel in the ocean, set in a ring of sparkling coves, bays, and lagoons and containing an exciting assortment of pirates, Indians, and mermaids. The scene was so inviting that my six-year-old self began exploring the possibilities of wishing upon a star. I wanted Peter to bring me some fairy dust to frost my happy thoughts. I'd have joined the Lost Boys in a heartbeat.

Peter never showed, but I had already fallen victim to the allure of islands. Once I learned to read, my cluttered bookshelves bore testimony to my preference. I whisked through the adventures of Robin Hood, Paul Bunyan, and Pecos Bill and enjoyed every tall tale, but for sure-fire daydreaming material, I turned to *Treasure Island* or *Robinson Crusoe*, or even *The Adventures of Tom Sawyer*. It wasn't Tom, Huck, and Joe hiding on an island in the middle of the Mississippi, swimming, fishing, and watching the river traffic float by; it was Tom, Huck, and me.

Classic literature aside, there has never been a shortage of reminders that islands breed romance, mystery, and adventure. Few people haven't heard of Fletcher Christian, Nellie Forbush, or McGarret, Five-Oh. Ian Fleming wisely sent James Bond to Jamaica and other Caribbean islands for many of his missions. Game show announcers excitedly describe grand prize trips to Bermuda, the Bahamas, or Hawaii in tones usually reserved for the announcement of a new pope.

My love affair with islands and the sea had ultimately led me to climb aboard the USNS *Vanguard* shortly after my 23rd birthday. The *Vanguard* was a ship that NASA built in the '60s to complement the existing land-based global tracking network in preparation for the Apollo moon missions. I had been too young to participate in those glorious days of space exploration, but on the *Vanguard*, I consoled myself with ports of call in the islands of Hawaii, Trinidad, Tahiti, the Seychelles, and Truk Lagoon as we provided coverage for both earth-orbit and interplanetary satellite launches.

The *Vanguard* not only carried me to the islands of my dreams, it was responsible for introducing me to the girl of my dreams. Tall, slim, and lovely, Gloria Tucker had the same desire to travel as I did and had decided her ambition was worth the difficulties inherent in breaking the ship's all-male tradition. To her relief, the vast majority of the ship's two-hundred sailors welcomed her aboard; the unmarried crewmen, of course, accepted her unanimously.

Six months later, our crewmates' smiles had lost a little of their brilliance; it was my arm that Gloria held when we walked down the dock. For two years it seemed that there could be no sweeter deal than the *Vanguard*, where Gloria and I enjoyed free room and board, banked generous pay and bonuses, and sampled life in dozens of ports around the world.

A long-lived career aboard ship, however, was not in the cards. With the constant downsizing of NASA's post-Apollo budget, the value of the *Vanguard*'s returns began to diminish. Bendix Field Engineering, the company that owned the tracking station contract, transferred as many of the ship's crew as they could to other stations. Gloria and I took this cue to marry and try our hands at playing house. Unfortunately, the house we chose to play in was on a mountainside in Quito. Pronounced "Key-toe," the city is the two-mile-high capitol of Ecuador and was, for us *norteamericanos*, the closest approximation to reasonable housing that could be found within seventy-five miles of NASA's tracking station in the Andes Mountains.

The experience all but wiped us out, both financially and physically. Our first mistake had been to ship a planeload of goods to our new mountain home before reading our company's guidelines for overseas relocation. Bendix reimbursed us for only a fraction of what we spent. At the same time, we learned that the cost of living was much higher than we had expected; for rent and groceries, we paid close to what we made.

We still might have been able to manage if we had at least kept our health. We didn't. Gloria and I both succumbed to an Ecuadorian version of Montezuma's revenge, a chronic ailment that was fairly common to the inhabitants of the area. Gloria, however, became so sick that, while she hadn't exactly been knocking at Death's door, she certainly found herself cruising through his neighborhood.

Broke and sick, we felt our only answer was to transfer to another tracking station, one that would put our health back in the pink while getting our checkbook out of the red. Ascension Island had to be the answer.

During the course of our tracking station careers, Gloria and I had often found ourselves working with people who had visited Ascension, people who had made the arduous trek to the remote middle of the Atlantic Ocean. A few degrees south of the equator between South America and Africa, Ascension was classified by Bendix as "overseas hardship" duty, which encompassed some broad territory, but basically meant employees working there would not be exposed to many of the amenities to which they had previously become accustomed, no matter where they had lived before. From many descriptions, a stretch in the maximum security wing of San Quentin prison would be preferable to a stay on Ascension.

By all accounts, Ascension Island had little in common with any of the islands I had visited in the Caribbean, South Pacific, and Indian Ocean. There were no vacation resorts, no lazy lagoons, and no waterfalls. Indeed, there was precious little of anything, especially vegetation. For that reason, although the United Kingdom's official name for its tiny possession is

Ascension Island, those familiar with the place more often refer to it as the "Rock," a clue that the island has less in common with Hawaii than it has with Alcatraz.

But scenery wasn't as important to me as Gloria's health was, and from what I could tell, there was nowhere else on Earth that could match the island's salubrity. Ascension boasted pleasant temperatures and fresh ocean air. It was a thousand miles from any sources of pollutants. Drinking water was distilled on the island and subject to US health standards. Food, flown in from Florida twice a week, was also subject to US standards. Ascension could be Gloria's sanitarium.

As for money, none of our contacts had ever disputed the fact that a person could make a pile of money on Ascension. Besides the overseas bonus and the guaranteed weekly overtime, food and housing were provided free of charge. Best of all, if we stayed eighteen months, our income tax calculations became exceedingly simple; we kept everything, Uncle Sam got nothing. Gloria and I pulled out our map, searched the South Atlantic for our new home-to-be and marked it, not with an "X", but with a dollar sign.

Of course, we had heard our fair share of gripes about Ascension, too. One common complaint was the boredom. With no television and just three radio stations to choose from, most Americans turned to the only barroom on the US Air Force base for their daily dose of escapism. Others focused on fishing and scuba diving in the ocean or hiking around the mountains.

The island's extreme remoteness exacerbated the boredom. With US transportation limited to the biweekly, five-thousand-mile flights out of Patrick Air Force Base, Florida, there could be no such thing as a relaxing weekend getaway. Bendix did, however, provide for a two-week (unpaid) leave-of-absence for every three-month stay on the island.

Boredom and cabin fever certainly conspired to take their toll on the islanders, but the number one challenge to Ascension's workers was significant enough to eclipse all other concerns. Unmentioned in the tracking station's orientation brochure but understood by all who contemplated the move was the plain fact that the island had very few women on it.

One source gave the ratio of men to women as ten to one, but that statistic was misleading, as it included the married women who lived in the two tiny British communities and who were rarely seen by the Americans. The ratio of men to women at the American base probably approached a hundred-to-one.

Ironically, it was this feature of Ascension life that nearly quashed our plans. The "overseas hardship" classification meant Ascension was not a family assignment; the room and board benefit and the free transportation to and from the island applied only to company employees.

Unfortunately, our company had never been in the situation where two of its employees had married and wanted to work together at one of the overseas hardship facilities. There were too many intangibles to consider, not the least of which was the morale of all the single workers. The picture of a young married couple strolling gaily through the midst of a flock of young, hard-working, hard-drinking, lonely Romeos was more than Bendix management wanted to consider. There was no policy governing this circumstance and nobody appeared eager to initiate one.

Nevertheless, with Quito slowly draining the life out of us, we had to make a move, even though the roster at the Ascension tracking station only had room for Gloria. I sadly packed my wife off to the South Atlantic and prepared to brave the Ecuadorian parasites by myself.

Three months later, Bendix gave me my ticket out of Ecuador, but instead of sending me to join my wife on Ascension, they sent me back to sea; the *Vanguard* had one more trip to make, a long South Pacific cruise to support the launches of the two Voyager spacecraft, the magnificent machines that eventually beamed back breathtaking pictures of our outer neighbors in the solar system.

Finally, six nail-biting months after my wife and I had reluctantly agreed to split up, my manager notified me that my transfer request to Ascension had been approved. Bendix gave me no explanation for this sudden change of heart, nor did I ask for one, as I suspected the outcome had ultimately been decided by a coin toss and any invitation to revisit that decision might result in a sudden flip-flop.

The message was delivered with little fanfare, as if nothing out of the ordinary had occurred. I, however, felt like I had just been dealt a royal flush for the last hand in a six-month poker game, a game against a con man who had suckered me into wagering all my current and future holdings, and a few pounds of flesh, besides.

With all the right cards in my hand and my young wife waiting for me, it was easy to discount all the harsh descriptions I had heard about life on the Rock. I cleared my head of all the stories that had compared the place to Devil's Island and dreamed once again of Neverland.

"Hey, Dan!" Bob was snapping his fingers in front of my face. "You with me now?"

Neverland quickly evaporated. I shook my head to clear it and looked back at Bob. "Yeah, I'm back. Sorry."

"I didn't know if it was too much Scotch or too little Gloria," he said. "By the way, how's your headache?"

Amazingly, my head felt absolutely normal—right down to the twinge in

The Devil's Ashpit

my jaw that I'd been living with since Quito. Dr. Bob was a miracle worker. He not only rid me of the headache, he also helped me diagnose my problem as a toothache.

During what I knew would be my last few weeks in Quito, I had decided to visit a dentist. I'd discovered a broken filling in one of my molars and I thought I should get it fixed prior to setting sail on the *Vanguard*. It seemed like sound reasoning at the time.

Someone at the tracking station recommended a Dr. Lopez. She turned out to be an attractive, thirtyish woman with the cheekbones and black hair typical of Ecuadorians. Like many of the professionals I'd met in Quito, her English was very good.

"Hmm. That is a very big filling," she said. " I could replace it, but it would just crack again. I recommend putting a crown on it."

I didn't know what a crown was, but it obviously fit over the tooth. This sounded much more appealing than having a drill grinding into my tooth to replace a filling, just millimeters from my nerves.

Of course, I was dead wrong. I didn't realize that Dr. Lopez would have to grind out the old filling, clean out the hole, and then file down the whole tooth in order to get a crown to fit over it. I was young, inexperienced, and completely ignorant of dentistry—especially Ecuadorian dentistry. I told her to proceed.

Dr. Lopez dove into my mouth without hesitation, and without offering me a shot of Novocain. The first bite of the big grinder against my molar told me that perhaps the crowning of a tooth was more involved than I had first suspected. But surely the pain would be short-lived, otherwise she would have offered the painkiller. I said nothing, thinking that every time she pulled her drill out would be the last. Every time she put it back in, I died a little.

Finally, with the temporary crown in place, I walked home, exhausted, soaked in sweat and still wondering, *why didn't she give me a shot?* It dawned on me that the key word was *she*. I may have been the victim of the dentist's gender in combination with the South American geography.

That is, I was in the land of *machismo*, sort of the forerunner to the "Real Men Don't Eat Quiche" movement. Dr. Lopez had not offered me a shot because it had never dawned on her that I would want one. Obviously, the vast majority of her patients were her countrymen, and no self-respecting Latino was about to admit to a woman that she was hurting him, even a woman with a drill.

When I returned to Dr. Lopez for the permanent crown, she showed me what looked like a big gold nugget. Once the crown was in place, it *felt* like a big gold nugget. When I complained, Dr. Lopez polished the crown for a few seconds. My bite was still wrong and I told her so, but she refused to take any more off the crown.

"It just feels big," she said. "You'll get used to it."

Instead, I got used to hammering that molar with every movement of my jaw. I also got used to tilting my head to pour all hot and cold fluids into the opposite side of my mouth. And finally, I got used to the dull ache, the very thing that I had wanted to avoid in the first place.

As my date with Bob had just kicked off the weekend, I had no recourse but to return to my motel room and open the slim Cocoa Beach telephone book to the yellow pages listing for dentists. I propped it open with a bottle of Scotch I bought to keep me company until the offices opened on Monday.

I was extremely upset at this new development, worried that my dental problem would cause me to miss my Wednesday flight, thus postponing yet again my reunion with Gloria. On top of that, I was still stinging from my last disappointment. When I had finally received my transfer notice to Ascension Island, the *Vanguard* was still a week away from docking at Hawaii. From the moment I accepted the offer, I pictured myself running down the gangway as soon as it touched the pier and catching a cab to the airport. I was easily the happiest person on the ship.

The admin supervisor, however, had a different set of priorities. I didn't get my paperwork until we'd spent a week at our dock in Pearl Harbor. And since the *Vanguard*'s support requirements were over and the ship was headed for the mothballs, it was a week with nothing much to do. Not many people would complain about spending a week in Hawaii, but my circumstances were very much out of the ordinary. As a result, I was the only person on Waikiki Beach wrapped in a scowl.

In Cocoa Beach, though, I begrudgingly had to admit that the admin supervisor's plodding pace was a godsend. If I had made the flights I had originally been hoping for, my toothache would have occurred on Ascension and it would have forced me to head right back to the airfield for a medevac. I would have been making three of the grueling thirteen-hour flights in the space of a few days.

Monday morning finally came and I forced myself to shake off the fog left over from my alcoholic weekend. I picked up the phone and all of my fears vanished; the first dentist on my list sent me to a specialist who squeezed me in for a root canal during his lunch period. The term, "root canal" gave me pause, though. I was as ignorant of that procedure as I had been about crowns, although I remembered periodically hearing the phrase, "That sounds about as attractive as a root canal!" Uh-oh.

Well, it just so happens that root canals have a bum rap. A root canal *ends* the pain, so the person who *needs* a root canal is the one to be pitied. If there was pain involved in the procedure, I didn't notice; it was minuscule compared to what I'd been suffering. As a bonus, the doctor finally ground the crown down to adjust my bite and sent me on my way with a prescription for pain pills. I was so busy with my travel preparations, however, and I was experiencing such relief (in every sense of the word) that I forgot to fill it.

And then came Wednesday, *my* Wednesday, the Wednesday that I had been fixating on ever since I got my travel package on the *Vanguard* the week before. And what a day it was; although it was mid-September, the famous Florida sun hovered in a cloudless sky, showering the land with rays so intense that they illuminated every speck of dust floating in the atmosphere. The resulting reflections from these otherwise invisible motes appeared as a faint haze that dulled the colors of the surrounding landscape. Heat waves further transformed the scenery, their cumulative effect over acres of asphalt serving to melt the trees, towers, and buildings on the horizon into a blurry, wavering potpourri.

I stood with my fellow passengers in a loose formation outside the main hanger of Patrick Air Force Base, which is just a few miles south of where I'd been staying in Cocoa Beach. Although I had been living in the tropics for the last three months, I was unprepared for the heat emanating from what seemed to be square miles of broiling decks and runways. We each adjusted our positions every few seconds as we tried in vain to find the remnants of an ocean breeze. The Atlantic was only a hundred yards in front of us but was hidden behind Highway A1A and a strip of undeveloped dunes—these becoming something of a rarity since the blossoming of the Space Coast had been piling up condos and bars all along the beach.

Fifteen minutes earlier, the hanger's loudspeakers had announced that our plane was ready to be boarded. My fellow travelers and I had stepped out of the too-cool waiting room and into the wilting heat of the unprotected boarding area. There, a security guard stopped us and, after telling us to wait, he disappeared into the hanger.

"It's not the heat, it's the humidity," announced one of the passengers as he cleaned his sunglasses on his shirttail.

How original...and how wrong, I thought. It's the heat, the humidity, the sun, the air, the ground, and the effects of walking out of a waiting room that had a thermostat setting that could douse a fire. For me, it was also the extra surface area caused by my 190 pound frame, which appeared to contain more heat sensors and sweat glands than most everyone else around me. I rapidly became drenched with perspiration.

Hoping to catch a cooling glimpse of water, I looked behind me towards the Banana River, actually a great saltwater lagoon that serves as the base's western boundary. It was no use. Light rays reflected, refracted, and polarized by the intervening layers of superheated air ultimately combined and canceled each other out, leaving a wide black impenetrable void where ground and water should have been. Above and beyond hovered the blurry coast of Merritt Island, supported only by the mirage.

Wilting under the staggering heat, I recalled an article written by a local who believed that a direct hit from a hurricane would dredge a path right through the air force base and provide watersports enthusiasts with another access to the Banana River. As I stood on the runway, sweat soaking my pants, shirt, and dripping from my hair onto my ears and neck, I thought the prospect of turning Patrick Air Force Base into the Patrick Intracoastal Waterway seemed particularly inviting.

I turned my attention towards our plane. This would be my first flight on a military aircraft, and the C-141 Starlifter cargo transport squatting on the runway provided the clue that this flight would be very unlike the few commercial jaunts I had taken during my short professional career. What struck me most about the plane that was to fly me five thousand miles down range was the apparent affinity it had for the ground. The plane's wheels were barely visible, with the result that the dull gray belly seemed to droop perilously close to the asphalt. The hatch on the side of the fuselage was so low that the crew members needed only a short stepping stool to ease their entrance.

Furthermore, the fuselage was designed to hang under the middle of the plane's wing. On the ground, of course, the body of the plane bore the weight of the wing, complete with fuel tanks and four jet engines. This load caused the wings to sag like those of a tired albatross. The cumulative effect was to make this droopy low-rider look like it was trying to hug the ground. I wondered if I should be doing the same.

This was the same type of plane that had taken Gloria to Ascension six months before and although she hadn't supplied me with the details of a Military Airlift Command (or MAC) flight, she did repeat the advice many of her coworkers had given her on how to ease the discomfort of the trip. Alcohol was the common denominator of each of these suggestions, the only difference being the amount to be ingested. A sober flight was not among the recommendations.

I was glad I hadn't followed the advice, however well-intentioned; my rapidly dehydrating body was already on the brink of collapse. The additional effects caused by a bloodstream full of alcohol would have been too much to bear. Of course, once I was airborne, in-flight jitters might cause me to have a change of heart. By then, however, it would be too late. MAC flight loadmasters wouldn't be serving drinks, and our carry-on bags had already been checked to ensure we wouldn't be helping ourselves.

At last we got the signal to board and our little group shuffled forward to select our accommodations for the next thirteen hours. By the time we reached the hatch, I was somehow first in line, as one-by-one, the other passengers had slowly fallen in behind me. After I vaulted myself into the plane and took a step towards the passenger area, I discovered the reason behind my companions' apparent generosity; the atmosphere inside was even worse than what we had been enduring on the exposed runway. Once the huge cargo doors in the tail were closed, the Starlifter's interior was rapidly approaching the temperature required for baking pottery.

My lungs searing with every breath, I walked slowly towards the rear, my hands outstretched for protection while my eyes worked to adjust to the darkness. Two small bright disks glowed from either side of the plane, illuminating a few rows of rear-facing bucket seats. I plopped down beside one of the two windows and with the help of its light, watched as the rest of the passengers took their seats.

Gradually, the darkness ebbed and more and more of the plane became visible as my eyes adjusted to the dim overhead bulbs. In front of me, a cargo net served as a divider, separating the passenger compartment from four pallets piled high with boxes and canvas bags. More cargo nets held the pallets in place. Along the colorless aluminum fuselage ran the vents and the plumbing and conduit connecting each of the plane's subsystems. Again, the crew had applied cargo netting liberally, using it to hold an assortment of supplies against the sides.

Sitting only inches from the uninsulated aluminum skin of the airplane, I could feel its heat even through the super hot air and my drenched clothes. Suddenly, there was a loud roar of rushing air and I was showered with a cloud of ice crystals. Air conditioning. Within seconds, my damp clothes became an extremely efficient conductor for the frigid wind blowing down on me and I covered myself with one of the blankets piled on the empty seats.

After ten minutes and no fluctuation in the volume and temperature of the air pouring out of the vents, I had just begun to pull another blanket around me when the air suddenly stopped. I breathed a foggy sigh of relief, but the atmosphere in the plane seemed to defy physical laws; the cold, clammy air slowly warmed up, then skipped the mid-seventy degree comfort zone and landed in the high eighties. From there, the temperature resumed its steady climb until, with another roar and shower of ice crystals, the air conditioning kicked in and the cycle repeated itself.

A trio of loadmasters in olive drab Air Force jump suits began to make a number of trips between the galley and the passenger area, making preparations for the flight. As they solicited each of us for the dollar to pay for our optional lunch, I realized they were acting as flight attendants. I was quite amused to see that one young attendant, although dressed in jump suit and combat boots, still displayed enough attributes to reveal she was a very good-looking girl. She must have been a knockout in civvies.

The howling winds of the air conditioning had just announced the beginning of yet another Arctic Circle experience when the pilot pushed the throttles forward to roll us out to the runway. With no insulation in the fuselage to deaden the loud, shrill whine of the engines, our compartment seemed to amplify each frequency and focus it right into our ears. At takeoff, the unimaginable happened—the engines got louder.

Soon after we were airborne, my favorite attendant moved up and down the aisles offering each passenger what looked like a treat from a box in her hand. My eyes lit up when I recognized the soft pink peppermints that had been my grandmother's favorite candy. I grabbed a couple and was about to flick them into my mouth when I saw my neighbors rolling theirs between their hands and pushing the resulting cylinders into their ears. Despite their appearance and their heady peppermint smell, the stuff wasn't from Grandma's candy jar; it was earplug wax.

Privately embarrassed, I imitated the rest of the passengers. Unfortunately, the earplugs merely changed the tone of the all-encompassing noise. The wax did effectively block out the engines' high-pitched scream, but in its place I became more aware of a low frequency rumble that bypassed the middle ear and penetrated deep inside my skull.

I quickly regretted not having taken the advice of my wife's friends, specifically the ones who had suggested that a MAC flight was best experienced while unconscious. Then, only minutes into the flight, I caught myself glancing at my watch. I resolved not to look at it again until we landed for fear that the thirteen-hour countdown was going to be too much to bear.

Instead, I began to tick off all of the various legs of the trips I had made since Gloria had left for Ascension. I remembered the feeling I had on the *Vanguard* when we left the Atlantic Ocean—Gloria's ocean—and traversed the Panama Canal. As the ship exited the Miraflores locks and entered the Pacific, Gloria and I were officially oceans apart, and our separation increased with each turn of the propeller. Ultimately, the *Vanguard*'s western course to its assigned launch support position took me through the point where I had the unhappy distinction of being on the exact opposite side of the globe from Ascension. On that day, I made the glum observation that Gloria and I were literally a world apart.

Once my *Vanguard* support ended, though, I had been steadily drawing closer to my wife. The first leg was the most agonizing, as it was a 3,000 mile journey at a top speed of fourteen knots. Then, after my 5,000 mile flight from Hawaii and restless weekend in Cocoa Beach, I had just one more 5,000 mile hop to make. I tried not to think in terms of the thousands of miles or even the thirteen hours, but in terms of one last hurdle.

I closed my eyes, as if cutting out all visual clues of my surroundings would help diminish the roaring audio and I tried to envision my reception at the flight's end, where, after six suspenseful months, my wife and I were going to be together again. Just this one last hurdle and home would have a new name—Ascension Island.

Chapter 2

Beginnings

One would suppose that Ascension Island's extreme isolation, its hostile terrain, and its meager water supply would have ensured that the island would remain deserted until the end of time, visited only by shipwreck survivors or others similarly desperate for the sight of land. Why would anyone care about a pile of rock, ash, and cinders 1,000 miles from the closest appreciable land mass (roughly the distance from Miami to New York City)?

And yet, as of this writing, Ascension is the destination for routine flights from both the US and the UK, is a monthly port of call for a cargo/passenger liner, and is host to five communities. This astonishing development warrants a brief study of the island's history...

The Mid-Atlantic Ridge is a submarine mountain chain which, true to its name, bisects the ocean that separates the continents of the Eastern and Western Hemispheres. At some point in history, a series of underwater eruptions on this range built layer upon layer of rock higher and higher until ultimately, the pillar breached the surface. A boiling, steaming river of the earth's crust poured out of the ocean and reached towards the sky.

When the last of the lava flows had solidified, a mountainous thirty-four square mile area of volcanic debris, roughly in the shape of a triangle, lay exposed to the atmosphere. Although the area is minute in comparison to the thousands of square miles of surrounding blue ocean, the remains of forty-four major cones in that space bear testimony to the concentrated violence of the cataclysm.

This wretched, ruinous speck of land remained unseen and uncharted until 1501, when a Portuguese nobleman named Juan Da Nova set sail for India to procure a share of the lucrative spice trade for King Manuel. In the interest of speed, Da Nova had decided not to hug the African coastline as he sailed towards the Cape. Instead, his heading through the middle of the South Atlantic attempted to follow the route pioneered some four years earlier by Vasco Da Gama on a similar quest for the king.

The crude navigation tools of the day, however, put Da Nova's four ship armada on a slightly different heading than that recorded by Da Gama. Consequently, a few hundred miles south of the equator, a perturbation appeared on the horizon, breaking the smooth monotony of the South Atlantic waters. As Da Nova drew nearer, the small land mass eventually took shape and lay before him; a number of giant mounds of rock and ash, the highest of which disappeared into a trail of clouds.

Da Nova named the island Conception in honor of the day of its discovery, but made no attempt to land. Surely there was nothing on this fire-scarred mid-oceanic eruption that could compare to the rich cargo that awaited him in India. Da Nova sailed on.

The name Conception was short-lived; by 1503, some unknown adventurer (or cartographer) had renamed the place Ascension.

Interestingly, both Conception and Ascension could be regarded as names befitting a chunk of earth found in the middle of the ocean. With their divine connotation, the names imply that the land was heaven-sent, which would certainly be the first vote of any sailor clinging to a raft and scanning the horizon for a miracle. Indeed, from a distance, it's not hard to imagine the island as a huge sandbox and the conical mounds the accumulation of grit sifted through a giant, playful hand. Ascension must surely be the Almighty's oasis for sea-weary sailors.

But closer inspection reveals the true nature of the emergence of the land. Walking across the island is like walking through the slag heaps and ash pits of all the world's coal furnaces. It's impossible to imagine this wasteland as the work of the gentle and caring God familiar to most religions. Nearly every feature of the island is pummeled with the fire-blasted hues of the rocks that arose from the earth's crust. Huge pyramids of rust-red ash appear randomly around the island and encroach upon slopes of black cinders. In many spots, twisting lava flows skirt cones of utterly lifeless ash, the monotony of their slopes broken only by competing shades of gray. Ascension Island couldn't be heaven-sent; it must owe its birth to the boiling rocks and the vicious temper of the Underworld.

For over three hundred years after its discovery, this harsh intrusion upon the open sea lay practically untouched, serving mainly as a rendezvous point and a source of turtle meat. Ships' captains also used Ascension as a post office of sorts; a bottle set in a protected area in one of the rocky shores served as the mailbox. The seafarers made their way ashore to retrieve the bottle, read its contents, and add messages of their own, usually detailing their ships' names, destinations, and cargo.

Aside from its primitive communications function, Ascension also served as an austere haven for victims of shipwreck and functioned as a prison for those sailors with the misfortune to incur the wrath of their captains. Anyone expecting a leisurely island experience during their Ascension tenure, however, would be in for a shock, for although it might seem that the bounty held by the surrounding sea ensured that inhabitants of the island would not starve, the meager fresh water supply was found far inland; those struggling to survive wasted precious energy hiking back and forth between the two necessities for life. At times, the struggle was for naught, as the springs occasionally dried up.

The year 1815 was a milestone for Ascension. The British, determined that Napoleon would not escape from exile as easily as he had demonstrated the year before, shipped the defeated emperor to the island of Saint Helena (actually spelled "St Helena" and pronounced "Saint hel-LEE-na"), another pinpoint of land some eight-hundred miles southeast of Ascension. In contrast to Ascension, St Helena can easily sustain a population, but is no less remote; the island's closest significant neighbor is Africa, twelve-hundred miles due east.

To dissuade any would-be rescuers, the British admiral charged with Napoleon's security ordered one of his captains to sail northwest from St Helena and claim Ascension for Britain. The sailors were to establish a settlement on the new acquisition and use it as a base from which they could challenge any ships that came within sight.

From that point on, Ascension Island has supported a population, although some would argue that "supported" may be too strong a word. Indeed, for most of its existence, the island and its tenuous settlement did not even rate the status of a colony. Instead, in 1816 the same admiral responsible for the island's occupation declared the land to be a British Sloop of War, and thereafter referred to his permanently anchored ship as His Majesty's Ship (HMS) *Ascension*. The admiral apparently made this move to simplify the day-to-day operation of the settlement; the edict meant that the inhabitants of the island were crew members of a warship in King George III's navy and were thus obliged to recognize their captain's orders as law.

In 1821, Napoleon died, removing the original reason for Ascension's occupation, but increasingly, the island had become important as a sanitarium for sailors in distress and an essential supply base for ships engaged in suppressing the slave traders operating out of West Africa. As a result, the Lords of the Admiralty continued to keep the HMS *Ascension* afloat.

The year 1899 was another milestone in Ascension history. The Eastern Telegraph Company, which later became Cable & Wireless Ltd., included Ascension in its plans for an underwater telegraph cable to link Capetown, South Africa with England. Subsequent cables to Argentina, Brazil, and

West Africa, and the eventual introduction of radio receivers and transmitters made the Ascension relay station a valuable asset to its owners.

It's uncertain what impact this new communications network had on World War I, but in 1922 the British Navy finally withdrew, leaving its facilities to the employees of the Eastern Telegraph Company. No longer a Sloop of War, Ascension returned to its former status of island, and with the issue of a set of postage stamps that year, the tiny outpost was officially recognized as a dependency of the colony of St Helena.

Twenty years later, the strategies of the Second World War made the biggest impact on the terrain of the island since the lava from its last eruption had cooled. Nearly two thousand men of the US 38th Engineer Combat Regiment unloaded eight thousand tons of equipment from their ships and began clearing space for campsites, roads, fuel tanks, radar stations, and most important, an airstrip.

In just three months, Ascension Island became a stepping-stone for pilots flying men and munitions to the Allied campaign in North Africa. Furthermore, throughout the war, the island played an important part in the hunt for German U-boats. US Navy bombers, acting on coordinates obtained via the cable links between triangulated listening posts at Sierra Leone, St Helena, and Ascension flew off to intercept the marauders. The post-war documentary *Victory at Sea* briefly praised the exploits of the participants in this tiny theater, claiming that, "Here, more submarines were destroyed than in any other comparable stretch of ocean."

As the war ended, so did the United States' interest in Ascension. Thus, in 1947, the last American withdrew, returning the island and incidentally, tons of abandoned war materiel, to the small party of Cable & Wireless technicians.

Ten years later, the Americans returned. Britain and the United States had signed an agreement that allowed the Department of Defense to install and operate a tracking station to follow the trajectories of missiles fired from Cape Canaveral, Florida. Soon afterwards, the National Aeronautics and Space Administration got into the act, beginning construction of a similar station to track an entirely different class of missiles, those containing human cargo.

The NASA tracking station was in operation in 1967 and served as a vital link in the network responsible for the safety and success of the Apollo missions, the pinnacle of which was reached in 1969 with the landing of Neal Armstrong and Buzz Aldrin on the moon's Sea of Tranquility.

Thus, Ascension Island, a barren, inhospitable heap of ash that had once served as a primitive mail box for lonely sailors had, in some four hundred and fifty years, become one of the most sophisticated communications centers in the world, relaying spacecraft telemetry and astronauts' voices to a world-wide audience.

Chapter 3

The Rock

My MAC flight had left Florida at noon. Flying away from the path of the sun over a featureless ocean, though, quickly negated what little advantage I thought I had gained by grabbing one of the window seats. We crossed five time zones in total darkness before I was rewarded with a slight change in scenery as the sky began to prepare for dawn. Thirteen hours after leaving Florida, I felt the plane make a wide, flat turn and Ascension Island gradually filled up my window.

I had known Ascension was small, but from my vantage point, the Rock was surprisingly squat and fragile-looking, as if a good storm might send its waters racing up the long, shallow slopes to overcome even the tallest peaks. The land that I knew to be studded with volcanic cones and twisting lava flows appeared dull and smooth, like a drop of solder on a workbench. The view was a trick of the lighting. Like a photographer's portrait set, the soft, cloud-diffused rays of the morning sun served to subdue the island's harsher features. The same light muffled the earth tones I knew to exist, providing me with a simple study in shades of gray, set against a black sea.

Watching this apparently lifeless slab reminded me of a theory on how the moon was formed. Some scientists believe the moon was once part of the Earth, bulging like a tumor on the equator. The Earth's spin gradually pushed the mass further and further away until the elongated connection snapped, flinging the moon into orbit. As far as I was concerned, the colorless moonscape below me was evidence enough that, not only was the theory correct, but I had found that broken connection.

Ascension disappeared from view for a few moments as we made our final approach. When it did reappear, just yards outside my window, the landscape held two surprises. First, the lifeless gray was gone; my new viewing angle brought back the spectrums of brown and red. Secondly, I had come to expect rock, lava, cinders, and ashes. The corrugated plains that began at the airstrip's edge and abruptly halted at the surrounding burned-out cones certainly contained each of these elements, but what startled me was the vegetation. The plains were dotted with small cactus plants and dry brownish tufts of some type of grass. This pitiful display of plant life would never be confused with the Hanging Gardens of Babylon, but I had expected an utter wasteland.

Our landing was otherwise uneventful and we taxied slowly back to a small hanger at the edge of a gargantuan parking lot. The vast parking area seemed wasted, as ours was the only airplane on the island, but then again, this was an airstrip that had been built during World War II. At one time, the area had been a jumble of airplanes, utility vehicles, and supply dumps.

My real interest in the hanger area was the sight of my young wife standing in the midst of a small group of welcomers. Aside from being the only female in the bunch, Gloria was further distinguishable by her flowery blouse and dressy slacks. Everyone else wore their work clothes: T-shirts and jeans or cut-offs.

My fellow passengers and I finally exited the plane and seconds later, I had my arms around my wife. After a quick embrace, Gloria suggested, "Let's get out of the wind." That these were the first words out of my loved one's mouth on this momentous occasion should have alerted me to their significance. Ascension's location, far from any land masses, puts it square in the path of the trade winds. Their effect on Ascension is to sweep practically every mountain, plain, or valley on the island with a relatively constant fifteen knot breeze. Inhabitants quickly become thankful for the swirling air; without it, the island would become unbearable under the tropical sun.

Gloria, however, hated the wind. It wreaked havoc on her long, flowing, chestnut hair, lifting random locks of it skyward while simultaneously sending strands to whip across her cheeks and eyes and wrap around her neck. Compromise was out of the question. Gloria would tie her hair in pigtails for a day at the beach, but didn't like the way she looked. She refused to consider any hairstyle other than the one that attracted me when we first met on the *Vanguard*. I couldn't blame her for that, but her obstinacy meant I was doomed to hear "Let's get out of the wind," a few times a day for the next three years.

Gloria led me a short distance to a small parking lot, where I half-expected to see a fleet of lunar rovers. Instead, the lot held a half-dozen vehicles that looked like they'd been salvaged from a demolition derby. Gloria was heading towards the worst wreck, an old Volkswagen van that I guessed she had borrowed for the occasion.

Although my wife had six months of experience on the island to my six minutes, she walked automatically to the passenger door, leaving the driver's side to me. This little bit of choreography slipped us nicely back into our pre-separation relationship, during which I had always been the chauffeur.

After all those months, I was once again behind the wheel with my wife beside me. I leaned over to give her a proper "I'm back from the war, honey" kiss and was a little taken aback to receive a "Thanks for stopping by, cousin" close-mouthed, tightly-puckered, peck on the lips. Well, okay; there were still some spectators around, and neither Gloria nor I had ever been into exhibitionism. We would have plenty of time together. I could wait.

As I turned the van around and headed out the only road leading from the airfield, we rode silently, with a contentment that couldn't be measured in words. This reunion, after all, had been in doubt ever since we had reluctantly parted ways in Ecuador.

After we had driven a half-mile, Gloria broke the silence.

"You're on the right side of the road."

I didn't know how to respond to that.

"Ahh...yes I am."

"Well, move over. The right side is the wrong side. We have to drive on the left."

Of course. Ascension belongs to the British. No problem; we had visited other countries whose inhabitants drove on the port side. Although there were no other vehicles in sight, I made the adjustment and noted, among a dozen other problems, how dangerously loose the steering wheel felt. Even on the straight, well-paved airport road, the van drove like a rudderless boat.

"Whose van is this? It's a piece of shit."

"It's ours."

"Oh."

Before I could apologize for ridiculing Gloria's investment, she assured me that she shared my appraisal. Our van, I would come to find out, was pretty much representative of the base's fleet of private vehicles, a fleet that consisted mostly of company-purchased vans and pickup trucks that, a few hundred-thousand miles past their warranties, had outlived their usefulness. The vehicles were already junk by the time the contractors decided to replace them, but the islanders, desperate for transportation, placed bids for every rolling wreck that became available. Through a variety of miracles, they always managed to coax another mile or two out of the junkers.

Our particular junker was giving me fits, and I struggled to find the right touch that would keep the van from bounding off the road and littering the surrounding rocks and cinders with huge chunks of our undercarriage. Gloria, meanwhile, tried to convince me that our van was much better than many of the other used vehicles that had been available.

Luckily, the airstrip was barely a mile from the American base and I

The Devil's Ashpit

soon saw a number of long, white, barracks buildings with a smattering of Quonset huts and boxy utility buildings. All were painted white and stood out sharply against the pure black cinders that comprised the grounds.

We approached an intersection and, anticipating an instruction to turn, I tapped the brakes. The van immediately swerved sharply to the right. In a second, although the steering wheel had never moved, we were cruising down the right-hand lane.

Fortunately, there were no oncoming vehicles, and indeed, I would soon learn that this was the normal Ascension traffic pattern; that is, no traffic. If the island ever had an "eye in the sky" for a rush hour traffic report, the pilot would have a tough time coming up with anything more exciting than a monotonous, "All clear."

But I was far from comfortable, trying to aim a one-ton deathtrap that came with its own peculiar set of rules. I found my years of driving experience actually working against me, as the drive train's characteristics totally invalidated the conditioned responses I had developed on the normal vehicles I had driven for nearly ten years.

Gloria, acknowledging my frustration, summarized the car situation.

"The Brits have the best cars. Their company ships them down here for free. We just have to stay on the lookout for a Brit who's leaving and try to place a bid on their car."

I hoped we wouldn't have to wait too long. Our lives depended on it.

As we drove through the deserted streets of the base, Gloria pointed out the mess hall and library ("Don't get excited, it's just a closet full of paperback books"), and directed me up a slight rise to see our barracks. Large black numbers had been painted on the corners of each of the buildings, and I learned that barracks number eleven was our new address. Nearby were the few highlights the base had to offer for the athletes—tennis courts, skittles alleys, and for the truly adventurous, a softball field.

The softball field served as an exclamation point to the austere surroundings. Although it sported a flat, smooth, regulation-sized surface and was rimmed with benches for the players, bleachers for the fans, and a high chain link fence for a backstop, an ingredient essential to the recipe for a real softball park was glaringly absent. The entire playing field was bare. Not a single blade of grass broke the monotony of the light brown, gritty, hard-packed surface. Even from the road I could tell the texture of the field was not conducive to diving fielders or sliding runners; it looked as though the field had been cut out of a giant piece of double-ought sandpaper. I guessed that it also contained a number of strips of epidermal tissue. A field of dreams? No way. It was more likely a field of screams.

Beside the ball field, a network of sidewalks wound their way through similarly hostile terrain. A sign pounded into the parched ground between the concrete implored its readers to "Please Keep Off The Grass." I assumed the sign was erected in humorous recognition of the islanders' plight. But no, Gloria told me that the sign was all that remained of a recent attempt to transplant a few square yards of sod from Green Mountain, the only place on the island where such a resource existed.

I parked our van near our barracks, and my wife and I walked across the street and sat together on a bench in the shade of the Volcano Club, the hub around which most of the base activities revolved. The Volcano Club contained a bar, a sandwich shop, a gift shop, a game room, and served as the foundation for the bleachers for the outdoor theater. Nevertheless, Gloria mentioned that despite the diversity of club activities available, the vast majority of the club's patrons merely planted themselves at or near the bar, leaving periodically only to answer nature's inevitable call.

When Gloria further informed me that many of these bar-flies hit the club every day after work and stayed there for eight hours, I expressed my disbelief; I found it inconceivable that people would subject themselves to the isolation and deprivation inherent with life on a volcanic island only to exchange their hard-earned cash for a numb brain and a sparkling clean urinary tract.

Gloria didn't bother to defend these alcoholics, but she did try to clarify one point.

"For all the time they spend in the club, nobody spends a lot of money there. The drinks are real cheap."

"How cheap?" I asked.

Gloria squirmed a bit on her side of the bench. "I don't really know. I've never had to buy one."

I burst out laughing. Married or single, young or old, attractive or homely, girls were a valuable commodity on Ascension and the men on the island naturally did what they could to initiate the chain of events that could lead to a few minutes of female companionship, even though they knew those few minutes would only be spent in the bar and not the boudoir.

I had experienced the same situation during our years on the *Vanguard*, where my shipmates and I had gone to great lengths just to be the recipient of a nod or a smile from one of the girls. The mere presence of a few women aboard the ship was a morale lifter, as that meant that there was a chance, however slight, for a romantic interlude during those lonely nights on the high seas.

Gloria gave my thigh a little slap.

"All right, Mr. Smarty-pants," she began, "Maybe I don't know how much a single drink costs, but it just so happens that I know the price of a case of beer."

"…Umm … four dollars? That's a dollar a six-pack," I said hopefully.

"Hah! You're off by four dollars."

"What? Eight dollars? That's no bargain. You can get a case of beer in Florida for that price!"

"Who said eight dollars?" She was taking great delight in one-upping me. "I just said you were off by four."

Turned out she wasn't kidding. Ascension Island certainly must have already ranked in the top ten of the most-alcoholics-per-capita list, yet the base's morale committee still decided that one way to boost the residents' lust for life was to supply free beer to anyone throwing a party. Well, to be precise, the beer wasn't for any *one*, but for any *four*. The saying goes that "two's company and three's a crowd," which may be true under certain circumstances, but by Volcano Club standards at least, four's always a party. The proof of that was in the little slips of paper the club printed up to track the requests. They read simply, "We confirm that we are having a party," and underneath were four lines for signatures.

As I tried to wrap my brain around the staggering concept of free room, free board, and *free beer*, a truck pulled up to our barracks, delivering my luggage. At last I could change my clothes. The driver and I unloaded my bags and followed Gloria to our room. Actually, my wife pointed out, the room wasn't "ours," but "hers." As an employee with some seniority (albeit only six months), she was entitled to a private room. New arrivals on the island had bunkmates until other rooms became available. Officially, I was to share a room at the end of the hall with a mechanic named Charlie, but I didn't even bother to see if he was in; my toothbrush would be going in Gloria's bathroom, not his.

Gloria's room was surprisingly spacious, especially when compared to the cramped quarters we had shared on the *Vanguard*. It was a simple room, with only a coat of cream-colored paint to cover the concrete block walls and nothing at all to cover the dark linoleum-tiled floor. The standard furnishings were a pair of vinyl-covered easy chairs, two Formica-topped end tables, and two single beds Gloria had pushed together and covered with a double-sized bedspread.

The room had a familiar sweet, spicy aroma lingering in the air and I quickly spied the source; a half-dozen scented candles that lined one shelf of a snap-together bookcase. The other shelves supported our stereo, our record collection, and a number of pictures and other knickknacks.

Opposite the bookcase, a large refrigerator hid the wall between two walk-in closets. The refrigerator came as a surprise. Since all meals came free of charge from the mess hall, the barracks rooms hadn't been designed as efficiency apartments. Nevertheless, base officials had considered the convenience a morale lifter and wisely included refrigerators in every room.

I naturally checked the contents of the refrigerator, as well as the two closets. Then, before Gloria could stop me, I opened a third door and walked into the bathroom, surprising our next-door neighbor as she washed her face. My wife and I had already corresponded concerning this petite, young technician and her petite, young boyfriend who had transferred together from another tracking station. After reading Gloria's descriptions of the couple and the news that, unmarried, they had easily obtained passage to the island while my wife and I had continued to wait and fret, a wave of non-benevolence overcame me and in my next letter, I referred to the couple as Mouse and Twerp. Gloria had quickly set me straight, though, as she was good friends with her neighbor and intended to remain so.

Thus, the natural embarrassment I felt at barging in on our bathroom-mate was topped off with a touch of shame as I remembered the nickname I had unfairly attached to her. Besides, I quickly saw that Gloria's friend was no Mouse.

Despite her surprise, No Mouse greeted me warmly, welcoming me to the island, the barracks, and even the bathroom, before leaving so I could take a shower. I locked the door behind her to prevent any more surprises.

A few minutes under the hot spray rejuvenated me, no small trick considering my internal clock was tolling 7:00 AM after a sleepless night aboard the cargo plane. The shower's high pressure was a pleasant surprise; I had half-expected the plumbers on the parched island to demand that all occupants take sponge baths.

Happy to be rid of the smell of dried sweat, I put on a fresh set of clothes and took a minute to adjust my watch. It was a black, waterproof diver's watch that I had bought in Florida in anticipation of all the time I was going to spend underwater. I spun the dial, leaving Eastern Daylight Time in favor of Greenwich Mean Time. I would never have to change hours again as long as I remained on Ascension; that close to the equator, the islanders had no need for Daylight Saving Time.

Adjusting my watch showed me that the local lunch hour was at hand, which didn't confuse my stomach's timer at all. I didn't care whether it was breakfast time or lunch time; it was simply time to eat. Gloria and I left for the mess hall to sit down for our first meal together in our new home.

Outside, the morning overcast was almost completely burned off, leaving only a few puffy white clouds that hung low over the center of the island, marking the unseen crown of Green Mountain. Early explorers often noted that Ascension appeared completely devoid of the color green. This was a reasonable observation, as prior to the British attempts to farm the island the only plant life was a small fringe atop the highest mountain, where the perpetual clouds hid the greenery while providing the moisture the plants needed.

From the American base, our view of Green Mountain was obstructed by South West Bay Red Hill, a mouthful of a name that was necessary to distinguish this four-hundred foot red cone from all the other red cones on the island. The harsh environment of this old volcano was apparently too much even for the hardy little breed of cactus I had seen near the airport. Thus, the scenery during our walk to the mess hall was limited to this steep, red incline to our west, and the black cinder "lawn" and white concrete block buildings to the north, south, and east. There was not a single spot of green in sight.

It was this casual walk through a stark, alien landscape that convinced me that we had finally realized our six-month dream. Back when we worked on the ship, Gloria and I had walked together to the mess hall a thousand times. Passing through the shadows cast by the ship's superstructure and satellite dish antennas was as familiar a journey to us as the trip most people make from their bedroom to their dining room. On Ascension, however, the new scenery was a radical change from the obstacles on the ship's deck and alerted me to the reality of our situation; we were embarking together on a new and exciting adventure. Overcome by happiness, I reached for my wife's hand.

She quickly pulled away. Seeing the shocked, hurt look on my face, she attempted an apology.

"I'm sorry," she whispered. "I just don't think we should."

Something was very wrong here. In the past, our time together had always been accompanied by plenty of touching, whether that meant holding hands, hugging, or just sitting side-by-side and massaging each other's knees. The one exception had been during our *Vanguard* courtship; we both felt that the entire ship was so tightly associated with the word "work" that holding hands on the main deck or in the movie room would have been just as gauche as necking on Gloria's communications console. On board, we had limited our young-couple-in-love act to the privacy of our staterooms.

But Ascension circumstances were quite different, with the station separated from the barracks by a good twenty minute drive. Then, of course, there was that little slip of paper called a marriage license, which in many countries entitles the bearers to indulge in any number of conjugal activities. So what was the problem? What could be more natural than a husband and wife holding hands as they walked to lunch?

Something told me this was not the time to press the issue. I was, after all, on Gloria's turf; it would be wise to follow her lead whether I liked it or not. At this point, I didn't like it.

We covered the remaining fifty steps to the mess hall in silence. There, we picked up our trays and went quickly through the cafeteria-style serving line. Although we had a good selection of dishes from which to choose, the food reminded me of the food we had been served on the *Vanguard*, that is, unremarkable. One giveaway was the mess hall's smell, or rather, its lack of one. On the other hand, the operation resembled that of the *Vanguard* in one other very important category; there was no cash register in sight.

The number of diners filling the tables was a surprise. I had seen very little activity around the base and assumed that all the inhabitants were working, but of course only the day shift personnel were away at the site. Correction: Sites. NASA didn't have a monopoly on the island. The Radio Corporation of America (RCA) ran a tracking station for the Department of Defense, and the US Air Force supported a small contingent of airmen to run yet a third facility. A division of Pan American World Airways also had a stake in Ascension; Pan Am workers maintained the base.

The mess hall contained representatives of one other group of individuals who, in general, were easily distinguishable from all the rest. The British had recruited and imported this group from their overseas territory of St Helena which, at a distance of 800 miles, was Ascension's closest neighbor. Upon their arrival at Ascension, these subjects of the Crown were dubbed "Saints," a sobriquet that fit in nicely with those nicknames already held by the two other major players on the island, the "Brits" and the "Yanks."

Saints possess an astonishing variation in physical features that they owe to their island's position and its natural resources. In the days when ships regularly sailed around Africa's Cape of Good Hope, St Helena was a common rest stop and naturally, the European, African, and Indian crew members fraternized with the locals. The average coloration that resulted from these international liaisons is black hair, brown eyes, and darkish, deeply-tanned skin, but there are representatives of both ends of the spectrum.

As I followed my wife to an empty table, I became aware of the attention she gathered from Yanks and Saints alike as she walked through the room. The motion of heads turning her way was as smooth as the trail a breeze makes when it crosses a wheat field, bending the stalks as it sails by. I would eventually learn to get used to this phenomenon, as the same thing happened wherever Gloria went. Almost everyone she passed would smile or nod. The rest just stared. No one ignored her.

After lunch, fatigue finally got the best of me. Gloria caught a ride to the site to work the remainder of her shift and I went back to the room for some sleep. When I awoke, it was after eight o'clock and the sun was gone. I was disappointed at not being able to see more of the island on my first day, especially the beaches, but Gloria suggested we could spend the evening hours in the Volcano Club, meeting my coworkers.

During our two-minute walk to the bar, I marveled at how conveniently the base was laid out. Although it was the same base Gloria and I had toured that morning, I had been concentrating on committing the layout to memory, not admiring the community planning. I was beginning to feel that, except for the scenery, the base was a little like a vacation resort, where all the facilities a person needed were within a very small radius.

The Devil's Ashpit

The proximity of the bar especially delighted me, not because I was that much of a booze hound, but because our last hardship assignment had been the *Vanguard* and alcohol hadn't been allowed on board. Of course, our little version of Prohibition had caused drinking to become much more attractive than ever and as a result, my shipmates and I labored to keep a huge stock of liquor on board. Feeling like teenagers smuggling girlie magazines into their bedrooms, we salty dogs sneaked our bottles aboard in laundry bags and boxes of souvenirs.

Such shenanigans clearly would not be required on Ascension. With the Volcano Club right across the street from the barracks, there was a steady stream of pedestrian traffic flowing through its doors. And not only did the bar stay open to accommodate the workers on each of the three shifts, it sold its wares at ridiculously low prices.

In the Florida saloons I had just left, patrons were grousing that the price of beer had hit a dollar a can. At the Volcano Club bar, a dollar bought four beers. Mixed drinks cost ten cents more, but the bartenders were so liberal with the alcohol that even the weakest drink had a double helping of liquor. Gloria remarked that the bartenders' efforts to please the girls often resulted in mixed drinks that were so heavily laden with the hard stuff that they were undrinkable.

Inside the club, I noticed immediately that the place was cut from the same mold as half of the no-frills bars in the States. There were no pretentious brass railings or etched windows to distract the drinker; just a wide, clean bar and comfortable-looking barstools. A maze of tables effectively blocked access to a small dance floor and an equally small corner stage. The stage was empty, but a jukebox filled the room with the high-fidelity harmonies of the Starland Vocal Band singing their hit, "Afternoon Delight." Lights shone only in the bar area, where they illuminated the rows of liquor bottles, causing the glass to shine like the contents of a jewelry display case while highlighting the famous labels.

The only missing ingredient, conspicuous by its absence, was a television. By stateside standards, ten television sets should have been hanging from the walls and ceiling, bombarding patrons with five channels of sports events. Instead, the Volcano Club's wood-paneled walls held only a variety of aerospace memorabilia—faded pictures and plaques supplied by NASA, the Air Force, and the island's defense contractors.

The Volcano Club was proof that a bar could not only exist but thrive without a television. The question of a cigarette machine, however, was another matter. Although half the bar's regulars had stepped outside to watch the evening movie, the remainder all appeared to be in one of the stages of lighting, inhaling, nursing, or stubbing out cigarettes. Plumes of smoke rose from fifty ashtrays, curling upward to join the cloud already clinging to the ceiling.

If I wanted to live on Ascension, I learned, I would have to get used to smoke, ashtrays, and smelly clothes. Cigarettes on the base were just as cheap as alcohol, and the attractive price helped offset any health concerns the bored residents may have entertained.

Mindful of the hovering cloud, Gloria and I chose a table next to an open window and we had just pulled our chairs out when a young Saint in a white shirt and bright green vest materialized, holding a drink in his hand. A small earring sparkled from one ear.

"Here your drink be, Gloria," he said. His speech was quick and high-pitched, as if he had recorded the sentence at 33 $^{1/3}$ RPM and played it back at 45. He solicitously wiped off my wife's already spotless corner of the table, placed a coaster in front of her, and presented her with what I knew was her favorite drink, a rum and coke with a wedge of lime on the rim. I noticed a napkin had been carefully wrapped around the glass.

Gloria introduced the Saint as Topper, the only bartender to heed the girls' pleas for drinks with less joy juice than mixer. While Topper left to get me a beer, Gloria admitted that a few small gifts may have gone a long way to helping Topper remember the preferred formula for Cuba Libres.

"Did you see his earring?" she asked. "When he comes back, see if you recognize it."

Gloria had lost a few earrings in the past six months and since an unmatched earring didn't do her much good, she decided to place her orphans somewhere where they would. Judging by Topper's devoted service and his attention to detail, her investment appeared to be a wise one, a point made abundantly clear when he returned with my can of beer and plopped it down in front of me, jarring it so hard a fountain of foam began to belch out the top. I wondered if I had something with which I could buy Topper's good humor, and considered the set of earrings I had brought for Gloria as a homecoming gift.

After asking my wife if there was anything else he could do for her, Topper told her that someone else had paid for our drinks. He then returned to his station behind the bar.

For the next two hours, visitors and drinks magically appeared at our table. I gave warm welcomes to a number of the friends-to-be, thinking I would be seeing them at the tracking station the next day. I soon began to notice a trend, however, in that once the well-wishers had said hello, they would turn immediately to Gloria and begin talking exclusively to her. During the subsequent conversations, it became evident that Gloria didn't know these party crashers. They were just lonely lechers desperate for a woman's company.

This was apparently nothing new to Gloria, and she handled each intruder the same way, making a minute's worth of polite small-talk as she gauged the man's alcohol consumption. Without fail, it seemed, her admirers were only a breathalyzer away from what in the States would be a night in the drunk tank. Gloria would then pointedly ignore the inebriate, who would watch us a few minutes more before shuffling back to a bar stool.

During one brief respite, Gloria confided that she hated acting rude to all of these people. But the alternative was worse; a girl who didn't mark off some territory and send out signals saying "keep your distance" was quickly overwhelmed by the sheer weight of numbers. This undesired attention was the main reason why Gloria seldom visited the Volcano Club; when she wanted to socialize, she would visit a girlfriend or an old shipmate in the barracks.

Just then, yet another party crasher sat down, spilling some beer on me in the process. This gent was approaching middle-age, as evidenced by his shining pate and a short, graying, beard. I was just about to experiment with a more direct appeal for solitude when the intruder asked me the names of all the other tracking stations where I had worked. I knew then that he was one of the Bendix troops.

At some point in the history of the tracking station network, Bendix had recognized that the type of worker that seemed to be attracted to the stations couldn't sit still for more than a year or two; no matter where they were, technicians began to find reasons to believe that life at one of the other sites was more appealing.

The company cooperated. By paying relocation expenses every few years, Bendix was able to simultaneously satisfy its employees and its NASA customer; workers remained in the network and the tracking stations continued to be manned by skilled, experienced people. The resulting workforce was a rather odd fraternity of cosmopolitan, blue-collar workers. These were people who, for the most part, held minimal post-high school credentials, yet had traveled to the ends of the earth and personally sampled many cultures and customs.

My fraternity brother introduced himself as Wayne Bibb, a globe-trotting technician who had decided that he could best serve his wife and kids by spending a few tax-free years on Ascension. As with any first meeting between two station-hoppers, our conversation centered on searching each other's network history for familiar names.

"What's Miles Komora doing now?" Wayne asked, "I knew him in Madrid."

"Don't know," I replied. "He was on the *Vanguard*'s last cruise, but I don't think he even bothered to put in a transfer request at the end of the trip. How about Paul Fee? I heard he went to Madrid, too."

"Oh yeah, I worked with Fee in the Canary Islands, but then I think he went to Guam. Do you know Steve Huff?"

I shook my head at what turned out to be the first of a string of unfamiliar names we fired back and forth across the table.

"Chris Weigel?"

"Short black guy?"

"Nope. Tall white guy. How about Paul Fratto?"

"Don't think so. Paul Nguyen?"

"Uh-uh. Debbie Borden?"

"Negatory. José Hernández?"

Wayne's face brightened. "Oh yeah, the Hoser. I hear he's on his way to Alaska. *¡Coño!* That's a long way from Cuba! Umm…how about Tom Laws or Mike Bruce?"

And so the mutual interrogation continued. Ten minutes later, we were old familiar friends. It was then that Wayne went strangely silent for a moment. I could tell he was struggling with himself, trying to make up his mind whether or not to share something with me. Apparently, I passed whatever test he had given me because he suddenly leaned forward and with a tentative smile, began to whisper conspiratorially.

"You know, Dan, we've had a joke around here ever since we heard that you were coming to Ascension. We'd tell someone, 'Hey, buddy! You better watch out, 'cause Gloria's husband's coming to town!'"

I could understand why Wayne had to think twice before passing on this bit of information with its message of implied infidelity. However, he wasn't done.

"Then today, once we had confirmation that you had arrived, we switched the joke to, 'Hey buddy! Gloria's husband's here, and he's looking for you.' Then the other guy would go, 'What? Why's he looking for me?' and we'd go, 'Well, I had to give him *somebody's* name!'"

Wayne saw the polite smile on my face, and thus encouraged, laughed uproariously at his zany antics.

"The best thing, though," he said after catching his breath, "is that we were telling the joke without ever seeing you. Then, when we found out you were such a big son-of-a-bitch, that made the joke even better!"

Wayne obviously figured I was a good-natured son-of-a-bitch, too, or he wouldn't have told me about this joke that the station shared at my wife's expense. Actually, I wasn't so much good-natured as I was understanding. Ten years before, my first full-time job had put me beside bricklayers who greeted each other every morning with a cheery, "How's your wife and my kids?"

Since then, I had spent my share of time in the company of men desperate for the company of a woman. Something in the hormones causes us to revert to the mentalities we had as sixteen-year-olds, when we heard and eagerly believed totally unfounded stories of classmates who were

The Devil's Ashpit

supposedly donating their bodies for impromptu sex education classes in the school parking lot. As we matured, the claims were not as extravagant, but no less titillating, as in,

"You know Patty Preston? Man, I'd love to do her."

"She's married, isn't she?"

"Yeah, but I heard that don't matter."

Wayne's story was also a continuation of the stories that had spread throughout the network a few years before, when Bendix had allowed girls to work on the *Vanguard* for the first time. No sooner had the company newspaper printed an article about women working on a ship than rumors began circulating of a highly profitable floating brothel. The entire ship's company knew better, but any of our shipmates who passed through Bendix headquarters or another tracking station never failed to return with fresh stories they had picked up involving ten-minute romances aboard the good ship *Vanguard*.

Wayne must have seen my thoughts reflected in my face, as he suddenly cut short his paroxysm of laughter, wiped his eyes, and leaned forward once again.

"I think you should know, Dan," he said seriously, "that Gloria was a perfectly-behaved young lady while she waited for you." He reflected for a moment. "Gee, maybe I should have said that first."

I assured Wayne that I hadn't taken offense. Although his humor was a bit crude, I knew he wouldn't have told me the story if he had had the slightest suspicion that he might be giving something away. Visibly relieved, Wayne excused himself and ambled off to the restroom.

While Wayne and I had been trading network stories, Gloria had been talking to another Bendix employee, a young man our age whose mop of sandy brown hair was almost shockingly thick, especially considering that I'd just spent the last half-hour sitting opposite Wayne's high and dry forehead.

This was Randy May, and when Gloria introduced us, he shook my hand with an eagerness I attributed to the location and the hour. I learned later, however, that Randy, or "Radar" as he liked to be called, approached most everything with the same alacrity. His wide, easy smile showed off a set of teeth that looked as though they would never need the touch of a dentist's drill. It was a smile that perfectly complemented his gregarious manner.

Radar quickly invited me to explore the mid-Atlantic marine world with him; Gloria had tipped him off that I was a diving enthusiast and would be looking for a diving buddy. I accepted, of course, and we made a date to meet on nearby Turtle Shell Beach the next day. I was ecstatic; although my last dive had been in the incomparable World War II ships' graveyard at Truk Lagoon six weeks before, it was impossible to subdue the excitement I felt at the thought of exploring a new underwater location.

I was in the midst of pumping Radar for every detail of his last spearfishing expedition when Gloria suddenly jumped out of her seat.

"Watch out!"

It was almost a scream and made me duck instinctively. A second later, she was trying to push my chair, with me in it, through our table. After knocking my sternum into the table's edge, she regained her composure and sat down again.

My heart was pounding at what had obviously been a close call. Gasping for breath, I asked Gloria what had happened.

"Somebody was trying to get by and you were blocking the aisle," she said.

I checked out the bar, looking for someone carrying a keg on his shoulder, or a tray of boiling coffee, or a grudge, or anything else equally dangerous. There was nothing out of the ordinary. Gloria had practically punctured my eardrum and knocked the breath out of me because my chair was blocking someone's path to the pisser. My heart was slowly returning to normal, but my wife's outburst had startled me into pouring a quart of adrenaline into my system.

"Don't you think you overreacted a bit?" I asked.

Apparently not. Gloria explained that she was trying to help me avoid a confrontation. She had watched the mating dances of the Ascension males for six months and had seen the bitterness that resulted when she rejected their offerings. Since I had arrived, Gloria had cause to worry that there would be some young buck horny enough, jealous enough, pissed-off enough, and drunk enough to lash out against the lucky bastard who had come in to wrap a protective arm around his girl.

But Gloria wasn't just considering the possibility that I might get my butt kicked; she was thinking about the consequences of fighting on the island. Ascension's security enforcers had a method of discouraging such behavior. They didn't call in crime scene investigators and they didn't compare the wounds. It didn't matter who had the broken jaw or who had the bruised knuckles. They simply placed all the participants on the next plane to the States. Obviously, Gloria's startling reaction had been caused by a vision of our Ascension future being whittled down to a single day.

When I applied these puzzle pieces together with Gloria's afternoon display of seemingly cold behavior, I had a fresh understanding of the hardship she had been enduring. Although this was the day her lawful wedded husband had joined her after six months of suspense, those months had been spent on Ascension Island, where she had felt compelled to suppress every word and deed that might be construed as a sexual overture. With four hundred sex-starved guys casting eight hundred hungry eyes her way, she had become ultra-cautious and withdrew into a very small shell.

Evidently, there was something about our long-awaited reunion that I had not considered; we had been separated so long under circumstances so peculiar, that to return to our previous relationship would require more than a little time, effort, and understanding. After thirteen months of marriage, I was going to have to woo my wife.

Chapter 4

Island Boy

Our evening in the Volcano Club ended without further incident and the next morning, after another price-is-right meal at the mess hall, we piled into one of the nine-passenger company vans for my first trip to the site.

During my years in the tracking station business, I had learned that NASA had gone out of their way to situate their sites in areas that were practically inaccessible to man. There was a reason for this; one byproduct of what we call civilization is an incredible number of radio waves. Some of these waves are well-behaved and limited to certain frequencies, which is why we can push buttons to tune in different AM or FM radio stations.

While we're tuning in the signal that's carrying our favorite Bach sonata, however, we are also trying our best to discourage signals from other stations. Designing a circuit capable of performing this task is relatively easy for electrical engineers. Where designers really earn their paychecks, though, is in their circuit's ability to reject the myriad of radio waves that are being generated by every spark plug, refrigerator, air conditioner, or other electric appliance in the neighborhood. Furthermore, while commercial radios are built to lock in on the signals broadcasted by powerful transmitters measuring thousands of watts, NASA's radio receivers must pick up signals from spacecraft capable of transmitting just a few watts. Electrical noise can easily interfere with such a small signal and valuable information can be lost as a result.

That said, I still thought the NASA site planners had performed their duty a little too enthusiastically when they designed the Ascension station. They observed that the island's three noise-producing settlements were all to the west of Green Mountain, Ascension's most prominent feature. There was the American base near the southwest shore, Georgetown on the northwest shore, and Two Boats, near the northwest foot of the mountain.

The simple solution was to build on the mountain's extreme eastern side. Any electrical noise that succeeded in breaching that mass would be very serious noise indeed.

On the other hand, I thought it likely that the noise output of our three puny towns was so feeble that any of the forty-three lesser volcanoes on the island could have served equally well in the capacity of a noise buffer. A station built behind one of these other cones would have been a lot more accessible than the Green Mountain site.

Nevertheless, the Green Mountain location afforded us a picturesque view of the island's southern perimeter during our daily drive. First, however, we had to get away from the base and across Donkey Plain. From there, our van climbed the saddle that linked Spoon Crater and Mountain Red Hill, from which we had a continuous view of Green Mountain's southern slopes. Down this expanse, black and gray lava grew in twisted, tortured, clumps interspersed with pools of rust-colored ash. The implied violence of these brutal slopes was abruptly softened by the rich, smooth blue of the surrounding ocean, an ocean that stretched so far that I sometimes thought I could detect a hint of the earth's curvature on the horizon.

Once past Mountain Red Hill (who named that place, anyway?) we were officially on Green Mountain's southern face and climbing steadily. It was during this part of the drive that most of us would make our closest daily approach to plant life in any abundance. Near the road, cactus and sporadic patches of a yellowish hardy weed called "greasy grass" grew nearly parallel to the ground, pushed uphill by the force of the southeast trade winds. Real vegetation flourished further up the side of the mountain, seeming to maintain a relatively constant one-hundred yard distance from the road.

The greenery seemed thickest at the mouth of Breakneck Valley, which held a stand of Norfolk pines. The giant trees stuck obtrusively out of the valley, as if planted intentionally to block access to the sheer cliffs beyond. I wasn't surprised to learn later that they had indeed been planted—not to improve the landscape, but to provide timber for ships' masts.

Just past Breakneck Valley and two-thirds of the way up the mountain's 2,817-foot peak was a break in the land, a table that jutted out from the eastern face of Green Mountain for a half-mile before plunging back down to the sea. It was not a very flat table, hosting such features as Devil's Cauldron, Power's Peak, and Cricket Valley. Still, on the lip of a massive trench called the Devil's Ashpit there was enough level ground to hold the buildings and antennas of NASA's Devil's Ashpit Tracking Station.

The Operations building, or as we called it, the Ops building, was practically identical to the one I'd seen at the Quito station, a large, white, squat matchbox trimmed in NASA blue and surrounded by a web of antennas. The latter were odd-looking devices that rode atop two-story towers and resembled giant death-ray guns from bad science fiction movies of the '50s. The names of two of these antennas in particular were just as ominous as their looks and fit in well with the hellish convention for naming landmarks on the island; these particular contraptions were referred to as the SATAN antennas, which only a few technicians knew was an acronym for Satellite Automatic Tracking ANtennas.

There was also a giant dish antenna, easily visible behind the Ops building and seemingly larger than its advertised thirty foot diameter. This was the S-band antenna and the station's bread and butter. It was part of a high-fidelity system that had provided spacecraft with command, telemetry, and voice links during the moon shots of the late '60s and early '70s.

My inspection of the grounds ended when our driver pulled up to the front steps of the Ops Building and we all piled out to relieve the midnight crew. I followed the crowd only to find that the interior of the building was completely different from its Quito counterpart. The entire front of the Ops building was devoted to office space for the NASA station director, the Bendix senior manager, a safety supervisor, and the administration office. Further down the main hallway, however, was a door through which I could plainly hear the familiar noise of hundreds of thrumming power supplies and blowers.

We walked into the din and my nose told me that the most important equipment in the tracking station was close at hand. In a second, I located it: Two coffee urns and a tray of doughnuts. Nearby, a bulletin board contained a number of yellowed posters depicting emergency exits, station policies, and the standard workers' rights notice, printed in English and Spanish.

This bulletin board was practically a twin of the one I'd seen in Quito. The one item missing was the "In Case of Volcanic Eruption" poster. Quito's NASA tracking station was built at the foot of Cotopaxi, an active volcano. I remembered the steps listed on the poster instructing us to close and lock all windows and doors and to close and lock the outside gate once all vehicles had exited the site. I also remembered feeling quite certain that a few seconds after Cotopaxi's first rumble, there would be no gate to lock since I would have commandeered the first NASA van outside the door and crashed through any and all barriers!

A second bulletin board at my new workplace contained more recently posted items and attracted much more attention. There was a notice for a pig roast to be held the next week at the Saints' Hut on Pan Am beach. Beside it was an announcement of an island-wide competition of something called Question of Arrows. Then there was a list of the upcoming professional football games tacked below the previous week's football pool results; fittingly, someone named "Coach" had walked off with the prize money.

The Devil's Ashpit

Something that made me feel right at home was the teletype machine and the looping, curling stack of yellow paper that slowly piled up against the wall. Teletypes are typewriter spin-offs that every station used in those pre-email days to print out the hundreds of messages transmitted daily by our controllers at the Goddard Space Flight Center. Similarly, we could use the same system in reverse to send station information and status reports back to Goddard. We referred to each of these messages as a *twix*, which was our way of pronouncing the acronym TWX, which stood for TeletypeWriter eXchange. Due to the sheer volume of teletype traffic, "twix" was easily the most-used word at any tracking station.

On the *Vanguard*, we had taken a spare teletype and connected it to a radio permanently tuned to a special Associated Press frequency, enabling us to read news bulletins from around the world. At my new assignment, I realized that the coffee-table teletype was serving the same purpose, although a glance at the paper scrolling off the machine told me that the Ascension system contained the same flaw as the one on the *Vanguard*; every once in a while, the teletype would confuse its "figure" and "letter" modes. This electronic hiccup always resulted in line after line of nonsense, along the order of,

"!@#$5L   %^&*&3.   >?^#$A/+   @)*2$$. $^%GG)KL   45# 99((*6$33!@,:=."

There was a quick fix for this that I'd learned one New Year's Day on the ship when a noisy AP news link kept reversing our teletype during the college football scoreboard. Luckily, a teletype technician had been on hand to reset the machine at each burp and we managed to come away with a list of the winners—essential to the managing of our own football poll.

Relieved to be faced with such a familiar chore during my first few minutes at a new station, I lifted the teletype's cover, adding the clatter of a few thousand moving parts to the noise in the room. I felt under the dancing chassis, flipped the offending lever, and closed the cover. Magically, the story in progress switched to English:

"... TO NAME THEIR NEW COLISEUM IN BILOXI AFTER THE DEAD KING.
ELVIS PRESLEY HAD PLANNED TO PERFORM AT THE NEW BEACHFRONT ARENA DURING ITS GRAND OPENING, BUT HIS SHOCKING DEATH ROBBED COAST RESIDENTS OF AN ELVIS MEMORY ..."

Ah yes, another Elvis story. I was used to that, even though a full month had elapsed since the King's untimely death. (A few weeks after my arrival,

I was surprised to find the teletype hammering out still more Elvis stories, this time in the context of comparisons between him and the just-deceased Bing Crosby. Little did I dream that decades later, Elvis would still be providing writers with a steady income.)

I turned my attention back to the bulletin board and a doctored "Doonesbury" cartoon. There, the relief I'd felt at finding something familiar in this otherwise alien environment quickly evaporated; penciled-in character names and modified dialog rendered the joke incomprehensible to outsiders and served to emphasize my status as Norman Newguy. I had the feeling it was going to be a long day.

It wasn't that long. Although I had a lot of new faces and names to remember, my duties were very similar to those I had learned at the Quito station. Furthermore, all of the equipment in the room differed from that of my previous assignment only by their serial numbers. In a sense, it was as though I had taken all of my furniture and moved it to a new house.

My job, simply put, was to send commands to spacecraft. To accomplish this, I used a computer christened with the somewhat officious-sounding appellation, "Spacecraft Command Encoder." Of course, every system and subsystem owned by NASA is known by two names, its formal designation and its acronym. Thus my computer's lengthy name was shortened to SCE (pronounced SKEE) and I was a SCE operator.

I stood at my SCE to orient myself. My immediate concern was to locate the communications (or *comm*) panel. The comm panel was essentially a telephone that allowed us to converse on any one of four lines, but at the same time, it gave us the option to listen in on the other three. With this set-up, I could, for example, keep Goddard controllers apprised of a problem on Net 1 (our "hot line" to Goddard) while simultaneously listening to in-house troubleshooting activities on any of the internal loops.

After I saw that the headset to the comm panel was within easy reach, I looked up to make sure the clock was in the same slot as it had been in Quito. The SCE's clock, like all of the clocks at all of the tracking stations, was connected to an atomic clock that was accurate to within a few microseconds of the world's standard. I would be using the clock's digital readout as my cue to press the Send button, thus issuing whatever command the spacecraft controller's schedule had me type into memory.

To eliminate time zone confusion among the worldwide tracking station network, all references to time were made as if we were all sitting in Greenwich, England. This city has been the basis for Greenwich Mean Time (or GMT) since 1884 when it was designated as the Prime Meridian (that is, zero degrees longitude). For brevity, we used Z instead of GMT (the Z standing for "zero degrees") and also used a twenty-four hour clock so we could drop the colon and the AM/PM. Thus, for example, after 1259Z our clocks rolled over to 1300Z instead of 1:00PM GMT.

The Devil's Ashpit

There were a number of these clocks placed in strategic locations around the station, and as I looked around to locate ours, I got another reminder of my new location. Each of my previous stations had a few places where a local-time clock was stacked on top of the GMT clock. Since Ascension Island permanently observed GMT, the local-time clocks were unnecessary and our station designers saved a few bucks by omitting them.

As I reacquainted myself with the SCE, the computer supervisor introduced himself. It was Coach, the winner of the football pool. Coach was in his mid-forties, but his slim build and easy stride reminded me of a younger man. From his athletic manner and his nickname, I deduced that Coach spent a lot of time outdoors. His general complexion, however, did not especially support this assumption, with the exception of his nose, which glowed with what appeared to be fresh sunburn.

While I tried to keep my eyes off Coach's nose, he gave me a few instructions concerning some station-unique procedures. Then he began to quiz me about my previous SCE experience. I could detect an underlying current of doubt, suspicion, and mistrust in Coach, which didn't surprise me in the least. All newcomers to a tracking station are subject to a breaking-in period while the coworkers size him up. On Ascension, I came to learn that the first report that a new troop was on the way was generally met with such welcoming comments as, "He's probably an asshole."

This was a rather natural reaction due to the steady influx of techs who scored "Does not work or play well with others" on their kindergarten report cards. I suppose Bendix had little choice; techs weren't exactly beating a path to the hardship areas when stations like Bermuda and Hawaii were still in the network. I imagined Bendix recruiters making little notes in the margins of their Ascension-hopefuls' applications in order to justify their stamp of approval: "Did not pick nose during interview."

Since the overall effect of working with an asshole was a negative one, the pronouncement that, "This guy's a zero," was actually a kind of promotion. It's just math. Sure, the "zero" wasn't going to contribute anything to the operation and maintenance of the station, but neither was he going to foul things up and put us behind. Net result? Zero.

This would explain Coach's comment a year later when he got the news that Steve Sypher would be joining us.

"Hmm. I wonder if he's a zero. Sounds like a zero to me," he said with a smile, pleased that the Sypher-cipher homonym fit right in with our method of prejudging.

"Now, don't forget, Coach," I countered, "A cipher can also be a secret code. I think we're still going to have to figure him out."

In my case, Coach would be doubly justified in questioning my experience. Despite my four-plus years of network experience, I didn't have anyone else on the station to vouch for me. Coach and a lot of other people were wondering if my only qualification was my marriage to Gloria.

I suddenly had a moment of *déjà vu*. I don't know if it was a word, a look or a gesture, but I saw myself talking to Coach, not on Ascension Island, but on the *Vanguard*.

"Excuse me, Coach, but were you ever on the *Vanguard*?" I asked.

Coach raised his eyebrows.

"Yes. I was there for a couple of hours back in '74. Al Docktor and I carried an atomic clock around to each tracking station to compare timing signals. How would you know that?"

"Because I was the ship's timing tech!"

Coach admitted that he didn't remember me, but then he and Al had probably met twenty timing techs in four weeks of non-stop travel. Then it was my turn to ask the questions, quizzing Coach on the details of his so-called "time travel." As we talked, I could see that I had already jumped the bottom two rungs of the "who's the new guy" ladder.

In just a few minutes, though, a Saint interrupted us and handed Coach a twix from Goddard; the UK-5 (United Kingdom-5) satellite was due to pass over our station in thirty minutes. The twix included a list of commands for the SCE operator and the time that each command was to be transmitted.

With satellite support imminent, Coach went back to questioning me about the SCE. Soon, he seemed satisfied that, while I didn't know the SCE from top to bottom, neither would I confuse its top with its bottom. Coach watched as I prepared for a satellite pass, loading the correct program into the SCE and running the pre-pass checks. When I mentioned that I had supported UK-5 from the Quito SCE and that nothing had changed in the interim, Coach ambled off, leaving me on my own.

As always, somebody in the Recorders section signaled the beginning of the pass.

"Recorders On"

Network operations procedure dictated that these giant reel-to-reel magnetic tape recorders be activated a full two minutes prior to the predicted "acquisition of signal" or AOS. Absolute silence followed this announcement, while everyone waited for the S-band techs to find the satellite's beacon and lock onto it. Then it came.

"Ascension has AOS, link one."

"Ascension has AOS, link two ... Ascension has two-way lock ... Ascension is 'Go for command', USB."

"Roger, Ascension," came the very British-accented reply from UK-5 Control, "We see your data."

At this point, the S-band receivers were extracting the UK-5 satellite's data stream from the carrier wave (much like a commercial FM radio). The

The Devil's Ashpit

S-band equipment fed this stream of 1's and 0's to the Telemetry section to clean it up and make sense of it (figuring out the byte and word boundaries) before sending it to the Computer section. The site computer rearranged these words into a stream that could be transmitted to satellite controllers at speeds up to 2,400 bits per second. In just a few years, this transmission rate would be considered laughably slow, but in 1977 we considered it blazingly fast, especially since the alternative was to pile all of our magnetic tapes into the belly of the next plane leaving the island.

Satellite controllers generally waited a bit to let the satellite rise a few more degrees above the horizon. This tactic allowed their low-wattage transmitters to get closer to our S-band dish with less atmosphere to muddle the signal. This gave me plenty of time to type in my first command. I watched the station clock and when it matched the time on the twix, I pressed the Send button.

"Command 202 uplink complete," I announced.

The first command to any satellite was generally an order to stop recording and set up for playback. The second command usually initiated the playback.

"Command 205 uplink complete."

"Roger, Ascension, we see your playback."

The satellite began downloading the data it had been designed to gather. The mission of UK-5, for example, was to hone in on x-ray emitting stars and to measure their energy spectra.

I could only imagine the difficulty involved in keeping track of the data these satellites delivered—never mind interpreting it! Someone, somewhere, was calculating the satellite's orbit and determining which tracking stations would be able to see the satellite and for how long. Since we generally supported satellites passes that lasted as little as one minute or as many as ten minutes, that Someone had to continuously estimate how much of their on-board recording could be downlinked versus how much still remained to be downlinked, versus how much room was available for more recording. It was a juggling act that I did not envy.

Meanwhile, I typed in my next command, double-checked the twix to make sure I had the time right, and waited. I assumed this command would tell the spacecraft to stop the playback. As I had done a thousand times in the last year, I pressed and held down the Send button two seconds before the time printed on the twix. In two seconds, I would let go of the button, issuing the command.

"Ascension, UK-5; stand by on that next command."

Oh shit.

"Roger, UK-5," I managed, "Standing by."

I stood there like the little Dutch boy, wondering if my finger was all that stood between life and death for the UK-5 mission. How would I abort a command that's already in the Send buffer? Could I pull the patch cord that sent my commands to the S-band transmitter? Could I reach the patch cord and still keep firm pressure on the Send button? Was my finger starting to tremble? Luckily, my anxiety was brief.

"Ascension, UK-5; you can issue that command now and follow up with the 212 command as soon as you're ready."

"208 uplink complete," I gasped, unaware that I'd been holding my breath. I quickly finished the job by issuing the 212 command. Apparently, all was well. UK-5 Control confirmed the commands and a few seconds later, we announced "loss of signal" as the satellite went over the horizon.

"UK-5, Ascension; we have LOS, all links"

"Roger, Ascension, thank you for your support."

Thus ended my first satellite support at my new job. I printed out the post-pass command summary and loaded the SCE for our next support, the third Small Astronomy Satellite—hence, SAS-3.

Just as I finished, the PA system crackled to life, announcing that lunch was ready. Since SAS-3 AOS wouldn't be for another hour, we emptied the building through a side door and took a dozen steps to the lunch room, which, with its own blue and white matchbox motif, looked like a miniature version of the Ops building. A sign above the door, however, eliminated any possibility of confusion, as it informed visitors to the NASA Devil's Ashpit Tracking Station that they were about to enter the Devil's Hashpit.

The Hashpit was much smaller than the base mess hall, but its interior suffered from the same Spartan decor. Government-issue tables and chairs occupied the dining area, which was separated from the kitchen by a row of warming trays and a professionally-lettered sign declaring, "KITCHEN PERSONEL ONLY." Someone had scrawled in the delinquent 'N', but had written it backwards, bestowing a forgiving childish charm to what had been a careless error.

A couple of Saints in white hats and uniforms hovered over the warming trays, casually rearranging their contents for better heat distribution, better esthetic appearance, or maybe just for want of something better to do. The servers chatted amiably with the diners, but their quickly-delivered Brit-like patois was largely incomprehensible to my inexperienced ears.

Standing in line with Gloria, my nose tingled from the sharp, delicious aroma of onions frying in butter. When we reached the food, however, there was nothing in the trays to compete with the onion scent. Even more discouraging was the food's appearance; not only were our entrées apparently odorless, but the warming trays had drained them of any vivid color they may have once had. Meats looked like they had been cut from sick animals, vegetables like they had been salvaged from a mulch pile.

The kitchen, it turned out, was pretty much a sham. All of our meals were prepared by the base mess hall a few hours beforehand, then loaded into one of the NASA vans for delivery to the Hashpit, where the "cooks" reheated each tray. This procedure placed all Hashpit meals into the same category as leftovers. The one exception was breakfast fare, which the Saints whipped up on the spot and, incidentally, explained the fried onion smell; one of my coworkers had ordered an omelet.

I followed suit and was surprised by Gloria's smile.

"You won't be doing that once you switch to mids," she warned me as a beaming Saint carefully added a pile of dark, soggy green beans to the dry cut of roast beef on her plate. Then she picked up a glass of iced tea and walked off to find a table while I waited for my omelet.

A moment later, I followed, eager to dive into the mound of fried onions, green peppers, and mushrooms that garnished the eggs on my plate. I also wanted to find out what Gloria had meant by her last remark. What did midnight shift have to do with eating omelets?

I forgot my question when I saw where Gloria was sitting; we'd be sharing our table with the operations supervisor.

Each of the shifts had an "Ops," as we called them, who monitored the station's preparations for each satellite pass and served as the verbal connection between our station and the satellite controllers in the real world. Monitoring the operations from his centrally-located console, the Ops was in the hot seat; he was the one who matched wits with the honchos at Goddard whenever a local equipment failure or, heaven forbid, an operator error resulted in a loss of spacecraft data.

Most all of the operations supervisors I had known in my tracking station experience had shared the same traits. For one thing, they were all intelligent. Secondly, they were self-confident, an understandable development for anyone so experienced in tracking station operations that they could field strip and reassemble one of the sites on a day's notice. Lastly, most of the Ops I knew acted aloof, imperious, or a combination of both, and deigned to speak to us underlings only in the line of duty. Thus, when I placed my tray beside Gloria's and across from the Ops, I was prepared to eat my lunch in an uncomfortable silence.

I had seen our luncheon companion in action that morning and had even talked to him a couple of times, delivering a terse, "SCE, go!" over the station intercom to let him know my computer was loaded and ready to send commands. Despite his equally brief dialog with my coworkers and the Goddard controllers, I had detected what I thought was a New Jersey intonation in his speech. This sound track accentuated his already acute resemblance to another Jersey native—a fortyish Frank Sinatra.

"Dan, this is Tom McWilliams. I think you two are really going to hit it off," my wife gushed.

It was only at that moment that I realized that our Ops was one of the people Gloria had described in her letters to me over the past six months. None of her letters, however, had ever contained an anecdote, a short quote, or any other clue into Tom's character, just the blithe assurance that he and I were "really going to hit it off."

Of course, Gloria's confident pronouncement had the deadly potential to dampen even the liveliest of conversationalists. It was as if Tom and I had suddenly been pushed on stage together to sweat in front of an audience who was anticipating a riotous flood of jokes, impressions, and witty repartee. Anything less than a spectacular performance would be viewed as a failure. In that respect, a quiet meal with an aloof and imperious supervisor began to look pretty good.

As Gloria leaned forward in her chair to catch our act, I cleared my throat.

"Hi, Tom."

(Sorry ladies and gentlemen, the show for tonight has been canceled. Please consult your ticket agent concerning a refund.)

Before Gloria could show her disappointment, however, Tom rescued the skit.

"Gloria says you went to the Volcano Club last night."

While I nodded my head, Tom continued.

"I'll bet you didn't hear this song," he said, and began singing:

> "In 1814, we took a little trip,
> Along with Colonel Jackson,
> Down the mighty Mississipp.
> We took a little bacon,
> And we took a little beans,
> And we caught the bloody British,
> In the town of New Orleans."

Smiling, I admitted I hadn't heard Johnny Horton's "The Battle of New Orleans" during our time at the club the previous night.

"Well, you're not likely to," Tom said, sticking a toothpick in his mouth. "The base commander had it taken off the juke box."

What? I loved that song since the first time I'd heard it. What ten-year-old wouldn't be impressed by such lyrics as

> "We fired our cannon
> Till the barrel melted down,
> So we grabbed an alligator
> And we fought another round.
> We stuffed his head with cannonballs

> And powdered his behind,
> And when we touched the powder off
> The gator lost his mind."

For me, the number had become an instant classic. So what did the Air Force base commander have against my song?

"I think it all started because someone got pissed-off at the Brits," Tom said, toying with his toothpick. "See, the Brits run a couple of clubs of their own, but we colonials can only get in by special invitation."

"On the other hand," he continued, "The Volcano Club is open to anyone who can drag himself through the door. The Queen Mum's finest often come up to the base to scarf down some American booze at American prices."

"One night, when a couple of the more popular Brits had bar-hopped their way to the club—actually, they don't call it bar-hopping, they call it pub-crawling—someone got the bright idea to punch up B-12, Battle of New Orleans."

I cringed, suddenly realizing that the Brits would probably not share our amusement at a song that celebrated their drubbing at the conclusion of the War of 1812. I was shocked at my countrymen's audacity, but also delighted and eager to hear more; I had always marveled at the mischievous exploits of the bad kid down the street who did things I'd have liked to have done if I had had the nerve.

Tom rolled his toothpick over to the other side of his mouth.

"There could have been an ugly scene, but these Brits were good-natured enough, or smart enough, or drunk enough, not to raise a ruckus. We all had a good time."

"After that, any time a Brit walked through the door, someone would yell out, 'We need a shot of B-12!' and the scene would repeat itself."

"One night, though, a different crowd came up from Georgetown and got the treatment. They didn't care for it and said so before heading for the door."

"But it was just before the last verse. Incredibly bad timing. The whole bar started to sing along."

I nodded. Of course I knew the words:

> "Yeah, they ran through the briars,
> And they ran through the brambles,
> And they ran through the bushes,
> Where a rabbit couldn't go.
> They ran so fast,
> That the hounds couldn't catch 'em,
> Down the Mississippi to the Gulf of Mexico."

"The Brits lodged a complaint with the base commander, whose justice was swift and sure. The next night, anyone wanting a shot of B-12 was treated to a Barry Manilow song."

At the conclusion of Tom's story, I decided that my wife had been right; Tom and I were going to hit it off, especially if all he needed was a straight man.

At the end of our lunch break, we all filed out of the Hashpit to return to work. Four hours later, the swing shift trickled in to relieve us. We briefed our replacements on the health of our equipment, reviewed the upcoming support schedule with them, then took their places in the vans to return to the base.

Coach followed Gloria and me into the van and as soon as we sat down, he nudged me.

"I forgot to tell you," he said. "During your first UK-5 pass, the assistant station manager must have heard you on the loop. He came running into the room and asked me why the hell 'that guy' is sending commands. I said, 'Well, I guess UK-5 Control asked him to.' He gave me a blank look for a couple of seconds and then said, 'Oh,' and walked out. I don't know what his problem was."

Then Coach paused and reflected a bit. "Make that *is*", he said. "I don't know what his problem *is*. Anyway, it's a good thing you didn't screw up."

"Agreed," I said, although I wondered whether Coach had watered down the exchange for my benefit. When I was sending those commands that morning, I still had that 'new guy smell' on me, so it was much more likely that Mr. Assistant Station Manager had asked him why the hell 'that asshole' was sending commands. Coach's confidence in me that morning served as a virtual air freshener hanging from my neck. I've always appreciated that gesture.

As soon as we pulled up to the barracks, Gloria and I raced to our room, where we traded our jeans for cut-offs and prepared for the beach. I had not seen Radar all day and I was hoping that he had not forgotten our date. With my mask, fins, booties, and inflatable vest stuffed into a laundry bag, we hurried to the parking lot. I had worried needlessly; Radar was waiting for us, his equipment already loaded in our van.

My first clear view of Ascension beaches came from the cliff on the westernmost lip of the base that guarded a rough crescent of coastal real estate two-hundred feet below. Turtle Shell, our destination, was one of three stretches of golden sand scalloped into this crescent, nestled between impossibly craggy, black, lava walls that seemed to have erupted right at the water's edge. An endless train of waves arose from the blue, shimmering sea beyond and repeatedly smashed against the lava, sending fountains of pure white spray skyward, each pattern different from the last.

The view was astonishingly pretty, despite the complete absence of vegetation—the palm trees, broadleaf plants, and other greenery one always expects to see in an island beach scene. I knew immediately that Gloria and I would be spending much of our free time on the beach.

There was something very odd about the sand, however. The entire beach above the waterline was pockmarked with what appeared to be hundreds of bomb craters. A number of treadmarks was also visible, as if a fleet of tanks or half-tracks had been patrolling the water's edge. What had happened here? Was there a military presence on the island that I didn't know about, shelling the beach and digging it up with landing craft?

Not at all, Gloria explained. The only assaults on the beach had been made by egg-laying turtles. These were no ordinary turtles, however. Ascension served as the birthing grounds for giant green turtles weighing five hundred pounds. The shell holes were the evidence of these jumbos' nest excavations and the treadmarks were the tracks left by their flippers.

The asphalt in front of me suddenly dipped and I saw I would have to wrestle the van down a steep series of curves before pulling onto the straight, level road that ran parallel to the beach. The van's steering brought us to the brink with every turn, but we made it to the bottom intact.

Once I straightened out the wheel, I saw something on the side of the road that made me snort with laughter.

A fifty-gallon oil drum had been converted into a planter, its dirt hosting a scrawny, gnarly, undernourished pine tree. Hardly more than a six-foot stick, a dozen dusty pine needles drooped from each desiccated branch. If this lone roadside sentry was someone's attempt to cultivate the island, their effort surely suffered from the most absurd results.

As we passed the tree, Radar snickered, too.

"You are now leaving Ascension National Forest," he said.

A minute later, I was parked on a slight rise overlooking Turtle Shell. The islanders had taken advantage of this scenic spot and had turned it into a rustic picnic area. A tin-roof shelter protected a couple of picnic tables and a concrete block barbecue grill. Because of the party area's convenient location, I expected to see the litter of previous festivities strewn around the beach, but this was not the case; the only adornment to the shelter's concrete floor was a thin layer of wind-blown sand. Even the nearby oil drum trashcan was empty. The site's cleanliness was a welcome change from the beer cans, broken glass, and most astoundingly, dirty diapers I had seen on Florida's public beaches.

Radar jumped out of the van and started rummaging through his gear. I hesitated before reaching for my bag; the craters on the beach in front of me were really huge. Furthermore, although the area encompassed by Turtle Shell was about the size of a football field, there was barely a square foot of sand that remained on the horizontal plane. There were craters inside of craters. The place looked like No Man's Land.

"Radar, what do we do if we run into one of those monster turtles while we're in the water?"

"The turtles don't come close to shore until nighttime, so we probably won't see one," he said, fiddling with the strap on his mask. "If we do see any, the females are real shy and will swim away."

"The females are shy?" I asked, "So you're implying that the males are *not* shy, aren't you?"

Radar was satisfied with his strap and looked up at me. "Don't worry," he grinned, "I already asked the turtle lady about that."

The turtle lady, I knew, was an attractive young Yank named Jeannie who was on the island studying turtles and pursuing a doctoral degree.

"She said the only thing we had to worry about with the bulls is that they might want to mate with us."

I couldn't believe my ears.

"Radar, a horny bull turtle sounds like a serious worry!"

"Yeah, I told Jeannie I wasn't too comfortable with that," he said, pulling his fins out of his bag. "But they don't call her the turtle lady for nothin'. She said if one of those bad boys started closing in, all we had to do was give him the sign the females use for rejection."

"Which is?"

Radar dropped his fins and jumped into a spread-eagle position, his arms and legs spread wide. It was the exaggerated pose of the human female's equivalent for, "Take me, I'm yours" and I briefly wondered if Jeannie had modeled it for him.

"And you were reassured by this advice?" I asked.

"Sure," he replied, his grin losing some of its brilliance. "You see something wrong with it?"

"Two things. First, you'll notice that while standing like that, you're making no effort to block any openings the bull might care to fill."

"Maybe worse," I continued, "What if the turtle lady's right and it is the sign of rejection? What are we going to do with five hundred pounds of pissed-off turtle? Looks like we're screwed either way, if you know what I mean."

Radar laughed and used one of his outstretched arms to slap me on the back.

"Can't knock it till you've tried it, buddy. Let's get wet."

Despite my misgivings, I followed Radar to Turtle Shell's main attraction, a short line of rocks that acted as a jetty, protecting a portion of the beach from the direct onslaught of the waves. Gloria, who had no desire to see the Ascension underwater world, told us to be careful and went off to explore the turtle holes.

The Devil's Ashpit

At the water's edge, Radar handed me one of the two pole spears he had brought, long slender aluminum shafts with a loop of rubber tubing on one end and a trio of barbs on the business end. He showed me how they worked; when I wanted to shoot a fish, I would hook my thumb through the loop and stretch it four or five feet before anchoring it by wrapping my fingers around the pole. That armed the spear. All I had to do then was point it in the right direction and relax my grip.

Conveniently ignoring the odds that my flimsy pole could stave off an attack by a five-hundred pound turtle, my jangling nerves began to calm down. With thoughts of grouper fillets filling my head, I donned my mask and fins and when Radar was ready, we awkwardly pushed off into the water. Floating in only three feet of refreshingly cool water, I slowly beat my flippers to overcome the push of the small waves that washed the shoreline. Meanwhile, I was blind; my lens had fogged over as soon as it touched the water. With my free hand, I tilted the mask slightly, allowing a spurt of water in to rinse the fog away and restore my vision.

I was amazed at the sight. But then, I've never adjusted to the shock of my first clear glimpse of the underwater spectacle; it happens every dive. I suppose it has to do with the sudden appearance of life and landscape in startling detail, where before there had been none.

The ocean's surface is the culprit, misleading the eye by creating an extremely effective diversion. The brilliance of the sun, the impetus of the wind, and the tint of the sky are all parts of a mysterious equation that assigns a unique personality to each square inch of the ocean's face, producing a mesmerizing border between the two worlds.

Turtle Shell's little bay added an extra variable to the equation—clear water. That is, water so sparkling clean that it rivaled that of a chlorinated swimming pool. Its limpidity allowed the sun to glint off thousands of hovering fish. Even distant rocks cast sharply defined shadows.

There was no coral; this province of Neptune's dominion was limited to the same brown and gray hues as the rest of island. The rock formations, however, were even more outrageous than their dusty counterparts above. Some of the more peculiar shapes had been molded as lava had boiled through cracks in the underwater crust. Undulating walls and tumbling pillars showed where molten rock had hit the water after spilling over from the shore.

It was these same rock formations, I knew, that would no doubt hold my interest during each sojourn in Ascension waters. Sculpted with deep pockets, overhangs, trenches, and pits, the rocks provided homes for grouper, the staple of the local sportsmen's diet.

Radar had promised me that these fish were so plentiful and easy to stalk that, in order to enjoy our swimming and sightseeing, we would probably want to wait awhile before spearing our supper.

Radar had also promised me that we would see a somewhat less desirable fish during our quest for grouper. These waters were crawling with moray eels. To many divers (this one included), eels are as repugnant as snakes and the sight of one elicits the same response. Radar assured me, however, that I had nothing to fear; although the rocks were full of eels, he had never seen one come out of its hole more than a foot or two. If I stayed three feet from each rock, my spear would still be effective, and more importantly, I'd be safe from the jaws of Mr. Moray.

Radar's assurances ran through the back of my mind while we slowly kicked our way towards the center of the bay. Then, in a sudden, sickening moment, his words became meaningless. A moray eel crossed ten feet in front of us, its black, spotted body rippling as it moved effortlessly through the water.

I instantly realized that all comparisons to snakes had been dead wrong. This eel was much worse than any snake I'd ever seen. It was nearly six feet long, and almost as thick as a person's thigh. I knew that a third of this monster's length and girth could be attributed to the magnification caused by my mask, but this knowledge was eclipsed by a more fundamental revelation; unlike a snake, whose slithering is pretty much limited to the horizontal plane, an eel is quite at home in three dimensions. And this moray was not cruising through the rocks, but swimming high above them, only a few feet below the surface.

Things got worse. The giant eel saw us and instead of diving towards safety, he turned towards us. Radar and I instantly dropped from the normal prone snorkeling position and threw our legs out in front of us, assuming a nearly supine attitude.

Backpedaling furiously, we watched the eel close the distance. From our head-on perspective, the side-to-side rippling of the moray's body was more pronounced and gave the eel the illusion of being even bigger than it really was. Worse yet, its mouth gaped in a sinister smile, treating us to a view of three rows of wicked fangs, the biggest and nastiest of which ran right down the roof of its mouth. In seconds, the moray was close enough to touch our spears.

Our spears! Why were we running from this critter when we could be turning him into a shish kebob? Or rather, when Radar could be turning him into a shish kebob; Radar was the experienced one, the great white hunter and leader of this expedition. Any shots that I attempted would probably be more of a threat to Radar or me than to the mass of flesh and teeth that was chasing us.

But Radar wasn't cocking his spear. He obviously knew something that I didn't. Perhaps he couldn't shoot because of the angle. He might end up wounding the eel and really getting it riled. Even if he did sink the spear deep into the moray's neck, I pictured the eel wrapping itself around the spear and using its leverage to pull itself off the barbs. What would the creature do once it was freed?

The grinning head remained a few inches beyond the tips of our flippers, possibly held at bay by our pumping legs. Although I wanted desperately to look behind me to make sure we were headed for the beach, I felt that once my eyes left the eel's, he'd make his move. Maybe, like a couple of gunfighters, we could stare him down, although gunfighters running backwards rarely had the upper hand.

We were in six feet of water and the eel still followed us. We made it to four feet and he never flinched. We were swimming backwards in two feet of water, our snorkels collecting water from the breaking waves, when suddenly, I felt the sand of the beach beneath me.

I instinctively glanced down at my sanctuary. When I looked up, ready to bid farewell to the moray with a flip of my finger, he was gone.

During our brief conversation in the Volcano Club the night before, Radar had neglected to volunteer one important bit of information; he, too, was a comparative rookie on Ascension, having spent only three weeks on the Rock. With perhaps a half-dozen spearfishing excursions under his belt, he was no authority on the behavior of moray eels, nor on any of the other predators that Ascension's deep had to offer. Furthermore, he had never speared a moving target, and wasn't about to begin by spearing an eel.

As frightened as I had been, I was determined not to let this encounter keep me from diving. I had spent most of my life waiting for a chance to live on an island in tropical waters and a chance meeting with a rogue eel was not going to keep me on the beach.

Of course, my heart was in my throat for the next fifty or so dives, but the thousand or so eels I saw on these dives behaved exactly as Radar had first predicted; they stayed in their dens. I gradually reached an uneasy peace with them and with myself; many frightening things lose their ability to terrorize once the element of surprise is taken away. Once I came to expect a moray eel in every rock, the actual sighting of one became an almost casual observance.

As it turned out, the free-swimming, attacking-moray scene was never repeated in my three years on the island. Nor did I hear of anyone else witnessing such aggressive behavior. By the time I left Ascension, I realized that this animal's actions had been so bizarre that I was on the verge of doubting my memory of the event. Moray eels just didn't do such things, and had I not looked down the eel's spiky-toothed mouth myself, I would have refused to believe anyone else's tale of a similar adventure, chalking up such palaver to diver's bravado.

Chapter 5

The Southern Cross

Over the next few days, Radar and I went back to Turtle Shell and even managed to bring back a few grouper, although it was Radar who speared all the fish. I hadn't quite discovered the trick to spearfishing. My prey, with an insouciant flick of its tail, easily outdistanced my rubber-propelled thrusts, and my borrowed spear began to show the results. Nearly every shot caromed off the ever-present rocks, scratching the pole and dulling its barbs.

Radar could offer no criticism other than the observation that I might be telegraphing my intentions a split second before my shot. I might also be aiming for the body. A skittish fish could dodge such a shot, but if I adjusted my aim and shot at the head, or even led the fish a little, that same evasive maneuver would cause the fish to rendezvous with my spear.

Whatever the cause of my empty catch bag, the solution would have to be postponed. The end of my first week on the island coincided with the end of the month, when practically everyone at the tracking station rotated shifts. If I had to switch my schedule, I knew I would need a few days to adjust to my new shift. Even worse, if I couldn't match hours with Radar, I might have to find another diving partner.

My biggest concern, however, was not whether I'd be seeing Radar every day, but Gloria. During my months of daydreaming about living on Ascension with my wife, the thought had never occurred to me that once we were living together, we wouldn't be working together.

Nevertheless, after a week on the island, I realized such a scenario was not only a possibility, it was a probability. Every month would find us playing a game of match with a three-sided coin. If we lost, the next thirty days would find us struggling to adjust our internal clocks, trying to synchronize our waking hours to serve both Bendix and our marriage. This was not the kind of life I had envisioned for us, and certainly not the kind of life I would expect to strengthen the bond that Gloria and I were just beginning to reestablish.

The day the new work schedules were to be posted, I was programming the SCE for our next satellite support when Coach brought me the news I feared most; Gloria and I were going to be assigned to different shifts. We had lost our first match game.

Coach apologized profusely, explaining that he and Norm Smith, Gloria's supervisor, had tried to keep us together, but the skill mix of all the personnel involved coupled with everybody's normal shift rotation made it impossible to oblige us. Sorely disappointed, I took Coach's schedule into the Comm room to show Gloria. She frowned when she saw me.

"Norm already told me," she said. There was no mistaking the irritation in her voice.

"At least they tried," I answered, "Coach said that he and Norm spent most of the day trying to work it out so we'd be together."

My wife smiled wryly and shook her head.

"No, Norm said that by eight-thirty this morning, he had put two different schedules together, one showing me on swings, and the other on mids. Then he told Coach to try to put you on either of those shifts, whichever one was easiest.

Now after...," Gloria glanced at the clock, "Five hours, Coach has his schedule. But don't think Coach took this long because he's trying to keep us together. He takes this long every month. Norm gets a real kick out of it."

Although five hours did seem like a long time to come up with a nine-man work assignment, I had to stick up for my boss. After all, there was a big difference in job duties between Gloria's section and mine. Surely Norm would have had the same difficulty if he was in charge of the computer section.

While I defended Coach, Gloria studied the eraser-scarred list Coach had given me. Suddenly, she made a face.

"Why's Bumpy going to midnight shift? And why's Cliff taking swings? Bumpy should be going to days and Cliff to mids. Not only is that the normal progression, but that'll put you on swings with me."

It was my turn to frown. Although I liked what I was hearing, I didn't want to challenge Coach based upon my wife's snap judgment. Nevertheless, she had sounded very convincing, and I wanted desperately to continue sharing my days and nights with her. I took her suggestions to Coach.

"No, no," he said, rubbing his red nose, "If you put Bumpy on day shift, then...okay, you can put Bumpy on days, but Cliff can't take midnight shift because...well, if I did that, where would I put you?" Coach asked.

"Swings, I guess."

"Hey, yeah," he nodded thoughtfully. "That just might work."

Although I came to respect Coach for the wide range of talents he possessed, it soon became obvious that schedule-making was not among them. Gloria proved to be right about that; Coach repeated this scene practically every month. When the new shift schedules were due, Coach would pore over his manpower listing for four or five hours. Then he would show me the fruits of his labor, apologizing for not being able to work me onto Gloria's shift. I would then take Coach's schedule to Gloria, who, after no more than a minute or two's perusal, would send me back to Coach with the new schedule, revised to our benefit. Gloria's scheduling acumen was so acute that in our three years together on the island, we never had to work different shifts.

I was no stranger to shift work, but Ascension marked the first time that I would work a normal three-shift schedule as a matter of routine. Back at the Corpus Christi tracking station in Texas (my first Bendix assignment), our schedule had been derived from the trajectory of Skylab, our one-and-only tracking assignment. That orbiting laboratory had grouped its appearances over our station every twelve hours in a pattern that slipped an hour or so every day. We had manned our equipment accordingly, beginning our eight-hour shifts at 2:00 AM one week, 4:00 AM the next week, and so on.

The *Vanguard*'s work week had been considerably easier. During my first three months on the ship, our assignment was to serve as a 24-hour communications hub for weather monitoring ships, which we managed with standard shift-work assignments. After that, I worked day-shift almost exclusively, as our prime directive had returned to the support of rocket launches, of which only a few had required more than a single night of sacrifice on our part.

If the *Vanguard*'s schedule was a piece of cake, the Quito station's schedule was a castor oil casserole. In an attempt to give us fewer workdays, our managers dreamed up a timetable filled with a mixture of eight-hour days, twelve-hour days and a flip-flop to midnight shift at the end of every week. This oddball arrangement was supposedly to our advantage, the goal being to reduce the number of days we would be subjected to the adrenaline-filled three-hour round trip commute. We were all for that; the recklessness of Ecuadorian drivers coupled with the weather and road conditions through the Andes Mountains took a frightful toll in human lives. (Indeed, the reason I got the Quito job offer was to replace a technician killed a few miles from the station when he rear-ended a dump truck that was travelling through the fog with no lights.) But the crazy, confusing, hours had been a constant source of frustration. Certainly, everybody had bitched about the schedule, but nobody could come up with a crowd-pleasing alternative.

Those marathon work weeks at Quito had been especially grueling, considering my health at the time. But once I thought about it, I realized that not one of my work experiences that had involved nighttime hours had been particularly enjoyable. Loading computer programs at 3:00 AM was just as attractive as it sounded, and my performance during the hours of 10:00 PM to 6:00 AM was hardly top-notch; one night I fought to stay awake between the keystrokes of a critical spacecraft command sequence. The commands went through, but feats like these had me convinced that I was a borderline narcoleptic.

I theorized that my circadian rhythm was permanently etched in each chromosome, with subroutines in my genetic code directing my body to work and play during the daylight hours and to unwind, relax, and sleep after dark. If this were so, two out of every three Ascension months promised to be very miserable months indeed.

On the other hand, how could I account for the many nights my shipmates and I had run down the gangway, hit the town and, at four in the morning, cried out in dismay when the bartender flicked the lights to announce last call? Apparently, that genetic code wasn't as rigid as I had supposed; I had been able to patch the appropriate subroutines whenever I felt it would serve my purpose. Well, it would most certainly serve my purpose to adapt to shift life on Ascension. I started working on that code.

The evening of our last day-shift of the month turned into a celebration of sorts; John Lacewell had invited us to a dinner party at his house. John was the site manager, making him the top dog among all Bendix employees on the island. John looked to be in his early forties and except for his leonine mane of prematurely gray hair, he reminded me of early Hollywood leading man Victor Mature.

By the time I arrived in '77, John had already served several years and was so popular with the islanders that he had a piece of the Rock named after him; "Lacewell's Ledge" is a lava formation at the water's edge that serves as a perfect accommodation for fishermen on an otherwise unfishable cliff. Anglers walk down the face of the cliff on the nature-provided staircase-like path to a flat, roomy ledge just a few feet above grouper-filled water. Okay, Lacewell's Ledge is just a fishing hole, but John is the only Yank I know to have been honored in this fashion.

John's top managerial position alone qualified him for invitations to all of the British clubs, but his wide smile and gregarious nature kept him in constant demand. He was equally entertaining as either host or guest and at any function could reliably be found at the center of a ring of admirers. There, John would make a great show of lighting a cigar and citing Rudyard Kipling: "a woman is only a woman, but a good cigar is a smoke." Despite the ringing overtones of male chauvinism in the quote, the women in the audience loved it—perhaps because John always said it in Spanish, first.

I suspected the Brit clubs kept party lists on hand for their patrons, preprinted with the name "John Lacewell" at the top followed by a number of blank lines for the host to fill in. And thanks to the NASA station director Steve Stompf, John was able to reciprocate. As a goodwill measure, the Brits had long ago reserved a house on the southern outskirts of Georgetown for the lone NASA overseer. Steve found a kindred spirit in John and since the NASA house could easily accommodate two, he invited his Bendix counterpart to move in. Then, because of John's long-since-established popularity, he notched another landmark to his legacy; the NASA house immediately and forever after became known as "Lacewell's House."

The dinner party John had invited us to promised to be a real treat for me. It would be my first party outside the base, my first party with a largely Brit crowd, and my first trip to the fabled Lacewell's House.

Unfortunately, it turned out that I couldn't follow a single conversation in that largely Brit crowd. I was disoriented from the very first "Cheers!" that was shouted by an empty-handed Brit to the similarly empty-handed visitor who preceded us through the front door. Up to that moment, I'd only heard that word uttered beneath a canopy of glasses full of alcohol.

That first *cheers* triggered a flood of similarly unfamiliar usages as well as uniquely British pronunciations, idioms, and oddly-placed inflections. For a few moments, I couldn't tune in to any conversation in that noisy room, neither Yank nor Brit. Then as I grabbed some wine glasses from the bar, I found myself beside a couple of ladies whose speech was clear…yet incomprehensible.

"I 'adn't seen 'im in donkey's ears. Enne slaps me bottom! I was gobsmacked! Wot an oss! Well, we'd always beene at sixes and sevens. I wrote a mental meemo to strike him from my shedule permanently! Now, 'scuse me, I really need to go Jimmy. Where's Lacewell's loo?"

As I carried our wine back through the crowd I was suddenly reminded of my first visit to Gloria's grandmother outside of Meridian, Mississippi. As we sat and rocked on the front porch, Gloria and her grandmother did some catching up. I, on the other hand, sat there sniffing the country air and counting the magnolia blossoms; I couldn't understand a word that Grandmother was saying even though I had the advantage of hearing Gloria's side of the conversation. Periodically, Gloria would turn and address me.

"Dan, Grandmother wants to know…"

I'd give the answer and then go back to sniffing, counting, and waiting for Gloria's next translation, which I expected to be along the lines of, "Dan, Grandmother wants to know if all Yankees are as stupid as you."

The Devil's Ashpit

Then, to my dismay, Gloria excused herself and stepped inside to use the bathroom.

"Now Dan," Grandmother said, "Kinyu*tek*abaht"

The rising-then-falling inflection in her voice told my Pittsburgh-raised ears that this was a comment, not a question. But my first tracking station experience in Texas taught me that the opposite was true in the southern states. So I decided this was a question. With any luck it was a yes/no type of question and with any more luck, she was not asking me if I was a bedwetter. I mentally studied the sounds as long as I dared, and then I went out on a limb.

"Yes!" Say it with conviction.

With that, Grandmother rose from the rocking chair and went to the kitchen. And then it all became clear. Can…you…take…a…bite, which is the Meridian equivalent of Are…you…hungry. I eventually caught on to Grandmother's speech, which gave me hope that I'd soon be able to decipher Brit-speak.

At Lacewell's House, I was certainly ready to take a bite; we were used to walking to the mess hall within minutes of piling out of the vans, so the extra hour was starting to tell. When we had first walked in, I had been a bit concerned that the meal was going to be much, much, later because I didn't smell anything but cigarette smoke. I did, however, see a Brit hovering over a big pot on John's stove and moments later, the chef declared his meal was ready.

We all picked up a bowl and stood in line, where I heard the word *spaghetti* being bandied about. Soon, I was heading back to my table wondering what in the world the chef had ladled into my bowl. Remembering the allusion to spaghetti, I did indeed spy a knot of spaghetti noodles shining whitely, just under the surface of the pink water.

I had also caught the phrase, *sauce from scratch*. On Ascension, I reasoned, scratch must have meant ketchup and water—and a cut-rate brand of ketchup at that. After a sip, I decided that the only ingredients the soup had in common with ketchup was Red Dye No. 2. The "spaghetti" was uncontaminated by any tomatoes, meats, cheeses, or spices—not even salt—yet the room echoed with the oohs and ahhs of supposedly satisfied palates. I have never mastered the art of insincerity. Instead, I gamely tackled the concoction and hoped my expression was more smile than grimace.

We nursed another glass of wine and although we hated to be the first to leave, we simply had to get back to our room, for the spaghetti soup was as filling as it was tasty. I could barely wait to dig into the peanut butter and crackers we had squirreled away. We finally said our goodbyes and left to another chorus of "Cheers!"

The following day, we enjoyed the luxury of sleeping in for the first time in a month. Our introduction to our new afternoon start time turned out to be a rather mild adjustment, although it was hard to shake the nagging thought that four o'clock was the time to begin thinking of the beach, not the work bench. I quickly discovered, however, that working during the off-hours had its attractions also, not the least of which was the slower pace; with all the day-shift managers gone, the atmosphere at the station was more relaxed. Ironically, despite the slower pace, I noticed that the total work output of the techs on evening shift was at least that of the day crew.

After just a couple of nights of work, Gloria and I noticed the subtle alteration of our sleep pattern, slipping our wake-up time a little further past sunrise each day. This change helped stave off those head-rolling, neck-jerking nod-off sessions I was struggling with as the midnight crew came in to relieve us.

Our gradual ability to stay awake to the wee hours, however, presented us with another dilemma—late night boredom. Nighttime on Ascension provided us with even fewer choices of entertainment than the meager allotment we had sampled in the daylight.

Of course, the Volcano Club was always open, but I wasn't ready to park myself on a barstool every night. Neither did a moonlight stroll tickle my fancy. Unless we wanted to spend all of our time peering through the gloom for toe-crunching rocks and ankle-biting cactus, the only safe place to walk was the unlit main road, which did not afford a particularly scenic view even in daylight. In the darkness, what would be the point?

Instead, we spent nearly every evening in our room rediscovering our record collection. Old favorites and forgotten gems made it to our turntable, stirring up memories that we shared between sips of wine. It was a pleasant, comfortable way to spend an evening, but would our albums and conversation keep us entertained for a whole month?

One night, Gloria had an idea. We would walk down to Turtle Shell beach and watch for the big turtles coming ashore to lay eggs. If the huge reptiles didn't show, we could just lie in a turtle hole, drink wine, and watch the stars.

Gloria picked the *vin du soir* from one of the dozen or so bottles she kept on a closet shelf and we left for the beach. As we stepped into the shadows beyond the base's dimly lit perimeter, I was pleased and more than a little excited to feel Gloria's hand slipping easily into mine. This small gesture of familiarity was the latest of many promising clues I had noticed over the weeks, all of which indicated we were on the path to eventual reconciliation. Gloria's smiles had been coming easier, and she had actually laughed at some of my jokes, something she had hardly done even *before* we were married. Our trip to the beach was also a good sign, as it was the first activity Gloria had suggested that did not include her Ascension friends.

I squeezed my wife's hand gratefully as, with the aid of an occasional beam from our flashlights, we walked down the steep road to Turtle Shell. There, we carefully scanned the area, peering through the starlight for the smooth, round silhouette that would indicate the presence of a turtle. We knew we had to keep our flashlights off while we searched; turtles in the actual act of egg-laying are oblivious to their surroundings, but until that moment, they are easily spooked and will return to the ocean without finishing their nest and laying their eggs.

To our disappointment, the beach was empty. Resigned to yet another night of drinking and talking, I let Gloria pick out a turtle hole for us. She had often spoken in glowing terms about the cozy accommodations these six-foot diameter depressions provided and once I settled in beside her, I had to agree. Ascension sand, unlike the hard-packed silt I'd come to know on Florida's beaches, was composed of tiny bits of seashells that I could easily shift to suit my posture. I felt as though I had wriggled into the middle of a giant beanbag chair.

With the muted sounds of waves rushing up the beach and the feel of cool, contoured sand against my back, I looked up into the moonless sky and was dazzled by the spectacular view. Ascension's location, a thousand miles from the nearest significant civilization, also meant we were far removed from humanity's inherent pollutants. As a result, the sky's brilliance was unmatched by any I'd seen in my travels, as if layers of dirty film had been peeled off the celestial sphere. A shimmering blanket of stars twinkled against a backdrop so dark it redefined emptiness.

In this sky, the Milky Way really was milky. Where I had strained to pick out our galaxy's path in northern skies, my view from a turtle hole on an Ascension Island beach showed me an unmistakable swathe of stardust arching from horizon to horizon.

In this sky, constellations practically jumped out at us. The great hunter, Orion, stood astride the Milky Way, his club at the ready to protect the galaxy should Taurus ever decide to stray from its astral pasture. Gemini, Cancer, and Leo looked on, although each of these signs of the zodiac was oddly deformed; astonishingly, we had picked a night when Jupiter, Mars, and Saturn had each chosen to join those constellations, adding yet another dazzling point to their outlines.

Also in this sky, I saw the cynosure that had come to embody my lifelong fixation for travel to the tropics. Crux, better known as the Southern Cross, gleamed from its post above the horizon. This beacon for travelers to the Southern Hemisphere served as a heavenly reminder that I had indeed come a long way from my Pennsylvania roots.

I excitedly pointed out the formation to Gloria and tried to describe how it felt to realize a lifelong dream. Gloria and I had discussed our mutual vagabond tendencies many times before, but we had never done so in a setting that offered such dramatic proof of our distance from home.

Words failed me…but my memory didn't. One of the most dramatic television broadcasts of my youth was the World War II documentary, *Victory at Sea* and one of its most memorable episodes was entitled, "Beneath the Southern Cross." This episode, fittingly, concerned the war in the South Atlantic, where plenty of action centered around Ascension Island.

I had just started humming the sweet Richard Rodgers melody that accompanied that episode, when a dozen streaks of blue-white fire fell silently from the sky. Each of the meteors briefly flared orange and then red before vanishing as quickly as they had appeared.

This dazzling show had us eagerly searching for the next display, and we shouted and pointed and laughed like school kids when our vigilance was rewarded. The more we concentrated on the magnificent sky the better we were able to detect the slightest movement. That's when we started picking out satellites.

At first, we saw only the brighter, faster, low-orbit satellites moving steadily from horizon to horizon. Then we saw the dimmer, slower, higher-orbiting spacecraft. Soon, our eyes were tracking six or seven individual points of light as they floated far above us.

Rather than intruding on our majestic planetarium, the sight of these machines apparently drifting on the same level as the countless stars was even more awe-inspiring to me than the events of the night when human beings set foot on the moon. The significance as well as the reality of the moon landing had been blurred by the setting; I had lain on my living room couch, watching history unfold on the television.

In comparison, my unimpeded view of the satellites came from a desolate rock nearly five thousand miles from home, and more importantly, I saw the orbiting spacecraft with my own eyes, not via the television set. Furthermore, the soundtrack was not the intrusive commentary of television announcers, but the timeless crash of ocean against land. It was an introspective, existential moment, and the thought formed that although our planet was an infinitesimally small and insignificant part of the cosmos, we at least had our handiwork flying amongst the stars.

My musings were interrupted by a hand burrowing under my T-shirt and fluttering across my chest. Gloria had turned on her side and lay with her head on my shoulder.

"You still like me, right?" she whispered.

I knew then that I had been too strict in my interpretation of the "no contact" policy my wife had imposed on me the day I had arrived. When I had understood that Gloria needed time to shed the sexless persona she had worn as a shield during her six months on the island, I had not only refrained from public displays of affection but, sensing her tense response to my admittedly overeager advances during our first moments in seclusion, I had reined in my emotions in the privacy of our room, as well. Gloria could only interpret this behavior as uncaring aloofness, but nothing could be further from the truth. My actions were only guided by my belief that if I didn't lick the icing, I'd be less tempted to eat the cake.

Whether or not my recipe for reestablishing our relationship had been the correct one remained to be seen, but I had felt my wife and I were becoming friends again, and while stroking her hair, I told her so.

"Well, thank God," Gloria responded. "Then I can assume that those twelve boxes of rubbers in your drawer are for us?"

So she had found my cache. When I was unpacking my belongings that first day on the island, our awkward reunion had made me suddenly self-conscious of the condoms I had bought for our overseas stay. I had hidden them in my dresser, covered by a few pairs of jeans.

I gave Gloria's hair another stroke and assured her that the thought of cruising for chicks on Ascension hadn't crossed my mind. She, however, wasn't finished.

"I can believe that," she said, "but why'd you buy so many rubbers? Getting a little optimistic, aren't we?"

My wife was referring to our plan to take advantage of the company's ninety-day policy, the one that allowed us to take a well-deserved Florida vacation every three months. In that light, I had to concede that stocking one hundred and forty-four condoms to cover those ninety days could, in some circles, be considered optimistic.

I took a drink from our wine bottle, wriggled a little further into the sand, and told my wife the story of my overzealous purchase.

In Gloria's last letter to me, she had listed a number of items she wanted me to either mail to Ascension or pack in my suitcase. The stuff she wanted was all readily available from any drugstore but was impossible to find in the tiny store on the base.

I tried to explain to my turtle-hole partner what I was feeling as I pushed my shopping cart down the drugstore aisles; six months of forced continence had played a major role in shaping my thoughts. This was especially evident when I saw a shelf stacked with condoms—hundreds of boxes of condoms in every style imaginable. The pile of lubricated lambskin and latex and all its implied pleasures sent my lust-filled mind reeling.

"In the middle of my drugstore-aisle fantasies," I continued, "A joke suddenly popped into my head, a joke I must have heard in sixth grade."

> "A guy walks into a drugstore on a Friday and buys a gross of rubbers. On Monday, he returns to the store with a complaint; he had opened one of the packages only to find the rubber was torn.

The pharmacist apologized. 'I'm dreadfully sorry, sir. I hope it didn't ruin your weekend.'"

Gloria giggled at the joke, much like I had done in the sixth grade.

"I guess that was the kind of weekend I was hoping for," I told her.

My wife became suddenly serious and began to apologize for not living up to my expectations, but I hushed her because there, under the sparkling eyes of all the constellations of the zodiac, I knew we had rediscovered the mutual comfort and complete enjoyment that we had been forced to deny ourselves for so long. Our second courtship was over.

Chapter 6

The Base

As our month of swing shift hours wore on, I came to the conclusion that, despite the opportunity it afforded for late night ocean-side liaisons, the four-to-twelve shift was going to be my least favorite duty, forcing us to accept the least desirable portions of sunshine and darkness in a twenty-four hour period. The only way to maintain a comfortable level of performance during the evenings, we felt, was to make the noon hour our wake-up call.

Unfortunately, this plan required a little cooperation from the rest of the base's inhabitants, which was not always forthcoming. In order to sleep in, we needed silence, or at least a little volume control. But we had two hallway noise generators to contend with: The day-shifters preparing for their morning ride to the station and, forty-five minutes later, the returning midnight crew.

The slamming of the last door was also the signal for the base's public address system to swing into action, its feedback-induced squeals echoing around the base like an air raid siren. The missile attacks, however, never materialized; the announcements only served to inform us of the opening of the base gift shop or some other equally underwhelming news.

These daily rude awakenings were every bit as irritating as they had been in my youth, when my mother's idea of a gentle wake-up call was to flick on the overhead light. Thus, in an attempt to maximize my uninterrupted REMs and lower my blood pressure, I began a nightly ritual of disconnecting the telephone and screwing in a couple of wads of earplug wax. I also hung three layers of thick black plastic in the windows to cut out the morning light. These safeguards successfully blocked out most of the disturbances, but there were times when I considered sleeping with some wire cutters under my pillow in case I got the nerve to silence our electronic town crier.

A careful survey of the base provided plenty of evidence that I was not alone in my quest for an environment conducive to sleeping; roughly two-thirds of all the barracks windows were blacked out, which happened to match the number of residents working the off shifts. Another clue, but one not so obvious, was the number of air conditioning units mounted in the barracks windows. Although the local humidity was perhaps a few percentage points on the high side, a small fan was all that was needed for comfort indoors.

Nevertheless, an air conditioner was considered a "must have" item, at least as much for its noise abatement capabilities as for its capacity to cool and dehumidify. An air conditioner allowed the occupant to close the windows, thus deadening much of the outside noise. Furthermore, as we became accustomed to the unit's steady humming, we became less sensitive to the louder sounds that penetrated our walls.

Just how much each individual cherished peace and quiet in the barracks was perhaps best exemplified by one of our neighbors who, on his way to the Volcano Club, spied a solitary blade of grass shining bravely from the midst of the black cinders that constituted the barracks lawn. Miles away, the fringe of grass on Green Mountain had produced a seed and surrendered it to the wind. Floating over miles of inhospitable rock and ash, the seed had come to rest just a few steps from our door where, remarkably, it had taken root.

I watched as our neighbor bent down to examine this miracle of nature. Suddenly, his hand darted out and plucked the blade of grass from its perilous foundation. He crumpled the stray stalk between his fingers, cast it aside, and resumed his trip to the bar. Seeing the puzzled look on my face, he muttered an explanation.

"Next thing you know, they'll be bringin' in fuckin' lawnmowers."

Sleeping through the tumultuous morning hours was difficult, but sacrificing four or five hours of Ascension sunshine every day was almost more than I could bear. Nor could we really enjoy our remaining free daylight; any activity we chose from noon to three-thirty was marred by the distraction of our impending shift duty. The resulting anxiety was a wide-awake version of my old "you forgot to go to school" nightmare, and my subliminal appointment calendar had me glancing at my watch every four minutes to make sure we wouldn't miss our ride to the station.

Trying to make the most of our available sunshine, Gloria and I made a point of spending our afternoons outside, where we went for long walks up and down the road that led to Georgetown. On our very first afternoon stroll, we decided to visit the "Lizard." To get there, we walked about half-way to Georgetown, where we came across one of the few roads on the island that pointed inland, giving motorists access to the volcano-rimmed valley that hosted the village of Two Boats. For the true adventurer, the road continued through Two Boats, and wound its way up the steep face of Green Mountain. Our destination, however, was only a hundred yards or so up the gentle incline that led to Two Boats. That's where we would find the Lizard.

The Lizard was an odd little pillar of rock that poked right out of the middle of the packed ash that constituted the berm of the road. Roughly twice the size of a fire hydrant, the Lizard was named for the dead-on bas-relief image of an iguana that had ridden the pillar's crest ever since the bubbling rock had emerged from the underground.

Although the unique shape and location of this isolated eruption made it impossible to miss, the Lizard had one more eye-catching feature: color. The entire rock and a few square yards of ash, besides, was covered with brilliant multicolored splotches of paint. Tradition held that anyone finishing their tour of Ascension duty without painting the Lizard would be condemned to a return trip. The tradition was so deep-rooted that the phrase, "painting the Lizard" was synonymous with leaving the island.

The Lizard was the highlight of that first walk, but once we'd seen it, there was no sense in going out of our way to view the little monument again—at least, not until we had our own exit papers and cans of paint.

Otherwise, our daily excursions were about as exciting as an hour on a treadmill. To be sure, none of the Ascension landscaping I had seen would ever make the cover of *Better Homes and Gardens*, but with nothing to break the monotony of volcanic ash and rock, the area north of the base was especially drab.

And lifeless. A small population of feral sheep and donkeys, descendants of the livestock imported in the early days of Ascension's occupation, was a common enough sight during our trips to the station, but even these creatures knew enough to avoid the barren plains on the Georgetown road. Not only was the rock and ash devoid of trees, shrubs, or bushes, but the familiar scraggly cactus plants dwindled and finally disappeared altogether.

There were none of the sounds one would expect, either. Comparable walks through the fields near my Western Pennsylvania home town were anything but quiet; there, birds twittered and insects buzzed and whined against a backdrop thick with the shrill chirping of locusts. Occasionally, a gust of wind awakened the leaves, and their rustling would cause me to scan the sky for clouds and sniff the air for rain.

On the Georgetown road, only the stiff breeze kept us company, pulling at our clothes and hair until Gloria ended our walk with her standard request.

"Let's get out of the wind."

And so we would. But to my relief, we didn't necessarily have to retire to our room, whose smothering cinderblock walls were already planting dream seeds of tunneling to freedom. Instead, we often joined our coworkers, a few of whom could always be found lounging in the sunny but otherwise protected ground between our two tallest barracks.

At first glance, this crooked circle of sun-bleached, peeled-paint benches precariously anchored in a thick bed of cinders could never be as appealing as matching patio furniture and manicured lawns, and correspondingly, could never provoke the same soothing, tranquilizing calm. But the balmy weather served as an equalizer, to say nothing of the camaraderie. Our similar, special circumstances on this alien, desert island created a common bond, and the only credential anyone needed in order to open practically any door on the base was an Ascension address.

Gloria, by nature of her XX chromosome pairs, would never have to suffer from rejection as long as she lived on the island. Thus, as we approached their circle, our coworkers delivered hearty welcomes, each one patting the bench beside him in hopes of bestowing an extra suggestion of comfort to the worn planks. The smile from the winner of this daily sit-beside-Gloria contest was so rewarding that I quickly learned to choose a seat opposite my wife. This strategy allowed our friends to book-end Gloria, thereby lighting female-proximity fuses in two gratified males for the price of one.

The topics raised during these sunny afternoon block parties were heavily influenced by our unique circumstances; we talked about what we knew best. Thus it was no big surprise to hear our fellow shift workers lamenting the noisemakers around the barracks.

One technician, Mel, was especially bitter about his situation. Mel had the misfortune to live on the first floor, directly under the Chief's room. The Chief, as everybody knew, was a drunk. Furthermore, he wasn't just a drunk; he was the town drunk. This was a significant distinction on an island where dirt-cheap prices encouraged drinking, and where the charge, "Alcohol abuse!" was levied only at people who spilled a few drops of the treasured liquid.

From what I had seen of the Chief, it seemed likely that he would remain the undisputed holder of his title as long as his liver held out. A retired chief petty officer, the Chief had developed his penchant for overindulgence during his naval service, where smoking and drinking were just as much a part of a sailor's life as chipping and painting. The Chief went through a pack of cigarettes like a Halloweener goes through a bag of M&Ms, and I wondered how the makers of Wild Turkey would survive if the Chief ever switched brands.

As town drunks go, the Chief had little in common with Mayberry's lovable Otis Campbell, who quietly locked himself in Sheriff Andy Taylor's jail following an evening of intemperance. The scrawny, aged, red-faced

The Devil's Ashpit

Chief had a lot more in common with Popeye's old man, Poopdeck Pappy. When the Chief was on a bender, the hallways echoed with his raucous sea chanteys and tall tales.

"Aye, she was a dark and stormy night, she was, and the…ACK!"

The hallways also echoed with cigarette-induced coughing fits that interrupted almost every performance.

The Chief, having slept one night too many on the cinders outside the Volcano Club, did most of his drinking in the privacy of his room. The identity of his daily companion, the receiving end of the Chief's songs and stories, thus remained a mystery until the lonely Chief began leaving his door open as an invitation to hallway passers-by. There lay Snoopy, our ancient mascot, curled up on a throw rug. Although the Black Labrador's graying head rested between his paws, his eyes followed the Chief's every move. Experience had taught him to watch for bombardment from above, as cigarettes, drinks, and the Chief himself took turns hitting the floor.

According to Mel, the Chief's downstairs neighbor, not only did these thumps and crashes reverberate through his room, but even worse, neither he nor the Chief owned air conditioners and the open jalousie windows directed every word of the Chief's nightly harangues into Mel's room.

Mel had every right to complain; if I were the one suffering from the Chief's constant barrage, I might have been caught thumbing through some mail order gun catalogs. Mel, however, coped with his bitterness by performing a wickedly accurate impression of the Chief. On a moment's notice, Mel's youthful face artfully parodied the Chief's wrinkled, cockeyed, drunken squint, and his deep baritone switched to a raspy tenor.

> "Ohhhhhh, Sailor boy, sailor boy,
> Don't you get too springy;
> The admiral's daughter
> Waits down by the water
> She wants to ride your dinghy…ACK!"

Another common topic of the day for the bench crowd was, more or less, shop talk. After all, our workplace was another one of our bonds. Thus our daily penance at the site was actually a blessing in disguise, providing us with tons of conversational fodder on an otherwise news-deficient island.

Shop talk among technicians is largely based upon the techs' love of a good mystery, although in the techs' world, the story is not so much a "whodunit" as it is a "whydontit," as in "Why don't the damn thing work?" A technician is Columbo with an oscilloscope, or Sam Spade with a voltmeter. His world has at least as many prime suspects, red herrings, and plot twists as any of Hitchcock's movies, and every technician I know has a few favorite troubleshooting tales he's just itching to tell.

Many of these stories are favorites because they beautifully illustrate some fundamental concept of electronics; envision an episode of *Mr. Wizard* entitled, "Mr. Wizard Visits a Tracking Station." Other stories are remembered for their confusing symptoms and contradictory clues that often have techs blaming sunspots or the *aurora borealis* (or in our below-the-equator location, the *aurora australis*) before they manage to find a more down-to-earth explanation.

No matter which of these two types of anecdotes rises to the surface, however, their common, unstated message is the same: *Could you have beaten this problem? I did.* The techs could be forgiven for this bit of self-congratulatory backslapping; they don't normally grab headlines for their heroics. On the other hand, the tracking station environment also gave us numerous opportunities to seriously foul things up. So when the "super-tech" stories began to dwindle, there were plenty of "stupid-tech" stories to fill the void. Unfortunately, every site seemed to have an Inspector Clouseau or four in their midst.

We had the Bendix recruiting department to thank for this abundance. I had already learned, much to my dismay, that our association with NASA was by no means an automatic endorsement of our technical skills. On the contrary, a large percentage of our work force were technicians in name only; although they had the requisite background for the position, they were actually just equipment operators with little knowledge of their boxes' internal workings. Few of these operators had any inclination to learn.

If our recruiters were a little lax at weeding out the technically challenged when staffing the stateside tracking stations, they were even less demanding when trying to fill vacancies at an overseas hardship site like Ascension. Despite my newcomer's status, I could already tell that our barracks hosted a sizable number of individuals whose only apparent qualification for the job had been a body temperature.

Still, it wasn't difficult to find a silver lining in this cloud. If there's one thing a technician likes better than solving a mystery, it's solving a mystery that had stumped somebody else. Thus, many a troubleshooting tale began with a common thread:

> "It happened during day shift, but nobody there could fix it. Swing shift couldn't figure it out, either. So when I came in..."

Even better than the stupid-tech who couldn't fix the equipment was the poor unfortunate who made a problem worse, or who, heaven forbid, created the problem in the first place. Our coworkers' competence was a big issue; since we graded ourselves on a curve, the more examples of incompetence we found, the better we looked in comparison.

> "Mitch said he'd soldered in a new transistor but the card still didn't work. Well, you should have seen this card. Mitch is one of those, 'the bigger the blob, the better the job' guys. This solder joint was so big you could have used it for a shaving mirror."

Of course, everyone who worked at the site was human, which leveled the playing field somewhat. With seven day workweeks, even the super-techs were known to suffer an occasional lapse. We carefully noted every goof for later embellishment.

> "The strip with the labels on it had slipped a little, so when Bear thought he was putting the patch cord into jack 27, he was actually putting it into jack 28. As a result, we lost some spacecraft data. Goddard wrote him up for that, saying he was one jack off. We always knew he was a jack-off, but now it's on record!"

Then again, there were stories manufactured solely for entertainment but prepared with a certain mixture of crudeness and technical savvy that seemed to be a specialty of tracking station techs.

> "Last year, Goddard sent us a whole pallet of new tapes along with instructions that they all had to be degaussed before we could use them. You know that big-ass degaussing machine behind the recorders? I bent over that thing all day, feeding it tape after tape. Killed my back. On the plus side, though, now my gonads always point north."

Our shop talk was just one of the subjects that bore repeating day after day. In general, our barracks-lawn bull sessions meandered along an uneven but predictable trail. It was as if some official guidebook governed our subject matter, and we rarely strayed from this Ascension agenda of topics that included working, drinking, diving, fishing, and vacationing.

Our interpretation of this guidebook, however, placed all of these topics on the back page; we devoted the front page to the theme that addressed the islanders' number one concern. That would be women. More specifically, Ascension women. Any discussion of stories that did not contain a local heroine was short-lived.

Often, the signal that the idle, pointless chitchat would be abandoned in favor of some serious babe talk came when someone, anyone, opened the door with a casual reference to a chance sighting.

"I was in the Georgetown store this morning. Eula was there."

The circle would suddenly turn introspective, and nodding heads paid silent homage to one of the recognized "queens" on the island. Nobody asked what Eula was wearing or how her hair was fixed. They were content with their own private fantasy of the blond, statuesque, beauty scanning a rack of canned goods.

Seconds later, another tech might offer that he had watched Janice, Eula's raven-haired, copper-skinned, Saint counterpart, playing skittles outside the Two Boats club. Another private moment would pass, as each male enjoyed a swift, delightful daydream.

Eula and Janice were attractive by any yardstick, but on Ascension, they were goddesses. And just as untouchable; they were married and, by all accounts, faithful. Whether it was because of their beauty, their fidelity, or their poise, the respect and reverence commanded by these first ladies was so great that during my entire stay on the island, I never heard a lewd or suggestive comment that came in the same breath as their sacred names.

A host of other married women didn't fare so well. After the veneration of Eula and Janice subsided, the circle would launch into the latest news on the island's adulterers. If all our peers' stories were to be believed, it would seem that Sodom and Gomorra had reemerged as Georgetown and Two Boats, with nearly every Brit household entertaining a Yank or Saint lover. As the tales progressed, I calculated that the paramours were spending more time in Brit beds than the Brits were. Another yarn or two, and I realized there weren't that many beds on the island.

Nevertheless, enough evidence surfaced over the years to support the conclusion that Ascension hosted its share of extra-marital activity. Okay, considering the 100-to-1 male/female ratio, maybe Ascension had more than its share. Imagine the temptation posed by all of the attention; the first time hubby appeared the least bit inattentive, what girl would *not* start thinking about the hundred guys professing their readiness to walk across hot coals for her? Most Brit wives were unemployed, which had to have amplified their boredom tenfold. With no television soap operas to while away the time, perhaps a real-life one was made to order.

I tried not to be swayed by my experience from four years before. In Corpus Christi, I met an ex-Ascension technician named Terry who was in Texas because his Georgetown indiscretions had resulted in an invitation to find employment elsewhere. He did. But when he left Ascension, he took one of the Brit wives with him.

While I was on the island, another departure occurred when a Brit husband found his wife had been having an affair with a Saint. To put some distance between the two lovers, the husband sent his wife back to England. This move actually benefited the adulterous pair in the long run, as the wife immediately filed the paperwork required to sponsor a Saint—her Saint—for English residency. He joined her a few weeks later.

A few other marriages disintegrated during my three years on the island, but nowhere near the number I would have guessed based upon the rumor mill. Either the gossip was greatly exaggerated or the Brit husbands were a very understanding and forgiving group.

While these accounts of bed-hopping Brit women may have been the fabrications of a sex-starved populace, our local Yank and Saint females should have been grateful for this diversion, for no matter how outrageous the accusations, the Brits, by virtue of geography, were generally able to distance themselves from the majority of the carnal minds that inhabited the base. Although the girls in the barracks had to endure the constant scrutiny of their neighbors, their reputations, in general, fared much better than those of their British counterparts.

That's not to say all the girls on the base basked in the same aura of respectability. Occasionally, an offhand reference to prostitution would bring knowing smiles to the faces of our coworkers, although in my experience, only one tech ever claimed firsthand knowledge of this service. Even then, I was suspicious of the motive behind this admission, as the tech in question used the incident to effect his release from his one-year contract. The self-alleged john claimed that his life was in danger; he had somehow incurred the wrath of the hooker's boyfriend/pimp and every minute he stayed on Ascension brought him closer to death. At least, that was the story he told me. I don't know what he told Bendix, but whatever it was, they let him paint the Lizard.

If our coworkers were to be believed, the girls on the base were all attractive, intelligent, charming, witty, and gracious to a fault. Of course, our coworkers were not to be believed. The girls in our tiny society were probably a good representation of any cross-section of twenty-two to forty-two-year-old working women, with the possible exception that Ascension girls were braver than most.

Which is to say that their looks and personalities ran the gamut. Yes, we had girls whose bath water could be bottled and sold, but we also had girls with, shall we say, lesser attributes. Nevertheless, neither beauty nor beast ever wanted for attention. Our tiny community was ideal in this regard; a girl's looks had little to do with her popularity.

For that matter, a girl's personality didn't have much to do with her popularity, either. We had loud, brash, demanding women; quiet, demure, unassuming women; and every category in between. We had saints, and we had sinners: One girl shared her meager supply of hard-to-get drugstore supplies with a new arrival; another girl poured sugar in an ex-boyfriend's gas tank.

But these traits were incidental compared to the main factor governing a girl's island esteem. That factor was presence. Just by stepping off the C-141 was enough to ensure a girl a spot in the Ascension book of legends. After her arrival, she continued to receive points simply by being seen. Her presence in the mess hall, at the movie, or in the club was satisfaction enough for many of the men on base, men who appreciated the reminder that humanity had its softer side.

Thus, more than any place I'd ever seen, it was Ascension Island that amplified the female's ability to cloud men's minds. Criticisms did surface, but their origins were firmly rooted in jealousy, as when a lady's choice in men was questioned. Quite possibly, few of the base residents wanted to risk the chance that their criticisms could be traced back to them, thus knocking them further down the already too-long list of potential suitors.

I would have thought that this atmosphere of adulation would have essentially guaranteed that any Ascension relationships would be long and fruitful. Curiously, this was not the case. Many of the lucky males quickly reverted to the "play the field" mentality they had fostered all their lives, perhaps without considering that the playing field had been drastically altered since they had left the States.

The most public example of this behavior occurred when one of our fellow Yanks decided he wanted to submit an article to the *Islander*, a twenty page, stapled pamphlet that served as our weekly newspaper. The article turned out to be a lyrical, moving ode to lost love. I thought it was a beautiful piece but I had to wonder if the author's current love, a Brit nurse, would share my opinion. She did not. She quickly assured the hapless Yank that his lost love was not hiding in the nurses' quarters and vigorously urged him to go out and find her. There was no patching that relationship.

Breakups among the singles occurred often during my three years on the island and I was astounded by each one. But perhaps my unique circumstances disqualified me as a judge. Who's to say I wouldn't have acted the same way if the situation were reversed? I considered myself extremely fortunate that I wasn't in a position to answer this question.

Chapter 7

The Ascension Diver

After thirty days of the four-to-midnight shift, it was time to move to the wee hours. Once again we were forced to weigh the advantages and disadvantages of the waking and sleeping hours. After briefly studying our choices, however, I felt there was no contest. We would work all night, play all day, and sleep all evening. The only hard part was staying awake for the first couple of days after a night of work. The bed was never so tempting.

One major downside to our new hours was the one Gloria had warned me about back during my first day at work when I'd ordered an omelet for lunch. Because we slept through the normal supper time, we found ourselves at the mess hall's 11:00 PM breakfast, spooning scrambled eggs onto our plates. Four hours later, the Hashpit offered us a choice: The colorless, odorless, sterilized contents of the previous day's warming trays; or eggs, any style. Shift's end at eight in the morning saw us lined up at the base mess hall again for...breakfast.

Nevertheless, once we got used to the diet and the hours, the midnight shift was our favorite. With our station duties behind us, we had a whole day of sunshine ahead of us. We could explore the beaches, sightsee, and even party if we wanted to; we'd have eight hours to sleep it off. I came to love the midnight shift. The only problem was, I still didn't have a steady diving buddy; Radar's motor pool job didn't involve shift work, so when I was working swings or mids, I rarely saw him. Oddly, on an island surrounded by beautiful clear water and an astonishing array of sea life, I had yet to find anyone on my shift who shared my enthusiasm for diving.

Two weeks later, I found one, or rather, he found me. Gloria and I had just started packing for a day at the beach when we were interrupted by a knock at the door. Standing in the hallway was my old *Vanguard* buddy, Dave Cramer, whom I hadn't seen since I'd left the ship. He hadn't changed his thick, stylish, swept-back hair, nor, apparently, his T-shirt; his wide-shouldered physique slightly deformed the "Boogie Till You Puke" motto that stretched across his chest. It was the shirt he had been wearing when I waved good-bye to him in Honolulu, our last port-of-call.

Dave became "Cramer" long before the inimitable Michael Richards made the Cosmo Kramer role his own in the phenomenal '90s sitcom *Seinfeld*. He periodically suggested we call him Crammit, but I refused to use a name that sounded like it was spelled with an exclamation point. A few coworkers met him halfway by calling him Crammer, but to me, he was always Cramer. (I wish I would have thought of "Cosmo", though…)

Although it had been some months since we'd last spoken, Cramer just stood there grinning. This was no surprise. Cramer was notorious for his long silences; on the ship, he'd often telephone, then wait for me to start talking as if I had been the one who had called him. I decided to put a quick end to the standoff.

"So, Cramer," I said, "Are you just going to stand there or are you going to amaze me with some profundity?"

"Oh no," he responded immediately, "My dad told me never to use profundity. He said he'd wash out my mouth with soap."

This verbal jousting was Cramer's way, and it made him worth keeping around.

On the other hand, many of Cramer's retorts were repetitive, and I eventually came to recognize that half of his repertoire had been gleaned from the finer moments of his favorite comedy troupe, Monty Python. Much of this humor was lost on me, however, partly because I had missed so many episodes of his heroes' television show and partly because Cramer delivered his lines in a fabulous and indecipherable imitation of the Cockney accent made famous by Eliza Doolittle.

For example, he not only translated the American phrase, "Just a minute, sir" to the British, "Half a moment, governor", but in the process, he further removed all semblance of refinement. The resulting, "Arf a mo', guv'na" was a far cry from the original and when inserted in the midst of a dozen other similarly altered phrases and delivered with the proper inflection, it was absolute gibberish.

The rest of Cramer's lines were riddled with sexual innuendo. I suspected that during those famous long silences, Cramer was analyzing all conversations within earshot, mentally scanning each sentence for words and phrases that could possibly be used in a sexual connotation. On the *Vanguard*, for instance, I would leave for the chow hall, asking, "Are you coming?"

"Pardon?" was his daily response, delivered with a tone of voice and elevation of eyebrows that expressed mock horror that I should probe into that most personal of sexual experiences!

Cramer was not averse to studying his surroundings for material, either. He pointed out portions of the female anatomy in each random design he encountered, be it cloud, rock formation, or coffee stain, while phalluses grew out of any object vaguely cylindrical. Cramer's world was a three-dimensional Rorschach test and it was his job to find the dirty pictures.

Although my friend was a few inches shorter than I was, he was in much better shape, due in part to his devotion to *tai kwon do* martial arts workouts. Cramer was also a real cutie-pie (or so Gloria had claimed in response to a picture I'd sent her), which hadn't bothered me at all when we went bar-hopping together along Honolulu's Kalakaua Avenue during our last cruise. Cramer's silver-screen smiles brought flocks of lovely admirers to our table. His wit kept them there.

What did bother me was Cramer's attire for the day we had spent on Waikiki Beach. Cramer had already served a stretch on Ascension and had become a bit of an anglophile, certainly where swimwear was concerned. English bathing suits (or bathing "costumes" as they called them) were those skimpy half-bikini, half-jockstrap strips of fabric that, at best, looked merely ridiculous wrapped around a guy's butt. I'm shamelessly chauvinistic in that regard; I believe peek-a-boo apparel is best left to the girls.

On this day, my bathing-costumed buddy and I had gone walking down the surprisingly narrow strip of sand that comprises Waikiki when we became aware of some shouts directed our way. Three college-age vacationers surrounded by crushed Olympia beer cans were pointing at us.

"FAGGOTS!" the boys screamed, "Look at the faggots!"

Just a few years earlier, this would have struck a nerve. In my small town, homosexuality had been such an alien concept that I had been shocked and disgusted when, just a week after leaving home, I was propositioned by a distinguished looking gentleman (and his sheaf of twenty-dollar bills) at an airport terminal. A dozen propositions later and I had to wonder why I was attracting such attention without a *Gay Is Great* bumper sticker on my car. It didn't help that every pick-up line I heard in those months came from men, not women.

By the time I got to Waikiki, though, I had long decided that the simplest answer was the best answer: Gay guys approached me because of my, ahem, rugged good looks. Girls, on the other hand, were girls and the only ones who initiated sexual liaisons were the type who charged for their services. Those girls who didn't charge yet jumped men's bones at the slightest provocation existed solely in the imaginations of the *Penthouse* letter-writer staff.

The beer-drinking vacationers, however, obviously didn't see things that way. Their leader suddenly jumped in front of us, his face twisted in hatred. He jabbed a finger into Cramer's chest.

"Listen faggot," he yelled, "You get the fuck off this b—"

The word "beach" came out in an explosive gasp as Cramer delivered a jump spinning back kick to the middle of the drunk's chest. The force of the kick actually lifted the drunk off his feet and sent him sprawling back to land amidst his buddies.

He shook his head and stared at Cramer.

"Holy shit!" he yelled, still flat on his back, "He's a *karate* faggot!"

The drunk's cronies, who had gone quiet after seeing their hero so easily tamed, started up again.

"Karate faggots! Look at the karate faggots!"

Although the taunts continued, our fans wisely voted against another face-to-face confrontation.

I was probably as shocked as the lead drunk; I had often heard Cramer talk the *tai kwon do* talk, but I had never seen him walk the walk (let alone kick the kick!)

"Now that," I said, "Was one fine demonstration. And boy, did he have it coming!"

Cramer's eyes lit up as he heard the magic word.

"Pardon?"

Although that incident had occurred only three months before, the circumstances surrounding the event were so contrary to those of my Ascension existence as to convince me that years must have elapsed, not weeks. In Hawaii, clusters of resort hotels had crowded the oceanfront, each striving to outdo the other with rings of palm trees and rich, tropical gardens that grew right to the edge of bikini-strewn beaches.

On Ascension, our base housing had as much in common with Hawaii's resort hotels as roach traps have with the Taj Mahal. Grounds-keeping consisted of sweeping the black cinders off the sidewalks, and the sighting of another human being on a beach was a rare occurrence indeed, never mind a bikini.

Nevertheless, I had come to recognize that these Ascension Island features were not altogether undesirable; there was something to be said in defense of untouched, unblemished landscape. While the tourist trade mentality in Hawaii meant that every island attribute had to be ringed by shops and asphalt, I knew the vast majority of Ascension terrain would remain undeveloped, and I was glad for it. This reaction, coupled with my difficulty in relating to my Hawaiian adventure, seemed to me to be evidence that I was adapting to my Ascension lifestyle.

Cramer's arrival on the island was an unexpected bonus. On the *Vanguard*, he had taken every opportunity to steer conversations towards his plans for his house in the high desert northeast of Los Angeles. I had listened politely, and then yanked the conversational steering wheel back in my direction. Since I had every intention of becoming an islander at the end of our cruise, I wanted to hear more about Ascension. Cramer obliged, sometimes relating a diving adventure, but more often, spinning a tale of romance. That figured; only someone with Cramer's looks and charm could fit the words "Ascension" and "romance" in the same sentence.

Evidently, the process of describing Ascension's attributes to me had also worked to convince my shipmate that he had left prematurely. Cramer postponed his California plans and put in his transfer request for his second tour of Ascension Island duty. When he arrived, his previous experience obviated the need for a break-in period and his supervisor immediately assigned him to our shift.

Gloria, Cramer, and I settled into an almost daily ritual of dining and working together. Also, at movie time, Cramer would let us know if the flick-of-the-day was worth watching. Not surprisingly, my martial arts buddy reserved his thumbs-up reviews for what we called "karate faggot" movies, which generally meant those that starred action-man Chuck Norris.

Cramer was also responsible for choosing the site for our daily swim. I was especially thankful for his help in this area; once I had started shift work I didn't have Radar to guide me to the other diving spots. I had memorized practically every feature of Turtle Shell's underwater topography and was even beginning to recognize some of the tenants. It was time for a change.

Cramer obligingly led the way to all the locations he knew that could reasonably be called dive sites; that is, oceanfront property that fit two conditions. First, the site had to be relatively accessible from a road. We wanted to spend our time swimming, not hiking over broken lava.

Secondly, we had to be able to enter and exit the water in comparative safety. This meant there had to be at least a small beach in the neighborhood. We often began our dives by jumping off rock ledges, but we didn't relish the thought of returning the same way; even Ascension's most sheltered shores received rude surprises from the currents that swirled around the island. A diver attempting to negotiate a slippery rock wall when one of these unexpected waves hit might find himself with a permanent reminder of the experience.

These criteria effectively ruled out dives from anywhere except the western face of the island. The remainder of Ascension's perimeter consists of untraversably steep cliffs. A detailed map showed some promising nooks along the northern shore, but without fail, these turned out to be protected by impenetrable fields of serrated lava flows.

By the time Cramer and I had run the length of the west coast, I came to suspect that the other coasts could not have hosted much in the way of variety. Not that our dive sites weren't distinctive; the underwater architecture in each bay seemed to carry its own fingerprint. The terrain ran the gamut from the smooth sandy bottom of Comfortless Cove to the trenches, caves, and spectacular flying arches off English Bay.

On the other hand, only the shapes of the lava sculptures were unique; their colors had all been dipped from the same drab palette. As my previous dives had all been in the coral-rich waters of the South Pacific, underwater Ascension's monotonous tones had nearly the same subliminal effect as watching color coverage of the Rose Bowl Parade before channel-surfing to a black-and-white movie in the 1930's *film noir* genre.

Still, monochrome can be a powerful medium, and the stark contrast of giant, sullen pillars of craggy rock against a backdrop of pure white sand was a formidable sight. Then again, there were the fish.

Ascension's real underwater drawing card was its fish population. I had been impressed by the variety of colorful submarine creatures in the Pacific, but the abundance of fish loitering among Ascension's rocks was absolutely staggering.

The most plentiful fish by far was a fearless, black, bony customer a little bigger than my hand. These were a type of triggerfish called, appropriately, "blackfish," and an army of these creatures surrounded the island. They were harmless, but so bold that it was a minor challenge for a diver, or even a wader to snatch one. The shallow waters just off the beaches held the greatest concentration of blackfish, and their bodies appeared as ugly dark splotches in the azure curl of every smoothly breaking wave.

A few years later, I saw blackfish while diving in the Caribbean. Oddly, they were a comparatively rare sight. I wondered if the mavericks I saw there were the few who didn't get the word that Ascension was blackfish heaven. On the other hand, there was the possibility that these fish weren't stragglers, but pioneers testing the waters before sending for their Mid-Atlantic kin.

Blackfish weren't the only fish with this strangely lopsided distribution. The foot-long "squirrelfish" looked like a leaner, red-and-white-mottled member of the snapper family. Again, the squirrelfish's Caribbean cousin was a loner, while the Ascension variety swam practically elbow to elbow.

Ascension squirrelfish didn't school, however. They gathered in deep pockets between the rocks and, for want of a better term, "swarmed." Perhaps fifty fish would form such a group, and each fish swam a series of figure-eights from one side of the pocket to the other, endlessly turning and repeating the cycle. Individually, their movements were organized, but collectively, they resembled a host of bees swarming angrily around their hive.

A repugnant-looking gray-black fish called a "soapfish" behaved in the exact same way. The soapfish was covered with unappetizing splotches of what looked like fungus. I caught one while fishing once, and the Saint I was with rubbed the side of the fish with his finger. In a few seconds, he had whipped up a thick froth, demonstrating how the soapfish had received its name. He threw the fish back in the water, where it left a trail of suds as it hurried back to the depths.

We saw a thousand blackfish, squirrelfish, and soapfish on every dive. In slightly lesser numbers were grunts, gar, puffer fish, trunkfish, and jacks. All these fish casually accompanied us on our dives, whether we meandered from rock to rock wearing our tanks, or just floated on the surface breathing through our snorkels. Years of exposure to us clumsy, masked intruders had taught our entourage that they weren't a link in our food chain.

Our escorts all knew we were looking for grouper. Unfortunately, the grouper knew that, too. I quickly recognized the pattern; once a grouper had me spotted, it would keep a wary eye on my movements. With nonchalant beats of its tail, it swam an errant course, easily maintaining a six foot distance from the barbs of my spear. Any move I made to close the gap resulted in a demonstration of speed that belied the fish's size as it effortlessly flitted past the next rock outcropping, then turned and disappeared.

Practically every grouper I saw was the same size, about twenty inches long with a wide, fat body. The grouper's big mouth, thick lips, and bug eyes may have been unappealing to some connoisseurs, but the fish was plentiful, its meat was excellent, and its girth made it easy to fillet. I had to learn how to catch them.

The answer came after one of my first dives with a scuba tank. Swimming slowly along the bottom, I was surprised at how many grouper I caught off-guard as they hid under rock ledges. I was even more surprised when they didn't move. They watched as though hypnotized as I crept up to the magic three-foot mark and easily gigged them.

I happily stuffed my first three fish into my catch bag, but I also felt a little guilty about the ease with which I had made each kill. Once I had learned about the groupers' belief in the invulnerability of their rock fortresses, the additional advantage the scuba gear gave me almost literally made the excursion as sporting as shooting fish in a barrel. Any more spearfishing, I vowed, would be done only while freediving.

This turned out to be a good decision. Our dive sites contained plenty of acreage in the twenty to thirty-foot depth range. My strategy was to kick slowly over the rocks, watching as my presence sent a dozen grouper scurrying for cover. I'd take my breath and dive, but instead of chasing the grouper that were still visible, I'd swim down to the closest pile of rocks that one of the fish may have chosen for a hiding place. With my spear cocked in one hand, I grabbed a corner of rock with my other hand and hung upside-down. From there, I slowly pulled my way to the bottom, checking each hole for my quarry.

Often as not, I'd find myself staring at a moray eel. That's when I'd push myself smartly backwards towards the surface and start reconsidering the silly vow I had made not to use a tank. The times I did get my fish, however, the subsequent meal wasn't my only reward. The taste was all the richer considering the difficulty of the hunt.

I could not have been happier about this aspect of my life. The knowledge that I was able to walk to the beach, swim a short distance, and spear my supper was satisfying beyond belief. I had thought that people who lived this kind of life existed only in the pages of *National Geographic*, yet here was a boy from the back woods of Western Pennsylvania enjoying the same experience.

Just when I told myself that life couldn't get any better, Gloria suggested taking a few cooking utensils with us the next time we went to the beach. We could have a picnic. If I was fortunate enough to spear a fish, we'd be eating it within minutes of bringing it from the water.

We loaded our supplies into the van and drove a few hundred yards past Turtle Shell to Saint's Hut, a ramshackle, open air shelter that had been built at the southern tip of the long crescent of sand that marks South West Bay. There, I started a fire in the grill while Gloria laid out the rest of our supplies. Then I donned my mask and fins, grabbed my spear, and jumped into the water.

Gloria had chosen this site because of its location almost immediately at the base of a curving one-hundred foot cliff, which gave us some protection from the wind. The water in much of South West Bay, however, was shallow, averaging four or five feet; I would have to swim for about ten minutes to get to the deeper water that the grouper preferred.

I had just entered the water when I began to feel twangs of anxiety, the same twangs that must have been first felt by prehistoric men who were afraid to return to the cave empty-handed. My spearfishing success rate was about eighty percent; not a bad record, but not a guaranteed fish dinner, either.

I didn't suffer long. While scanning the rocks for eels, I caught a glimpse of an oversize grouper's tail sticking out from an undersized hole in the rocks. I quickly pulled my upside-down spearing act. In a split-second, my mission was complete, and I returned to the shore. As I climbed up the beach, I held my fat grouper high for Gloria to see. I had been gone for only three minutes.

I pulled off the fish's skin and with my fillet knife, I carefully cut the meat away from the bone. Gloria then coated the huge slabs of meat with a flour and spice mix. She gently lowered the first fillet into the hot grease of the frying pan.

Gloria screamed.

Before our picnic, Gloria had always handled our fillets in the comfort of our barracks room, a few hours after I had shot and cleaned the fish. By then, all the life had drained out of the grouper's muscles and nerves.

I, on the other hand, had filleted a couple of dozen fish within minutes of spearing them and had become accustomed to meat that quivered as I cut it. It was still eerie to hold a piece of disembodied, twitching flesh, but I didn't think to warn Gloria what would happen when she laid this just-cut fillet in the hot grease; the results would set new standards for the term, "fresh fish." Luckily, when her fish had twitched, she had dropped it into the pan and not on the ground.

Gloria and I continued to spend as many hours as possible picnicking on the beach. Often as not, Cramer would join us. The routine was always the same; Cramer would bring a bottle of wine, I would bring a fish, and Gloria would bring her cooking skills. After a dozen of these parties, I thought I'd let Cramer know that we could switch duties once in a while, that is, I'd spring for the wine and he could bring in the fish.

I was just about to suggest this change when it dawned on me that, as many times as Cramer and I had snorkeled together, I had never seen him spear a fish. Where the pole of my mail-order spear was scratched and dented from its break-in period, Cramer could have displayed his unblemished spear on a dive shop's showroom wall.

Gloria confirmed my suspicions.

"I guess you don't talk to Cliff too much," she said.

Gloria explained that Cliff had been complaining about Cramer ever since their first day as roommates, when Cramer caught Cliff setting a mousetrap. Cramer wouldn't allow it, calling it a senseless killing. Then he wouldn't let Cliff squash a spider he found in the closet. Cliff drew the line at cockroaches, but Cramer still intervened when he could, catching these unattractive barrack decorations when he could and throwing them outside.

"It seems our Cramer is a regular little St. Francis of Assisi," my wife said.

I had to admit, it certainly seemed that way. But it was hard to picture St. Francis practicing jump spinning back kicks at the gym.

Although Cramer couldn't bring himself to spear a fish, he accepted my thrice-weekly fish kills. In that respect, I suppose ours had evolved into a kind of symbiotic relationship; Cramer provided me with a dependable dive buddy, and I provided him with fish dinners.

Cramer and I almost exclusively relied on our snorkels for our visits to the sea. At least once a week, however, we strapped on our tanks to explore the island's deeper trenches. We had made probably a dozen dives before the dive club caught up with us.

I was not a certified diver. That is, I had not taken a training course from an accredited scuba diving school and thus did not hold the cherished "cert" card. In the States, this omission would have kept me from filling my scuba tank at reputable dive shops. On Ascension, it meant I had to accede to the rules laid down by the Ascension Divers club.

On an island whose inhabitants recognized no laws other than two or three of the Ten Commandments, the Ascension Divers had somehow worked themselves into a position of authority. As a result, the Air Force had given the club control over the compressor they kept at the airfield; anyone wanting to fill scuba tanks had to first have the permission of the club.

Luckily, this permission wasn't hard to get, or so the club members told me. To win the coveted Ascension Diver's cert card, a diver had to either produce a card received from an accredited diving organization, or show that he could put on a tank, submerge, and surface without requiring hyperbaric therapy. Of course, the diver also had to attend a majority of the club's monthly meetings and fork over a few dollars in dues if he expected to continue using the compressor.

Instead of joining the dive club, I had been relying on Cramer's membership to get my tank filled. There were few secrets on the tiny island, however, and the club's president chided Cramer and me for not following the rules. I lamely defended myself with the excuse that shift work made it difficult to contact any of the club's officers to schedule the required checkout dive.

This excuse was quickly rendered invalid when I suddenly found myself on the dive schedule. The club secretary, a Brit named Tooley, would meet me at English Bay after work.

Cramer wouldn't be going with me. As much as he liked the Brits, he didn't like diving with them. On land, they were witty, articulate members of the upper crust. In the water, he had seen them become bloodthirsty savages, as if they were hosts to the spirits of Britain's infamous crop of pirates. The island's waters were one vast treasure trove and the Brits were there to ransack it.

At least, this was Cramer's view following a dive he had made with two Brits the year before. The divers had found a large, shallow cave swarming with "bullseye." Although the bullseye reminded me of red snapper, the dart players on the island had no doubt christened the fish after staring into their oversized eyeballs. The ring of fluid surrounding the black pupil was a bright reddish-orange and gave the eye the appearance of a target. The

The Devil's Ashpit

bullseye's entire body had the same smooth bright red-orange coloration and contrasted the fish prettily against the gray-black background of the rocks.

Unfortunately for the bullseye, the Brits prized the fish more for its meat than its appearance. Indeed, the fish was at the very top of their list of desirable seafood, and the flash of the distinctive reddish-orange color had the same effect on a swimming Brit as a matador's cape had on a grazing bull. Furthermore, the fish were about as smart as apples. They would hover in place and watch unconcernedly as divers floated in their midst and, one-by-one, speared the motionless fish and added them to their catch bags.

As a result, the sight of a bullseye was not the common occurrence it had once been, which in turn made Cramer's cave discovery all the more amazing. Cramer was delighted. Perhaps the fish were making a comeback.

The comeback would have to wait. Cramer watched in horror as his two dive partners went to work. The Brits speared thirty-four fish. When they were done, they hauled their booty back to shore, leaving the cave with only some suspended bits of flesh and scales as evidence of the population it had so recently hosted.

Once out of the water, the soft-spoken, easygoing Cramer became livid as he berated the Brits for the slaughter. The Brits, in turn, looked at Cramer as if he had just stepped out of a spaceship. No, Cramer wouldn't be going with me to English Bay.

I took my time leaving the base. For once I was not eager to get into the water. I was uncomfortable to be diving with a person I barely knew. I also resented the dive club's mandate that I had to take a test, no matter how simple. And, as if these reasons weren't good enough, Cramer had told me that Tooley was one of the Brits who had participated in that bullseye genocide. How would I react if he pulled a similar stunt?

I drove alone to the dive site. Located at the extreme northwest point of the island, English Bay is at the end of a stretch of asphalt second in length only to the road to the NASA station. The western third of the island is much more conducive to straight-line travel than the mountainous central and eastern thirds, and as a result, my drive along English Bay Road was much less demanding than the winding trip to the station.

A string of monster antenna masts told me I was getting close to my destination. These spindly giants and the miles of wire strung crazily between them were a part of the British Broadcasting Corporation's radio relay station. Just beyond the station was English Bay and the power station that provided electricity (and, incidentally, distilled water) to all the British facilities on the island.

As if my trip to English Bay—past Georgetown, down English Bay Road, under the BBC towers, and beside the British power plant—wasn't enough to remind me I was deep behind British lines, I saw the Union Jack flying on a pole by the power station. I got that queasy feeling that a lone stranger gets when he's in a strange land. Odd as it may seem on such a small island, I had actually done very little sightseeing during my three month residency. I did have more than a passing familiarity with each of the beaches and their corresponding underwater attractions, but I couldn't describe any landmarks in tiny Georgetown or even tinier Two Boats. Furthermore, during my previous excursions north of the base, I had always been accompanied by Gloria or Cramer. This time, I was on my own.

I tried to set my discomfort aside and, as there was no sign of Tooley, I took the opportunity to scout the beaches for the area with the best protection from the sea. Ascension's bays are not the tranquil, blue water pools that normally come to mind when picturing the typical island scene. None had a substantial breakwater and most were pounded at least once every day by the unbridled force of the surf. No one, not even the Saints, was able to forecast the magnitude and direction of potentially deadly waves on a given day on a given beach.

English Bay was not immune to these apparently random currents, but the four beaches along its meandering coastline afforded divers a variety of entry and exit sites. I picked out the calmest water, although it was choppy and whitecapped by the wind, and parked nearby. I wondered if Tooley would remember our date.

I had first met Tooley at a Bendix fish fry. His invitation had come by way of his wife, Wanda, who had grown weary of her daily Georgetown routine. After spending a few months sweeping cinders out of her living room and chasing wayward donkeys out of her tiny flower bed, Wanda had decided to enter the Ascension work force. Bendix had given her a job in the spare parts warehouse at the tracking station.

At the fish fry, Tooley had been friendly enough and always managed to keep up his end of the conversation, but the end he was keeping up was never attached to mine.

ME: Did you learn to dive before you came to Ascension?
TOOLEY: I got to go out on the fishing boat last week.
ME: (blinking, switching gears) Cool! What did you catch? I've heard that the Saints keep us well-stocked with tuna from that boat.
TOOLEY: Are you and Gloria members of the Exiles Club?

I blinked a few more times and switched gears a few more times, and finally, my eyes and gears wore out. I wandered off under the pretense of finding a fresh beer. Mentally, I slid Tooley into the bottom slot of my list of potential dive partners.

The Devil's Ashpit

Tooley's unorthodox thought processes apparently did not interfere with his sense of timing; he pulled up beside me only a few minutes after I'd parked. The sight of his shiny sports car caught me by surprise, as it would to anyone whose only exposure to vehicles over the past three months had been the junky trucks and vans parked at the American base.

We immediately pulled out our gear and began to prepare for our dive. Eager to show my proctor that this test was a waste of his time, I quickly and smoothly attached my backpack and regulator to my air tank, careful to perform all the little checks Cramer had taught me. I especially wanted to avoid the common mistake of mounting the regulator upside-down.

We donned our tanks. Then Tooley picked up his spear and pulled his flippers and a nylon net catch bag out of his car.

The catch bag sent off warning bells in my head. After my first couple of dives, I had learned that an underwater storage container was seldom essential equipment. The only time I used one was when I was spearing fish for a party. Otherwise, the meat from one grouper was more than enough for three people, and I didn't need a bag for one fish. I asked Tooley if he was planning on collecting shells.

"Not bloody likely," he said, "I haven't seen a good one in donkey's ears. But you never know when we might be able to spear a couple of lobster for the gang."

Spearing lobster? That was about as sporting as wiping out a cave full of bullseye. I tried a tactful approach.

"You know, I read that in Florida, you're not allowed to spear lobster. You have to catch'm by hand."

"Interesting," Tooley replied. "And I just read that in Lisbon, the word *señorita* means "hooker." How very odd."

Was Tooley deliberately trying to avoid the point I was making or was he just being scatterbrained again? As distasteful as I found this whole situation, I needed Tooley's blessing if I wanted to get certified. I didn't say anything more but made a show of picking up my spear and tossing it back into my van.

Ready at last, I followed Tooley as he walked across the sand and stepped up onto a lava rock plateau that separated two of the bay's beaches. I wasn't very comfortable with this move, as I assumed it meant we would be entering the water by jumping off the rock ledge. We would have to time our leap to avoid the waves that were crashing into the wall and showering us with a thick rain of seawater. Our entry would be far easier and safer if we just walked into the water from the beach. I shook my head and wondered how many indignities I would have to bear and how many foolish orders I would have to follow to become an Ascension Diver.

Tooley didn't walk all the way to the ledge. He stopped at the edge of a deep cut in the rock that had resulted in a cove the size of a backyard swimming pool. The resemblance to a pool ended there, however, as the sea raced through the narrow slot that fed the cove and whipped the trapped water into a white, boiling frenzy. I watched in fascination as currents and eddies collided and threw bits of flotsam against the cove's jagged walls. The raging water was an unbelievable display of nature's angry power, and I was a little apprehensive about standing so close to it.

Tooley spat into his mask and reached into the closest whirlpool to rinse it out.

"Here's a good place to jump in," he said.

This was when I came to the conclusion that Tooley wasn't scatterbrained. Tooley was fucking nuts.

And because I didn't argue with Tooley, so was I. I decided that this all guts, no brains approach to diving was undoubtedly part of my test. I wordlessly prepared my mask, pulled on my gloves and fins, and holding my mask tightly against my face, I sent a telepathic goodbye to Gloria. Then I jumped into the maelstrom.

I immediately felt myself twisting, turning, and hurling across the cove at great speed. My mask was useless in the white water, and, completely blind, I instinctively thrust my hands out in front of me to protect my head. Anticipating a crash into the rocks on the far side, I was surprised when my feet hit something solid behind me. I kicked off, hoping I was pointing in the direction of the slot. A second later, my arms absorbed the shock as I hit one of the walls. I clutched at a handhold, but the surging water tore me away and I soon hit my feet again.

I bounced from wall to wall in that fashion a dozen times before the Furies of the cove tired of playing with me and shot me out the slot like a torpedo. My vision instantly returned and I looked back just in time to dodge Tooley's spear as he, too, came shooting out of the slot. I wondered how long he had been in the cove with me, and how many times he had come close to puncturing me with those exposed barbs.

At least the worst was over. All I had to do for the remainder of the dive was follow Tooley and breathe.

Ignoring me, Tooley kicked towards an underwater chain of rock clumps and began inspecting each one, presumably looking for lobster. He was oblivious to his surroundings and never looked up from the rocks to get his bearings. Nor did he ever turn to see if his dive buddy was still in tow, or for that matter, still alive.

Suddenly, Tooley brought up his spear and shot it into a hole in one of the rock walls. When he pulled the lance out, a lobster was impaled on the tip, its eight legs helplessly flailing against the water in a futile attempt to free itself. As Tooley stuffed the creature into his catch bag, I saw a great blob of orange under the lobster's tail. This was one of the reasons why Florida had a law against spearing lobster; the overeager hunter could easily spear an egg-bearing female and seal the fate of as many as half-a-million unborn lobsters.

I had to admit that I wasn't in Florida. I was diving with a Brit in British territorial waters. Ascension was Tooley's island, and if his countrymen had declared any local fishing rules, limits, or seasons, I had never heard of them or seen a list. Certainly, no rules were enforced.

Nevertheless, I thought it was up to us islanders to practice some restraint. I fervently wished I could do something to spite Tooley. I couldn't do anything overt, however. I had already gone through hell to get certified and I didn't want to turn the whole exercise into a waste of time.

Then it came to me. I would catch a lobster with my hands. That would show Tooley that it was possible to do the right thing and still be rewarded. The best place to start, I decided, was in the rock Tooley had just left. I had often seen multiple lobsters congregating in one hole, and it would be just like Tooley not to notice the poor female's neighbors.

As Tooley's search took him further down the wall, I swam up to the hole that had just yielded the female. Immediately, a pair of antennae began to emerge. I was in luck. Not only had I found another lobster, but it was curious and was walking out to see me. All I had to do was remain still until the big bug walked out far enough for me to grab it by the body, or "gearbox", as Cramer called it. It was important to get to the body; grabbing the lobster's legs and antennae would leave me with just that, a handful of legs and antennae. A lobster would sacrifice these body parts in order to keep its head and tail intact.

I watched and waited, gloating at my opportunity to show up the boorish, thoughtless Brit. I was a second away from making my move when I bumped my head on the rock overhang. Or at least, I thought I bumped it. Almost instantly, I realized that I hadn't moved, therefore, I couldn't have bumped into anything. Something was bumping me. Maybe it was another lobster in the hole above me, tapping me with his antennae. What a stroke of luck! In just a few moments, I'd be swimming up to Tooley with two lobsters, one in each hand.

No sooner did I complete that thought when I became aware of pressure, and then, pain. I jerked my head back and looked up into the same kind of ugly, toothy mouth that had sent me racing for shore on my first Ascension dive with Radar.

The moray eel was hanging out of an opening a foot above the lobster hole and six inches in front of my face. All thoughts of lobster, revenge, and cert cards flew from my mind. To my surprise, I saw my fist come up to deliver a quick punch to the eel's nose.

The moray disappeared in a black, speckled flash, pulling itself backwards into its den as if something had yanked it by its tail. I stared after it, shocked to think that my head had been inside that horrid mouth.

A streamer of green water trickled lazily down into my field of view. Puzzled, I waved my hand through it and watched as the line of green broke apart, swirled, and gradually dissipated. Another green line, however, trailed behind the first. I suddenly flashed back to chapter one of *The Deep*, by Peter Benchley, where he states simply, but ominously, *Blood is green underwater*. That's a great way to start a book, I had thought. It wasn't such a great way to end a dive.

I caught up to Tooley and after some difficult underwater coaxing, I got him to follow me ashore. There, with blood streaming down the side of my face, I explained why I'd cut the dive short.

I checked out my wounds in the van's mirror and pieced together what had happened. The bloody sore spot on the top of my head held barely discernible puncture wounds where the eel had anchored its wicked looking upper teeth. The inch-long razor cuts on my temple were the results of the moray's lower jaw raking across my skull. The injuries were superficial, but a wave of nausea washed over me nonetheless as I replayed the incident in my mind.

Tooley, on the other hand, talked excitedly as he scrubbed the eggs off the lobster he had speared.

"Ravaged by a moray eel. How exciting! I must tell Wanda that one of her Yanks fought with an eel."

"No, you must not, Tooley," I responded immediately, mimicking his speech. "Gloria's already harping on me about being careful in the water. If she finds out I was bitten by an eel, we're going to have an argument. I'm going to tell her I cut my head on some rocks."

Tooley giggled at my predicament. He tossed his equipment into his car and brushed some of the clinging sand from his legs and feet. Then he jumped behind the wheel and stuck his head out his window to say goodbye.

"Good luck with the missus. And be sure and ring me up so we can schedule another checkout dive. Cheers!"

I watched, speechless, as Tooley drove off. I couldn't believe what I'd just heard. I had shamelessly kowtowed to that stupid, dangerous, insensitive clod, only to be denied my certification. I resolved then to have nothing more to do with the dive club until I took a scuba course from a stateside dive shop. Then there would be no question about qualifications. I would be allowed to use the club's compressor to fill my tanks without having to put my life in Tooley's hands again.

A bigger problem awaited me back at the base. Over the past couple of weeks, too many of my fellow divers had been telling Gloria stories about the dangers of the deep. I had enjoyed the tales, noting that they had all happened, not to the story teller, but to "this guy I read about."

My wife, however, had begun to suggest I give up diving. In return, I began to suggest that she be a little more circumspect when listening to these secondhand accounts. Despite my assurances that I wasn't placing myself in danger, Gloria still exacted a promise from me that I would quit diving if I ever saw anything bad happen.

The rock story went over well. Gloria fussed over my cuts, dabbing them with an antibiotic ointment to ward off infection. Remembering the sight of the gaping mouth and its uneven, vicious teeth, I would have much preferred a tetanus shot, but if I made too big a deal about the gashes, Gloria might get suspicious.

Once I was all cleaned up, Gloria mentioned that we had about an hour to get to the party at the Exiles Club. That was bad news. I had forgotten all about the affair, which would bring together practically all of the couples in Georgetown. Tooley would almost certainly be there. Even if he had kept his mouth shut, and I suddenly remembered that he had made no such promise, there would be plenty of other people at the party; any one of them could casually mention that my wound looked more like the result of banging my head against teeth, not rocks.

I decided to hide my lie in plain sight. I made a show of inspecting my cuts in my wife's makeup mirror.

"You know what's funny, Gloria? Tooley had to laugh when he saw these scratches. He said that they could look like teeth marks, if you could believe an eel was trying to swallow my head."

Gloria paused in the middle of curling her lashes. She glanced at my head.

"Yeah, I suppose so."

She went back to her makeup, unimpressed with Tooley's sense of humor.

With that seed planted, I felt somewhat safer as we left for the party.

The Exiles Club was a well-crafted two-story stone and concrete building with a superb view of Georgetown's beaches. The interior was as cheerfully decorated as one might expect from any of the pubs in London's Piccadilly Circus. Of course, the decorations were considerably enhanced by the presence of the bar, which always boasted at least two brands of fine English draught beer. Careless Yanks, used to guzzling the comparatively weak American beers served at the base, often found themselves at the mercy of the club's deep, overstuffed chairs after only two pints.

Yanks, however, were a relatively scarce commodity in the Exiles Club, or for that matter, in any of the three Brit clubs. It was common knowledge that the only Americans to receive invites to the Brit clubs were the supervisors and the girls. The same rules applied to the Saints, also, although they were well represented as bartenders and waiters.

As a non-supervisor and a non-female, the only reason the Brits allowed me to pass their hallowed doors was because I was Gloria's date. Gloria and I both admitted to each other that the Brits' overt discrimination against our friends and countrymen was detestable. But we couldn't bring ourselves to act on our principles. We liked the British clubs. On an island with so few amenities or privileges, our idealism had been washed away by a few too many spilled drinks by the drunk and disorderly patrons of the Volcano Club. Yes, I felt guilty, but I was also pleased to be a member of Ascension's tiny In-crowd.

The squeal of paper-thin brake linings announced our arrival at the Exiles parking lot. Gloria and I muttered a simultaneous "Thank God," as had become our custom, followed by a less appreciative oath as we waited for the engine-knocking to die down. We exited our van, me by kicking my door open, Gloria by holding hers up, and measured the millimeters that separated our front bumper from the stone wall of the Exiles Club. It was time to get serious about finding another vehicle.

The exciting drive, however, had taken my mind off my little predicament and I felt a sudden surge of lightheartedness as we climbed the stairs to join the party. We were having an evening away from the barracks, away from the Volcano Club, and away, I'll admit, from my countrymen's lopsided ratio of males to females. Nearly all the Brits on the island came as a couple and the wives took these parties very seriously, breaking out their best gowns to show off.

Wondering if Eula and Janice would be coming and if so, what they would be wearing, I pushed open the door, allowing the setting sun to fire an orange and crimson barrage through the club. The rays hit Tooley like a spotlight. My stomach immediately flip-flopped. Tooley was standing by the bar, talking animatedly to a small group of Brits. I didn't have to wait long to find out what he was talking about. A tall, affable Brit named Roger came striding towards me.

"Cheers, Dan," he said. Roger twisted his head to get a better look at the cuts on my temple. "So that's where the eel bit you, hey? The dirty bugger."

My first thought was to find a weapon with which I could put Tooley out of my misery. But I had a charade to keep up.

"Eel bite?" I said, acting puzzled for Gloria's benefit. Then I laughed. "Oh, you've been talking to Tooley. Yes, that's where the eel bit me, all right."

With Gloria standing beside me and listening politely, I proceeded to tell Roger the details of the bite. But I hesitated often, hoping to make it sound as if I was making it all up. Roger probably thought I had a speech impediment or some problem with my short-term memory.

But my ruse was working. Gloria even began to go along with it, joking, "I told Dan there were safer ways to feed the fish."

The Devil's Ashpit

I was naturally relieved that, so far, things were working out so well. Still, I knew my actions could easily evolve into one of those situation comedies, the kind where a stupid lie has the protagonist turning handsprings as his fabrications escalate, compounding his problems until his ultimately ridiculous story collapses.

At the same time, I was suffering from tremendous pangs of guilt; I had never before lied to my wife. In the States, she had even joked at my scrupulous honesty, calling me "Honest Abe" whenever I helped a waitress with her math or informed a motel manager that he had neglected to charge us for a phone call we had made from our room.

The shame brought on by my pretense was too much to bear. I took Gloria's elbow to steer her to a corner where she could hear my confession. She and Roger, however, had been having fun at my expense and, as I led her away, she gave him one more laugh.

"I told Dan that if anything happened to him, he wouldn't be diving any more. Well, that's it. I guess I'll have to beach him, now."

On the other hand, I thought, *Gloria's having a real good time with this "fictional" eel story; let's see how long it will play.*

It played a long time. It had to; Tooley must have taken a page out of Paul Revere's book, as absolutely every Brit who walked through the door came over to talk about the incident. That fact alone should have made Gloria suspicious; even islanders starved for news wouldn't make a big deal out of a diving injury caused by rocks.

The denouement of my little farce came with the arrival of probably the only Brit on the island who hadn't heard the story. Tooley's wife, Wanda, quickly corrected the oversight. Unfortunately, Wanda had a rather shrill voice, making her easy to pick out in a crowd; in truth, she always sounded as though she was addressing a crowd. Gloria overheard her telling the eel story to the latecomer. My wife turned to me quickly with a look of concern on her face.

"Dan, you need to talk to Wanda and set her straight. She's telling that guy the eel story as if she believes it."

The time had come. I got that pit-of-the-stomach feeling like when I confessed to my father that there was indeed a correlation between my snowball-throwing expertise and my brother's bloody nose.

"Actually, Gloria," I said, "Wanda's telling the true story. I lied to you because I didn't want you to worry about me and because you said you'd make me give up diving."

Gloria's mouth fell open. Then I saw her hand coming at me, fast. I didn't move, knowing I deserved a slap in the face. But instead of a sharp sting, I felt a soft caress.

"Oh, you poor thing," she gasped, "Let me see those bites."

She clucked solicitously as she inspected my cuts in this new light. Then we talked. Gloria finally decided that if "Honest Abe" had taken such measures to hide the truth from his wife, then he must feel pretty strongly about this diving stuff. She wouldn't take that away from him.

I couldn't believe what I was hearing. While the whole island population had known the truth about my little adventure, I had lied to my wife about it. I had expected her to feel humiliated that she was the last to hear the truth.

"You mean I'm off the hook?" I asked incredulously.

"No, Honest Abe's off the hook," she said. Then she held up her little fist. "You ever lie to me again and you'll be *hanging* from a hook!"

I had been through a lot in the space of a couple of hours; I had lied, suffered tremendous mental anguish, confessed, and had been absolved of my sin. At the same time, I had learned that, while Gloria had always teased me about my adherence to a strict code of ethics, she ultimately felt that honesty was still a pretty good policy. The eel bite was probably the best thing to happen to our marriage.

Chapter 8

That's Entertainment

Whenever I tell someone that we had to work seven days per week on Ascension, I get the feeling that people think we worked seven days, took our two-day weekend, then worked another seven days. That was not the case. We worked every day. We worked weekdays and weekends and didn't give a hoot whether holidays were on Friday or Monday to give us extended weekends; we worked just the same. For variety, we worked days, swings, or mids.

We didn't have many excuses not to work. For example, hardly anyone got sick. Some of our coworkers endured perpetual hangovers, of course. But a day off wouldn't have helped these sufferers, since their hair-of-the-dog cure never varied.

Nor did anyone miss work because of car trouble. Our fleet of company vans showed their age, but they were much more reliable than any of the private vehicles that had accumulated at the site. Besides, with the price of precious gasoline being what it was, it didn't make sense to drive to work in anything other than a company van.

None of us missed work because of family problems, of course. We didn't need to take time off to nurse a sick kid or meet with a teacher. We didn't need to buy groceries or a new lawnmower blade or a bucket of paint. There just wasn't anything that needed doing that couldn't be done before or after work. And since every spot on the island was within seven miles of every other spot, we didn't need a vacation day to take a trip to the beach or to take in a change of scenery by driving up Green Mountain.

One of the biggest reasons for our excellent attendance records, I suppose, was that there was just no point in missing work. What would we do with a free day that we wouldn't be able to do every other day? The Ascension Island social and recreational calendar was practically identical from one week to the next.

Of course, there were a few random social events that shift work prevented me from attending, but nothing on the island was ever really new and exciting. If I missed a pig roast on the beach, I could catch the next one. If I had to work during the premiere of a Brit variety show, I could sit in on one of the encore performances. Nothing was a once-in-a-lifetime event.

The technology of the mid-seventies also had a hand in helping to keep absenteeism low. Ascension, the communications link between four continents and dozens of orbiting satellites, had no means of collecting television signals and distributing them to island residents. Nor, it seemed, was anybody inclined to initiate such a system. For one thing, we couldn't simply pick up a catalog and write a check for a home satellite television terminal; nobody was marketing a simple, affordable setup at the time. To install such a system would have required a major cooperative effort among a group of people who, in all likelihood, would be gone by the time the network was in place. Ascension was not a place where couch potatoes could while away the hours by channel-surfing through the video pipeline.

Video recording and playback technology had been available for some years, but the only videotape players I had seen up to this point were suitcase-sized monsters sitting in company training rooms. The home Video Cassette Recorder or VCR industry was still in its infancy and only the very well-to-do bothered to listen to the arguments over which format was better—beta or VHS. "Too much TV" was only a phrase we islanders came across when reading articles in our week-old newspapers imported from the States. None of us could envision stores that would exist solely on the revenue of videotape rentals.

Similarly, we didn't know what Jobs and Wozniak were up to, out there in Silicon Valley. IBM had not yet coined the phrase "Personal Computer" or PC. The only video game in existence was the laughably rudimentary "Pong," and nobody thought enough of that game to include it in their luggage when they left the States.

Along those lines, we did have a tiny population of ham radio operators and electronic tinkerers. For the most part, however, we were composed of some mixture of the three main categories of personalities nurtured by the island's resources. We were each, to varying degrees, "aquatic," "athletic," and "alcoholic".

These groups were not mutually exclusive; many of our activities combined two or more categories. For example, cases of beer were as essential to most fishermen as were their fishhooks, and swimming through rough waters on many of my spearfishing expeditions was keeping me in pretty good shape.

Ultimately, however, it wasn't the presence or absence of distractions that kept us walking out to the company vans every day. I believe the

The Devil's Ashpit

majority of our coworkers felt the same way as Gloria and I did; if we were going to spend another day on Ascension Island, we wanted Bendix to pay us for the honor. We were working towards a goal, and every day we worked was another step towards the completion of that goal.

Every day we didn't work was counterproductive. Taking one day off meant the loss of our double-time day, subtracting a hefty sixteen hours from our normal sixty-eight hour paycheck. Anyone taking a two-day break would be declared insane; a two-day break lopped off your time-and-one-half day *and* your double-time day. This 41% pay cut was simply too much to trade for a couple of days of nothing much to do.

As much as I loved the ocean access and temperate climate, I wouldn't have been on Ascension if not for the money. After only a few months, Gloria and I began compiling a list of things we missed most. Gloria's number one desire was to lounge in a bathtub for an hour. Then she wanted a filet mignon. Tops on my list was a real magazine rack to browse through, after which I'd treat my taste buds to a salad with chunky blue cheese dressing. A hardship assignment brings out strange desires in a person.

Whatever the reasons we gave for voluntarily spending eight hours at the station every day, the fact remained that we devoted a large portion of our lives to the business of tracking satellites. When we returned to the base, the last thing we wanted to do was sit and contemplate the next day's work schedule. We wanted to play, instead. Well, at least the "aquatics" and "athletics" wanted to play. Luckily, the island had a limited number of games and activities from which we could choose. Each, of course, had its merits and demerits.

The game of darts was one sport popular at each of the clubs. The game's small playing field, minimum equipment requirements, and easy-to-find players in the midst of a pub crowd made it the easiest to organize. But the Brits and the Saints, comprising the plurality of Ascension's population, owned the game. For the most part, the Yanks let them keep it.

While our stateside game-o'-darts experience had been limited to wobbly, one-size-fits-all darts aimed at pressed cardboard dartboards, the Brits and Saints were fingering nickelled-tungsten darts while judging tailored weights and custom flights. They let fly their missiles into boards of genuine hog bristle. Brits studied their dart trajectories with the same intensity that Apollo astronauts monitored their lunar descents.

Cricket and soccer were also very popular with our neighbors, but again, there was little, if any, participation from the Yank sector. My excuse stemmed from something I read in an issue of the *Islander*. One article carried the results of a "duel on the cricket pitch." At one point, "the pace bowler hurled the ball in bouncers, googlies, yorkers, tempting shorts, and full tosses." This was a compliment, I believe. Then, however, the tide appeared to turn, as "the bowlers took their eyes off the stumps and lost their accuracy."

This game was a little too strange for me; I could handle learning a few rules, but not a whole new language. I think a lot of my coworkers felt the same way.

Then there was soccer. Stateside promoters had made a number of attempts over the years to bring the world's favorite spectator sport to US audiences, but viewers wouldn't have it. For one thing, the game seemed to follow the strategy of a rock fight.

Much worse, however, is the unfortunate habit soccer fans have of referring to their sport as "football." This assertion is blasphemy to anyone vaguely familiar with the Knute Rockne story. Those who saw the movie know that Knute didn't ask a bunch of skinny, bare-legged, funny-talking sissy boys to win one for the Gipper. Knute was the general of an army of bone-crunching, stiff-arming, red-blooded Americans. It doesn't matter that soccer's following must outnumber that of the National Football League by a thousand to one and that those "sissy boys" would certainly run rings around 95% of the NFL players. The Yanks' fierce pride insists that "football" is the private property of the North American continent.

Jingoistic tirades aside, the Yanks had a couple of other very good reasons for not wearing cricket or soccer jerseys. First was the location; the only suitable field for these sports was near Georgetown. Americans attempting to make games or attend practice sessions had to find a ride.

The bigger reason, however, was the same excuse we used for any of the sports that required more than six or seven people to field a team; our seven-day work-weeks and rotating shifts either limited our participation to one month at a time, or they so complicated game schedules as to cause the organizers to quit in frustration.

This was certainly the case in what should have been the Americans' showcase, softball. Despite the convenience of a softball field beside the Volcano Club, we found it was practically impossible to get twenty players together for a game.

If a single game was practically impossible, a softball league was absolutely impossible. The game gradually evolved into a sideshow for our holiday celebrations; that is, we held one-day softball tournaments as a portion of the festivities. Still, we had to be careful that the day's schedule didn't span the four o'clock shift change; the vans might take away more players than they brought back.

On the other hand, perhaps we would have tried harder to find a solution if the softball field had been a bit more conventional. Our grassless field was advertised as consisting of "hard-packed" sand, but if the

The Devil's Ashpit

foundation *was* sand, it was so hard-packed as to feel like asphalt. A thin layer of loose sand gave the illusion of softness. The illusion disappeared once you set foot on the surface.

The field was such an enemy to the epidermis that a well-deserved fear of injury steered the games. Since nobody was going to wear full bodysuit protection in the eighty-plus degree heat, the game was played as nearly vertical as possible. That is, nobody reached too far to catch a ball, or leaned too far forward when running after a ball. On offense, a slight change to the International Softball Federation rules helped keep base-runners vertical by allowing them to overrun second and third bases without fear of being tagged out.

These limitations really served to diminish the game, as the quest to maintain one's balance became the primary goal and winning one's game came in a distant second.

The one outdoors British game that did catch on at the base was "skittles." Skittles is essentially bowling, with a few important differences. The version of the game we played incorporated a gutterless alley about twenty-five feet in length. Curbs along each side of the alley kept the grapefruit-size bowling ball in bounds—and in play. Bouncing the ball against the curb was legal, though not usually desirable. The skittles themselves differed from bowling pins in that they had a fat middle that tapered to the flat ends. Being symmetrical, there was no need for a "this side up" decal. Indeed, more than once I saw a skittle fall over only to land upright again, which does not count as a knockdown!

The diameter of the heavy rubber bowling ball was a few inches less than the spacing of the skittles pins. Since the nine wooden pins were set in an evenly-aligned diamond shape, it was possible for the ball to pass completely through the stand of timber without touching a single pin. Score for ball number one: zero.

This was the catalyst for every drunken spectator to scream with delight. "Down the hole!" they'd shout, spilling their beer as they toasted the bowler's bad luck. But unlike bowling, the bowler had three balls for every frame. (The Saints were especially quick to remind us of that fact: "Never mind, mates, 'e's got three balls, or so I've 'eard!")

If the two attempts to pick up the spare met the same fate as the first ball, the chant changed to "Funny face!", which was meant to encourage the scorekeeper to add some decorations to the big zero he was about to enter on the chalkboard located near the alleys. At the very least, the zero grew eyes, ears, a nose, and a dunce cap. The public had equal access to the board and often added further enhancements to the low-scorer's frames.

The game was sufficiently difficult that an eight-frame score in the sixties was usually good enough to win the individual the game's high-roller award. On the other hand, one poor player who scored a fifteen (yes, that means he knocked down only 15 pins in 24 tries!), suffered the ignominy of seeing his scorecard published in the *Islander* under the title, "For The Record Books." Three Funny Faces (the touched-up zeros) and two Christmas Trees (touched-up ones) were instrumental in winning the low-roller honors.

At the other end of the spectrum was a perfect game, 216 points. A bowler would have to knock down all nine pins on each of twenty-four tosses of the ball. Based on my Ascension skittles experience, the perfect game would have to wait until the Second Coming; out of the few hundred games I watched or played, I saw only one strike. The girl who made it got so excited that she threw her next two balls out of the alley.

Of course, the cheerleading Saints didn't help matters; we had to forgo the courteous silence we enjoyed at stateside bowling alleys when approaching the line and delivering the ball. The Saints' favorite device during these crucial seconds was the bellowed admonition to "Keep your cheeks togetha!"

Sound advice, I thought, but it never improved my score.

I enjoyed skittles, but to guarantee a court, Gloria and I had to join the island league, and to join the island league, we had to play the league's schedule. This meant that Gloria and I couldn't just play the alleys right outside our barracks; we often had to rush from work and drive our deathtrap to the matches in Georgetown and Two Boats. This little inconvenience was enough to dampen my enthusiasm. Fortunately, I found another team sport that was much more convenient.

Ideally situated between the barracks and the mess hall was a volleyball court. The location was doubly blessed: First, a steady stream of potential participants walked by the court at each mealtime; Secondly, the distance from the Volcano Club significantly weakened the mysterious magnetism built into the club's barstools. I'm sure the court would have lain abandoned had it been built across the street from the club rather than the mess hall.

There was a down side, however. For any one game, at least half of the participants were Saints. The Saints played as well as any of the Yanks, but had the extremely annoying habit of reverting to their soccer roots whenever the ball fell below waist level. A boot-clad foot (few Saints owned tennis shoes) invariably shot out to intercept the ball.

The court had few barriers around it, so stray hits or kicks often sent the ball bounding for great distances. Another Saint would run to retrieve the ball and, of course, yield to the temptation to show off a good power kick. The other Saints waiting at the court immediately broke into an impromptu game of cutthroat soccer, jostling among themselves for control of the ball.

Unfortunately, they were quite good, and we Yanks weren't fast enough to grab the ball back. We were reduced to standing with our hands on our hips, pleading like frustrated kids for the return of the ball.

The introduction of tournaments helped to speed up the game, as the players were no longer just working off their meal before going to the evening movie. Now everyone had a specific team, and with it, a team standing. Soccer melees were quickly discouraged by members of the team with the lower score, the referee, and the teams on the sidelines who were waiting to play.

Volleyball leagues, however, fell victim to the inconveniences of shift work almost as often as did the leagues in all the other sports. Then we went back to pick-up games and pseudo-soccer time-outs.

Few people from outside the base played volleyball, but people traveled from all over the island to play…golf. To play a round of golf on Ascension, however, required perhaps the most unusual adjustments a sportsman would ever have to make. Furthermore, of all the sports or games ever invented, only a golfer would possess the masochistic fervor to consider the challenge.

The One Boat Golf Club sponsored an eighteen-hole golf course laid out on the rocky plains a mile east of Georgetown. Armed with a good map, a keen eye, and a bit of an imagination, the golfer could tee off and chase his ball down the cinder fairways. The reward for keeping the ball clear of the frequent outcroppings of lava rock was first of all, the ball; the course chewed up golf balls like a diamond-tipped drill. Then there were the vicious ricochets. One golfer had a knack for hitting rocks head-on; he was fortunate if the abrupt 100 mile-per-hour about-face landed in front of him. Many of his swings netted him forty yard losses.

A golfer lucky enough to get past each hazardous fairway with his Titleist intact found not a "green", but a "brown" due to the mixture of diesel fuel and packed sand that surrounded the cup.

The course was as regulation as could reasonably be expected on this purely volcanic island, as the designers posted legitimate par expectations and built different sets of tees for men and women. To no one's surprise, sand traps abounded but (excuse the obvious) there were no water hazards.

Divot maintenance was much simpler than on other courses; the player simply kicked the sand and cinders around to even the course. Not all of the kicking on the course was aimed at smoothing out the rough patches, though. There were ample opportunities throughout the eighteen holes for the unwary golfer to step in some dung left by the sheep or donkeys that ambled across the course. Some golfers (but not all) would have preferred the water hazards.

And as if these hardships weren't enough, I had heard some golfers complaining that the constant wind that whipped across the plains was spoiling their game, but my golfing brother had taught me the Scots' axiom, "Nae wind, nae rain, nae golf." He translated this as, "If it ain't windy and rainy, you can't call it golf." Or to drive the point home, "Quit bitching about the weather and hit the ball." By Scottish standards, at least, Ascension golfers had nothing to complain about.

Surprisingly, there was never a shortage of players and the sports pages in the *Islander* reported results of a different tournament every week. The club functioned smoothly until one legendary month, when the weather conspired to ruin their carefully-crafted operation.

The island received an abnormal downpour that served to germinate the seeds that blow down from Green Mountain and lie dormant, often for years, awaiting just such an occurrence. The seeds took root in the moist ground and Ascension Island looked like it was on its way to becoming another Emerald Isle.

The members of the golf club were aghast. They voted to postpone the Ascension Open on the grounds that grass on the course presented an unacceptable hindrance to play. The rain had already stopped, however, and the scorching sun was too much for the flimsy shoots. They withered, died, and were whisked away by the ever-present wind. The golfers rejoiced and the tournament was back on.

I am not a golfer and hence can not understand the club members' devotion to the game as it had to be played on Ascension. I assumed the popularity of the game hinged upon the success of the tournament organizers to inject a little variety in the lives of the members, offering so many trophies, pools, novelties, and raffles, that practically anyone with a little perseverance could walk away a winner.

There was also the possibility that the club had such a loyal following because its only requirement for membership was not based upon ancestry or sex, but on the sportsman's fee and subsequent dues. One Boat provided a welcome change for the rank and file from the American base.

In all probability, however, I suspect the esteemed members of the One Boat Golf Club merely joined for bragging rights. Upon leaving Ascension, they would be entitled to boast to future foursomes that they had played on what was arguably the worst golf course in the world. There are few who would dispute the claim.

Yet another very popular game offered little in the way of cardiopulmonary benefits, although paradoxically, its players seemed to be subjected to more stress than they experienced in any of the other games. This was "Question of Arrows," a combination dart game and quiz show.

A master of ceremonies controlled the action, reading prepared trivia questions, judging answers, and keeping score. The competing teams each consisted of four players, but one player from each team stood near the dartboard. His sole responsibility was to throw darts. The resulting score determined the potential point value of the trivia question about to be posed to the other three members of his team. If a team answered incorrectly, the next group to answer the question received the points.

I first watched the game one evening in the Volcano Club recreation room. The host, a middle-aged, long time base resident named Carol, sat at a little table in a corner of the tiled room. From there, she faced the four teams of players from the base who had pulled their separate tables up to form a semi-circle around her. The dart players all sat together at another table, fingering their darts and drinking beer.

I was among the crowd of spectators pressing forward to see the dartboard and cheer for our favorites. Gloria and I were for the Bendix team, of course, and the rest of the crowd was equally divided among the other Yanks on the base, that is, RCA, Pan Am, and the Air Force.

I had always been good at trivia and proudly whispered to Gloria the answer to practically every question. The people in the spotlight, however, didn't fair so well; for example, when asked the translation of the word, *gesundheit* (German for "health") our team captain announced confidently, "God bless you." The RCA team, obviously surprised that their competitor's answer was wrong, went out on a limb with, "Go blow your nose." Pan Am and the Air Force passed.

Okay, so not everyone had the forethought to take high school German. But our base medic had apparently skipped biology, too. When Carol asked for the number of chromosomes in a normal human cell, I was shocked to hear the medic not only miss the answer, but give a guess of 45—an odd number. Living in Ascension's ovary-challenged environment, I suppose he had forgotten the basics of reproduction because *everybody* knows the answer is 46; half come from the egg and half from the sperm. I could understand forgetting a number, but at least he could have guessed an *even* number, because *everybody* knows that not only will you get an even number when you add two even numbers, you will also get an even number when you add two odd numbers.

Well, maybe not *everybody* knows it, which is why it was included in the trivia game in the first place. But my knowledge of these facts made me confident of my ability...and frustrated that I hadn't been able to help the floundering Bendix team. I also knew that these games were a prelude to an island-wide competition; the base was looking for the best representatives to face the stiffest of competition, the Brits. So far, our teams looked as though they had spent too many years with their heads buried in tracking station technical manuals and schematics. Their real-world knowledge was sadly lacking.

The next day at work, I talked my way onto the Bendix team with a quick, spontaneous duel at lunch time. I won a seat when I stumped the team members with a little movie trivia: What was Ben-Hur's number when he was a galley slave?

I also recruited Tom McWilliams, our friendly, funny operations supervisor, who not only tossed out Ben-Hur's number, but humbled me by quoting some of Jack Hawkins' lines as the Roman Consul.

"Your eyes are full of hate, Forty-One. That's good. Hate keeps a man alive. It gives him strength."

"Ah…okay, Tom," I said, "I guess you'll do."

A week later, our new team walked into round two of the base's intramural Question of Arrows. I thought we did exceedingly well in the face of some pretty tough questions. For example, Tom knew a trombone used to be called a "sackbut" and I knew the painting that ushered in the impressionist period was Monet's *Impression of Sunrise*. Coach was the third in our trio and easily fielded questions on baseball's Triple Crown, football's Super Bowls, and tennis's Grand Slams. We easily dominated the competition. We outshone everybody in every way but one—we had no points.

While putting together our Q of A dream team, we had neglected one crucial element. Our dart thrower had trouble finding the board. The other teams, however, enjoyed strings of twenty-point questions.

The stress caused by the resulting needlessly-close contest caused me to become increasingly irritated at things I had previously found amusing, like Carol's Connecticut accent and idiosyncratic mispronunciations. I rolled my eyes when I heard the clue "Who said, 'Genius is one percent inspiration and ninety-nine percent *preespiration*'" (Thomas Edison), but when she asked for the name of the city with the "world's largest man-made hopper" I was completely fooled. An image of a giant grain hopper popped into my mind and I whispered "Kansas?" to my teammates, thinking the giant wheat fields of that state would be a good place to start. Tom gave me a startled look and then smiled and whispered back.

"She thinks she's saying 'harbor', not 'hopper'. The largest man-made harbor. So the answer's Los Angeles. You need to work on your New England accents if you want to win at this game!"

Against all odds, we won. Then we replaced our dart thrower and went head-to-head with the Brits…and came in last, behind both the Georgetown and Two Boats teams. When I found out that the questions for the island-wide competition had been prepared by a Brit, I began to remember an awful lot of questions that had dealt with characters in Charles Dickens' books. Prominent figures in English history were also well represented.

Ultimately, however, I had to admit that the list of questions contained just as many references to cowboys and American generals. I also had to admit that we'd been whipped. The Brits knew their stuff.

Right about the time I was in the middle of the Question of Arrows tournament, I began to notice something odd going on at the station. All at once, a number of coworkers had begun to pepper their everyday conversation with very strange phrases. Where passing each other on the way to or from the Hashpit used to merit a simple nod or a grunt, Bendix employees now began shouting things like, "Howard Johnson is right!" or, "I'm gonna work up a number six on 'em."

There was something vaguely familiar about their talk, and it came to me one night when one of the Saints came out of the communications section, waving a handful of teletype messages and calling, "Candygram for Mongo! Candygram for Mongo!"

These were lines from what was to be the most popular movie ever to reach Ascension's shores. No, it wasn't *Citizen Kane*, *Gone With The Wind*, or even *Star Wars*. It was Mel Brooks' *Blazing Saddles*. I was puzzled at the movie's mysterious resurgence; it had been a few years since the Volcano Club's outdoor Beachcomber Theater had featured the movie.

Gloria knew the answer. A Bendix technician enjoying temporary duty in Goddard Space Flight Center, Maryland had gotten his hands on a 16mm version of the movie and used the video recording equipment available at Goddard to make a videotape. He already knew that part of our training equipment at the station included a compatible videotape player.

When the tech returned to Ascension, he brought his bootleg copy of *Blazing Saddles* with him and instantly became legend. At the same time, he considerably enhanced Mel Brooks' reputation among the Saints. Their eventual level of respect for the man's talents rivaled that given Gene Roddenberry by the Trekkies.

In truth, Mel's genius couldn't take sole responsibility for his movie's popularity among our little community. A large part of the credit must go to the medium itself. For most of our Saint work force, the television monitor kept in our training office was their introduction to video technology. Oddly, that same box became a symbol of success for many of the Saints. One young man who worked with Gloria took pictures of the television set—and its blank screen—and sent them to his parents on St Helena. He knew his family would be more impressed by the sight of their son standing next to a television than by a picture of him in a room full of satellite tracking equipment.

By the time *Blazing Saddles* arrived, the Saints had already devoured all of the training tapes available and were the station experts on soldering, fire prevention, and CPR. Suddenly, it was hard to find a Bendix Saint who hadn't watched the exploits of Sheriff Bart and The Waco Kid at least fifty times. Each viewing apparently did nothing but increase their enjoyment of the movie.

Thereafter, the Bendix Saints barraged everyone with lines stolen from the script. Any occasion would do. A Saint finding one of the men's room stalls occupied would shout, "What in the wide, wide, world of sports is goin' on in there?" Nobody reached into a pocket for any reason without first saying, "Excuse me, while I whip this out." And no Saint would walk into an all-male area without looking left, then right, then asking, "Where the white women at?" Of course, on Ascension, there were plenty of opportunities for that line.

The Bendix Saints selflessly shared their gold mine with the rest of the Saints on the island. Soon, there wasn't a Saint who didn't know the movie by heart. When Gloria and I said our final good-bye to the island a couple of years later, a Pan Am Saint at the airfield took our tickets, checked them, and handed them back. "Candygram for Mongo," he said.

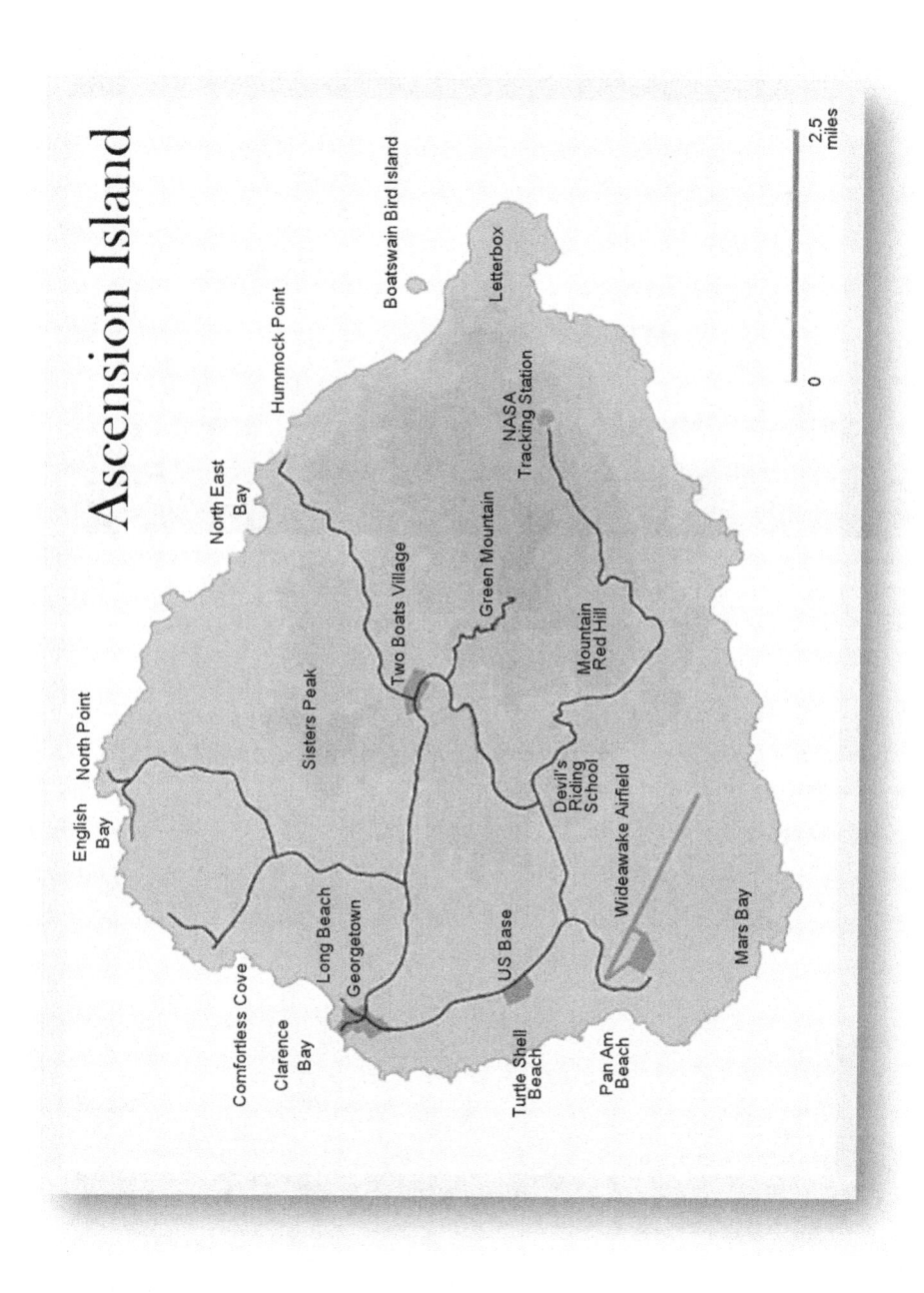

The Devil's Ashpit

Ascension Island. A rare view and a welcome sight to pilots after flying over thousands of miles of empty ocean. Pictured is the western tip and little Boatswain Bird Island, where several companies tried to profit by harvesting its rich deposits of phosphates and guano.

The Devil's Ashpit Tracking Station or "The NASA site" viewed from the west. At an elevation of 1,759 feet, it's still in the shadow of Green Mountain, which rises another thousand feet (off to the right of this picture).

The Devil's Ashpit

Gloria getting comfortable in a turtle hole on aptly-named Turtle Shell beach. Turtle Shell and Long Beach are the most popular breeding places for green turtles and the rarer hawksbill turtles. Each of these excavations holds perhaps a hundred golf ball-sized eggs.

Michael Benjamin shows off his grouper, one of the few we speared while diving with scuba tanks. The groupers' faith in their ability to blend in with the rock in their shallow caves was so unshakeable that there was no challenge in stalking them to within the three-foot range of the pole spear. Thus, we usually hunted these fish only while snorkeling.

Me, the Ascension Diver, intent on bagging a grouper.

He, the moray eel, intent on bagging an Ascension Diver.

The Devil's Ashpit

These periodic waves against the prevailing wind are called "rollers" and are shown here pounding Long Beach, the northern boundary of the Brit community of Georgetown. Their sudden occurrence is a challenge to anyone riding at anchor in Clarence Bay. No swimming on the west side of the island on this day.

Pan Am Beach is conveniently located immediately south of the American base. On no-swimming days like this one, residents resort to pig roasts, fish fries and scenery watching.

Ascension scenery circa 1979.

Pamela (Kerbow) Gates worked with me at the Corpus Christi, Texas site and then with Gloria and me on the Vanguard *before serving as Gloria's maid of honor at our wedding.*
This long friendship would explain why she was comfortable wearing a bikini when modeling for my pictures, while all of the other girls on the island considered swimwear in the style of Farmer John bib overalls.

The importance of the bikini is illustrated here. Cramer's legs were no match for Pam's and my underwater pictures underwent a dramatic improvement once she started modeling for me.
Most of the splotches at the bottom of the picture are an astonishingly abundant type of triggerfish called a "blackfish." They are harmless but have such a bad reputation as a "junk" fish that I once considered throwing away a grouper because I found a partially-digested blackfish in its belly.

The Devil's Ashpit

We were cautioned never to approach a turtle until it started dropping its eggs. Nobody cautioned the turtles not to approach night divers, though. Every underwater sighting spiked my adrenaline as our masks magnified the turtles' already impressive size.

Dozens of hatchlings crashed this nighttime beach shack party, prompting Saints David "DW" Ward, Donald "Duck" Joshua, and Barry "Bubba" Jonas to round them up.

Michael Benjamin helped me overcome my fear of eels. "Once bitten, twice shy" was literally true in my case.

This moray provided an impressive amount of meat. I thought it tasted far superior to grouper but local legend had it that eating eel was risky due to a supposed toxin.

Floating beside Mike is our catch bucket, suspended from an inner tube. Curious blackfish watch from below.

Michael shows the result when eel meets steel.

The Devil's Ashpit

Encounters with dolphins made Hummock Point's difficult access well worth the effort.

Clouds of fish and easy access made this English Bay wreck a favorite destination.

Gloria pets Maui soon after the orphan was brought to the site. The donkey became a fixture outside the Devil's Hashpit mess hall, begging for treats. As he grew, he started demanding those treats.

The full-grown Maui stubbornly going his own way.
His own way took him to the One Boat Golf Club, where he stuck his head through the open windows. This time, he begged for drinks. Maui turned out to be a mean drunk, so his original sponsor led him up to the Green Mountain farm to dry out.

Gloria cozying up against Lizard Rock.

This pillar of lava was said to contain an image of an iguana. It was also said that "painting the Lizard" was necessary to prevent a return trip to the island, thus leading to so many layers of paint that a great deal of imagination is required to pick out anything that might resemble a lizard.

The picture below shows that Lizard Rock doesn't hold the monopoly on strange rock formations. This extrusion is on the path to a shallow crater known as the Devil's Riding School.

Emiline Jensen and Daryl Dabbs stand beside the most isolated plug for Disney World I've ever seen—on the west slope of Green Mountain. Gloria and I timed our second vacation to attend this couple's stateside wedding.

A different world. The view from the Green Mountain farm was a welcome change from the cinders, lava rocks, cactus, and greasy grass strewn over the majority of the island.

The Devil's Ashpit

My only offshore fishing trip. I thought it made more sense to pick out a fish while diving than to merely hope for a fish while trolling. Mahi-mahi, tuna, and wahoo thanked me.

As if we needed another place to drink, we added a shady nook to the end of our barracks. Here, Cramer prepares himself for the rigors of swing shift (just this once.)

Dan Kovalchik

Gloria and Dan

Chapter 9

Repatriates

Originally, Gloria and I had planned to take full advantage of the Bendix vacation policy that allowed us to leave the island every three months. We wouldn't necessarily go back to the States, however. Perhaps we would get off the C-141 when it made its stopover on the West Indies island of Antigua. From there we would catch a flight to Brazil, Costa Rica, Trinidad and Tobago, or Mexico. On the other hand, some MAC flights left Ascension bound for South Africa. Maybe we would go east instead of west.

After three months on the island, though, we reconsidered our strategy.

First, there was the matter of paid versus unpaid leave. Our constant use of the term "vacation" had lulled us into a false impression of the Bendix policy, making us think we would be getting vacation *pay* during our three-week break. This was not true. We didn't get any extra vacation days for working on Ascension. If we left the island every three months, most of our time off would be unpaid.

Secondly, the agonizing memories of our last MAC flights were still with us. The thirteen-hour marathon in a plane designed primarily for cargo was so physically and mentally exhausting that neither of us was ready to cope with the thought of another long-duration flight in so short a time period. Besides, whenever we took a vacation, we would have two such flights for which we had to steel ourselves; the departure, and three weeks later, the return trip.

The third reason to stay on Ascension was the hardest to comprehend: We were used to it. As I mentioned before, our day-to-day routine hardly varied and as a result, we had a certain inertia built up. Life was simple, with few decisions to make. Every day, we slept, ate, worked, and chose one of a half-dozen ways to entertain ourselves before restarting the cycle.

Of course, this simple life had a serious drawback—boredom. We got tired of seeing, hearing, feeling, smelling, and tasting the same things every day. The island and everyone on it suffered from sameness. As time passed, it became increasingly harder to extract any excitement from any of the avenues we had open to us.

On the other hand, the Ascension sameness wasn't *all* bad. Every day we enjoyed the same temperate weather, same crime-free environment, same isolation from the world's problems, same clean ocean, and the same good friends.

The final, and perhaps the determining factor for staying on Ascension week-after-week, month-after-month, was the satisfaction we got watching our checkbook balance grow. We had no rent to pay, no utility bills, and no food bills. Any expenses we incurred at the bars or the little commissary were all paid from an eighty dollar monthly allowance we each received for living on the base.

Any time we began to doubt our commitment or wonder if our lives were headed in the right direction, we pulled out our checkbook. We could turn to any page for reassurance, as the entries were practically identical:

Date	Chk/Dep	Reason
3/4	Deposit	Paycheck
3/18	Deposit	Paycheck
4/1	Deposit	Paycheck
4/15	Deposit	Paycheck
4/18	Check	Certificate of Deposit

Money kept us on Ascension. As long as we stayed, we brought in the cash by the fistful.

We were approaching our one-year-on-the-island anniversary when Gloria casually mentioned that she wouldn't mind taking a vacation. We could rent an ocean-side condo in Cocoa Beach and spend our time visiting relatives, tracking down our *Vanguard* friends, and just plain loafing.

Suddenly, all our rationale for extending our streak blew away in a cloud of red volcanic dust. My carefully maintained inertia left me just as quickly. Within minutes of Gloria's statement, I developed a near-fatal case of short-timer's disease.

Short-timer's disease, while purely psychosomatic, is always devastating. The victim exhibits bouts of weakness, malaise, and listlessness while coping with a mental state that varies between euphoria and severe depression. Translation: In the short time I had until starting my vacation, I didn't want anything to do with work; I daydreamed about being back in the States and moaned that we needed two weeks to make our arrangements.

While I daydreamed, I realized that I had dismissed all thoughts of a globe-trotting vacation. Bendix didn't expect to see us back on Ascension for six weeks and I had no intention of spending a single minute of that time anywhere but in the States.

Gloria agreed. We had sacrificed too much over the past year and didn't want to risk trading our known inconveniences on Ascension for the unknown inconveniences of another country. We wanted to get back to the States, where we could drive for eight miles without falling into the ocean. We would walk barefoot through every grassy field we saw. We would cruise through supermarkets, not bothering to buy anything, but just reveling at the variety of products and the sheer magnitude of the operation.

We were also going to attack every menu item of every restaurant in sight. Sure, Ascension food had come a long way since the early days of British occupation, when the cooks sometimes coaxed maggots out of their flour by placing decaying fish next to it. On the other hand, our meals were typical military mess hall fare. In an era where investigative reporters were citing the members of the Pentagon for wasteful spending, our little corner of the Department of Defense was surely pulling more than its share in the war on waste. At the Hashpit, the poor swing-shifters had to face supper's leftovers at eight o'clock that evening. The midnight-shifters had it worse; they were treated to the same food at four in the morning. These rubbery entrees had never left the warming trays from the minute they had been served. It was going to be my distinct pleasure to leave Ascension food behind.

My daydreams kept me alive throughout the agonizing two-week countdown. Finally, our C-141 arrived and twenty-four hours later, we were on our way back to Florida.

Our flight touched down at Patrick Air Force Base on a bright, warm, glorious September noon. Of course, neither my wife nor I were feeling particularly glorious as we stumbled out of the plane. The rigors of fighting the rugged C-141 environment had taken their expected toll.

We had ample time to recuperate, however, as the customs agents at the base restricted us to a hanger waiting room while ground personnel unloaded our luggage. As was the norm, we had to entertain ourselves for over an hour before someone called us to get in line for declarations and luggage inspection.

I was amused to see security guards holding the leashes of two German Shepherds. The big dogs ambled casually through the maze of boxes and suitcases that had been retrieved from our plane. Both animals wore friendly "pet me" expressions that seemed oddly hypocritical considering the job they were performing. Beware of smiling narcs, I'd always heard.

I knew the luggage search and the dog parade were standard procedure for all flights that arrived from overseas, but I couldn't help but wonder if anyone seriously thought they were going to find something on a plane returning from Ascension Island. The island barely allowed us the necessities of life; it sure didn't supply us with any extras, legal or otherwise. To think that we would make the Ascension-Florida trip to smuggle contraband or to act as mules for a drug cartel stretched my imagination, which up to that time, had always been pretty flexible.

On the other hand, the human spirit is a force to be reckoned with. I suppose that if word got out that flights from Ascension were not going to be subject to any more searches, drug lords would soon be fighting to establish the majority share in The Ascension Connection.

Gloria and I passed our inspection and quickly called a cab to take us a few miles north to Cocoa Beach. On the way, I stared at the tall shady pines and searched for coconuts atop the palm trees that lined the ocean highway. These trees grew out of lawns that were, for the most part, thick and manicured, but even those that lay untended reflected a shocking green. House after house sat amidst landscaping comprised of a thousand varieties of tropical trees, shrubs, and flowers. Accustomed as I was to the bleak environment of the barracks and the fragile, thirsty, donkey-nipped postage-stamp gardens tended by the Georgetown residents, the abundance of greenery in each Cocoa Beach setting was actually garish in comparison.

Our gawking was interrupted as the cabby stopped at a car rental agency. Gloria and I unloaded our bags under the bright sun and lugged them into the shady, air-conditioned office, where I was quite surprised to see a Brit. Actually, finding a Brit in tourist-choked Florida wasn't surprising. The real oddity was that my Ascension exposure to subjects of the Crown had given me the ability, at least in this case, to look at a person and recognize his Anglo-Saxon heritage.

Even more surprising was that I didn't make my judgment based upon the man's looks or even his speech; the Brit was turned away from me with a telephone pressed to his ear.

I had known he was a Brit from his posture. He stood like a Brit. More correctly, he stood in a casual, self-assured, just-shy-of arrogant stance. I'd come to recognize the pose through years of watching English actors portraying stuffy noblemen in old movies. And, of course, I'd also noticed a number of the Exiles Club patrons standing in that same way only hours before we had left Ascension.

I found myself becoming irritated at this faceless, nameless Brit and simultaneously wondered at my prejudice. Certainly, I had formed a low opinion of a few of the Ascension Brits, but the vast majority on the island were witty, personable, and very talented. I was especially impressed by their ability and inclination to organize and participate.

Even Tooley had won my grudging admiration in these departments. Aside from performing as a secretary for the Ascension Divers, he held offices in two other clubs, ran the projector for the Georgetown Cinema Club, and wrote and performed imaginative skits for the two variety shows the Brits had produced.

My irritation, I concluded, stemmed from the presence of a reminder of Ascension Island so soon after I had left the place. I'm sure I would have felt the same had I walked through the door and seen one of the Yanks who had just gotten off the plane with us.

Gloria and I had gone through the same emotion when we had traveled together on the *Vanguard*. Upon arriving in such ports as Sydney, Australia, or Mombasa, Kenya, my sweetheart and I would search the town far and wide to find a little out-of-the-way place. We wanted to bask in the ambiance of our new experience without having to share our space with the rest of the *Vanguard* crew, many of whom were becoming annoying after months together at sea. Nevertheless, no matter what size the city or how far we drove to get away from the ship, whatever tavern we selected for our *tête-à-tête* had already been invaded by our shipmates.

The clerk who had been waiting on the Brit finally turned her attention to us and soon, Gloria and I were loading our luggage into a brand new rental car. Our next stop was a real estate agency to sign a lease and pick up the keys to a condominium we had reserved by telephone from Ascension.

Gloria begged me to let her drive our shiny new car. Before answering, I looked up and down the street. The lunch hour traffic had all but disappeared, although I saw some cars lining up behind a stoplight a half-mile away.

"Do you think you can manage?" I asked.

I was only half-joking. I wasn't worried about Gloria's ability to switch back to right-hand drive; even after a year on Ascension, we had to make a conscious decision to pull onto the left side of the island's roads.

I was worried about the number of cars I saw. Although we had never truly acclimated ourselves to Ascension's left-hand drive, we had adjusted very well to the Ascension traffic, meaning no traffic at all. On the island, sharing the road with another vehicle was a rare event. Indeed, we became so accustomed to having the road to ourselves that the sight of another car would elicit a number of emotions, all of which served to raise our blood pressure. I'm not talking about a slow-moving granny in front of us or a tailgater behind us; I mean a car maintaining a half-mile distance as it followed the roads snaking around the volcanoes, disappearing and reappearing with each turn. After playing peekaboo for a minute or two, the aggravation became so intense that I just pulled off the road and waited for the intruder to disappear entirely. Then I would resume my journey.

I can't explain why this was such a problem. I only know that after I hesitantly broached the subject to some of my friends, I found out I wasn't the only Ascension driver who had developed that idiosyncrasy.

Standing beside highway A1A, Cocoa Beach's busiest highway, it was evident that we would be in for a very long wait if we were foolish enough to want the road to ourselves, even in the Cocoa Beach of the '70s. Gloria assured me, though, that she could handle the pressure. I'm not so sure that I could have.

As my wife drove, I contented myself with admiring the car's interior. Compared to the sparse accessories of our aged, sun-cracked, stripped-down Ascension van, the clean, smooth, loaded-with-extras interior of our new car seemed ridiculously plush. I was amazed that the rental agency had classified this luxurious vehicle in the economy class. Instead of feeling proud to be associated with such opulence, however, I found myself feeling embarrassed at such an ostentatious display.

At the realtor's, we ran into a problem with our new car; Gloria couldn't pull the key out of the ignition. She made sure the transmission was in Park, spun the steering wheel, and even set the emergency brake, all while twisting and pulling the key. It turned, but wouldn't come out.

"Shit!" she yelled, slamming the steering wheel in frustration, "Now we're going to have to return the car."

Something stirred my memory as I watched her working to free the key, something I'd read in a magazine that had found its way to the island a few months before. Something about new cars and new anti-theft mechanisms. I cast a stealthy glance at the steering column and sure enough, I saw a little post just aching to be pushed.

I offered Gloria my help. She not-so-politely declined. The vehemence in her answer, no doubt, was due to the stress built-up from the struggle with the recalcitrant key after the strain of our long night.

Stifling a smile, I tactfully agreed that only a master locksmith could get the key out. We would take the car back as soon as we finished with the realtor.

Thus appeased, Gloria turned to step out of the car. I, of course, was waiting for this moment. I reached under the steering wheel, pressed the release and pulled out the key. Gloria wasn't even all the way out of the car yet.

"Here, catch!" I called, tossing her the key ring before she had a chance to close the door. I was very amused at my cleverness but I also felt the first twinge of disorientation. Gloria and I had been out of the mainstream too long. We had very nearly been defeated by a simple year-old feature that had been added to that most American of possessions, the automobile. I wondered just how many other now-commonplace bits of Americana would be new to us. Could we actually suffer from culture shock in our own country?

Inside the real estate agency, we met Debbie, whom we had talked to when we had called from Ascension. I had pictured a pretty, friendly girl to go along with the pretty, friendly voice I had heard over the long distance lines, and I was not disappointed; Debbie was a voluptuous thirty-year-old with sandy brown hair. I found her so distracting that I could only nod and smile dumbly as she explained the lease agreement on the apartment we were about to rent.

People find it hard to believe, but the overwhelming male/female ratio on Ascension affected me, too. Of course, I didn't suffer the withdrawal pains experienced by most of the rest of the male population there; I not only had female companionship, I had what I thought was the best. But then again, I had considered girls to be a valuable commodity even before Ascension. As every Madison Avenue advertising executive knows, sex sells; it sells because men were put on the earth to, above all else, love and admire women. There's nothing like a stretch in prison or a little Ascension duty to reinforce that notion.

Debbie eventually folded up the lease and invited us to follow her as she drove to what would be our home for the next six weeks.

Home turned out to be a three-bedroom apartment in the Sunrise Condominiums, located directly on the beach. I was a trifle disappointed with my first view of the building; Sunrise Condominiums was a rather generic squat and boxy structure compared to its high-rise neighbors. The building's drawing card, however, became clear once we stepped inside; each unit boasted a two-story high glass wall that afforded a commanding view of the ocean.

I walked around the apartment, running my hands over the opulent trappings. Wall hangings, oil paintings, and knickknacks decorated the walls. A thickly-piled couch, love seat and armchair suite served as velvety room dividers. Strategically-placed mirrors gave the illusion of more windows and extra room. Not a single furnishing or appliance was remotely similar to anything in our barracks.

I began to feel the same stirrings of embarrassment I had experienced in the car. While I could have been satisfied with an apartment that didn't require us to push two twin beds together to form a double, this eight-hundred-dollar-per-month apartment was about the best Cocoa Beach had to offer. It was also about five-hundred dollars-per-month more than the apartments we had rented prior to moving overseas.

Gloria, on the other hand, appeared to have no such misgivings about our self-indulgence. She was unabashedly enthusiastic about our smartly decorated home. And when I saw that the master bedroom was in a loft above the living room, treating us to an impossibly magnificent spectacle of the condo's verdant grounds, the sun-bleached dunes and beach, and the shimmering, blue ocean beyond, I forgot my embarrassment. We deserved to live like this.

We signed our lease and handed over our check. We were in. Then Debbie remembered yet another of the apartment's features; flipping a switch on the nightstand in the loft, she told us, would open and close the two-story curtains bunched on either side of the glass wall. We could awaken at dawn, open the curtains, and view the sunrise from our bed. I couldn't wait for morning.

Although we had endured a stressful, sleepless night on the C-141, we decided to try to stay awake as long as possible on our first day back in civilization in order to get our bodies back into Eastern Standard Time. It wasn't hard; we were too excited to sleep. We were home.

Ever since our time together on the *Vanguard* tracking ship, Gloria and I had come to consider ourselves Floridians. This was despite Gloria's Mississippi/Maryland upbringing and my Pennsylvania mining country background.

I can partially attribute our allegiance to the Sunshine State to the role it played in our courtship and marriage. Gloria and I had met and become close while on the ship, but we didn't get serious until one long port stay in Florida. We had taken that opportunity to travel the state, tossing our hard-earned sea pay at the ticket booths of the expensive tourist attractions that dot the state. Our time together in Florida had been one long, carefree romp.

A somewhat less romantic reason for deserting our home states was the significance of Florida as the *Vanguard*'s home port, its dock between assignments. After spending long months at sea mixing varying quantities of adventure and deprivation, we used the words "Florida" and "home" interchangeably. The sighting of the Kennedy Space Center's massive Vehicle Assembly Building on the horizon was as welcome a sight to us weary travelers as the Statue of Liberty was to millions of immigrants.

Our excursions to Ecuador and Ascension Island had further reinforced the notion of Florida as home turf. The only link to the States from Ecuador was Miami, and many of Cocoa Beach's residents considered Ascension as merely a far-flung extension of Patrick Air Force Base.

All of these forces combined to tell us we were home. It didn't hurt our state of mind to know that most people considered our adopted home to be an ideal setting for a vacation.

We spent the remainder of the afternoon on the beach, showing off our deep Ascension tans to all the tourists. For supper, Debbie had recommended a nightly all-you-can-eat surf and turf buffet hosted by one of the swanky beach hotels. We found the place just after sunset, and I wasn't disappointed in Debbie's taste.

The hotel was decorated Caribbean-style. We toured the grounds, guided by the light of the full moon and a string of flaming torches planted along the flowered walkways. A steel drum band hammered out a calypso somewhere nearby. I recognized the tune as one I had last heard the morning the *Vanguard* had sailed from Trinidad.

The dancing yellow-orange flames led us to a huge thatched pavilion where we found the band, an outdoor bar, and the buffet.

The lavish display of food was yet another reminder of the austere lifestyle to which we had subjected ourselves over the previous year. The buffet tables ringed the three sides of the giant pavilion not occupied by the stage and the bar, and a small army of cooks and busboys tended an unbelievable variety of dishes that occupied every available square inch of space.

I saw that many of the attendants were more concerned with exhibiting the food than serving it. Whenever a patron removed a morsel from the meticulously decorated platters, someone hurried to repair the damage to the concentric circles of meats, overlapping triangles of pastries, or pyramids of scooped casseroles. Other intricately carved food in the cornucopia was clearly ornamental and not meant to be eaten.

The overall effect of this sight on a couple who had been exposed to a year-long succession of drably colored, unappetizing smelling, bland tasting offerings was predictable. Gloria and I attacked the buffet like starving refugees.

At first, I carefully reserved half of my plate for the steak and lobster that was being served at the end of the line. There were just too many attractive dishes to pass by, however, and even though I sampled only one out of every dozen platters, the reserved area gradually eroded until only a narrow sliver of space remained.

I fretted that my surf and turf might be limited to a fried oyster and a meatball, but then I saw that the entrée chef was using a separate plate for the slab of steak and the lobster tail! This was my go-ahead to dish myself a few more pounds of food onto my overloaded plate, creating a ridiculously huge mound of carefully structured helpings of all the major food groups, each with multiple representation. Gloria applied the same strategy.

In all, we carried enough food back to our table to comfortably feed ten people. For good measure, a roving waiter came by and set a bottle of wine in front of us.

Somehow, we got it all in, although there was certainly no room for an after-dinner mint. Gloria and I returned to our apartment, groaning at our foolhardy excess. As we prepared for bed, we made a pact to skip the next few meals and then to eat sensibly during the remainder of our vacation.

We were terribly uncomfortable, but consoled ourselves with the knowledge that we at least had Cocoa Beach's most comfortable apartment in which to recuperate. As if to demonstrate just how much comfort we were talking about, I climbed up to the loft and found the switch on the nightstand to close the huge two-story curtains. I called for Gloria to watch and flipped the switch.

Nothing happened. I flipped it a few more times and listened for the sound of the motor. Again nothing. I went down to the living room and checked behind the curtains to see if the motor was plugged in. It was. It just didn't work.

I pulled the curtains shut by hand and returned to the loft to turn in. I was disappointed, but after all, we would have never known about the curtain switch or even expected it if Debbie hadn't remembered it at the last minute. Furthermore, we probably would not have used it more than once or twice. For the rest of our stay, we would most likely be cursing the sun as it shone directly through a quarter-acre of glass, overheating our apartment.

Thus solaced, I threw back the bedspread. There lay disappointment number two. I stared with disbelief at what had lain hidden during our first day in our expensive apartment, an apartment that was the polar opposite of our dour Ascension Island barracks. The double bed that I was looking forward to sharing with Gloria after a year of awkward twin bed maneuvering on the island was not a double bed at all. Despite our eight-hundred-dollar-per-month rent, the bed in our stunningly decorated master bedroom was actually two twin beds pushed together.

It was a cheesy rip off. For all our work and sacrifice, coming back to the States was supposed to have been a perfect vacation. Instead, we found out that things still went wrong no matter how much money we put in the bank. The difference was, if something went wrong in a cheap place, we'd expect it. Apparently, renting higher-priced digs just meant we were setting ourselves up for a bigger dose of frustration.

We eased our bloated bodies into bed and resolved to make the most out of the rest of our vacation.

This promise had to wait, however, as the next morning found us vying for the bathroom, using the toilet to catch the effluent that exploded from both above and behind. This was the first of three days of sickness and repentance for our gluttony, or perhaps it was merely the shock to our systems of spiced foods, jet-lag, and exposure to bacteria outside the comparatively sterile Ascension environment.

After three days of misery, I forced myself to crawl out of the apartment; I had a softball game to play! A call to JD Lynn, a friend we'd met on the *Vanguard*, had resulted in an invitation to join him and twenty others who had some past or present link with the tracking ships that called Port Canaveral their home. JD would have been hard-pressed to form even one team if he had limited his eligibility requirements to Bendix and RCA workers currently serving on the ships, which were gradually being retired. But many former shipmates had stayed in Brevard County, finding work at Patrick Air Force Base or the giant Harris Corporation. And after a long post-Apollo drought, the contractors at the Kennedy Space Center had begun hiring in preparation for Space Shuttle operations.

JD picked me for one of his outfielders, which was a mistake. I stacked up error after error and it wasn't because of my weakened condition. The problem was the grass. You don't just pluck someone off the Rock and put them down in one of the meticulously-maintained outfields of the Cocoa Beach Sports Complex and expect him to keep his eye on the ball. The lush green carpet was just too distracting. Batter after batter got on base while I walked slowly and deliberately around the outfield, watching my feet bending blades of green, green grass and marveling at the feel of the cushioned step.

Any other coach would have gone apoplectic, but JD had spent his time on the Rock, too. He called time, observed that I reminded him of a dog trying to walk through snow for the first time, and moved me to the infield, where the brown sand would make me feel a little closer to home. It was a good move. I played better.

After the game, JD drove me to the local dive shop to sign up for a scuba certification course. I had allowed the Ascension Divers to deny me access to their air compressor for long enough. I still resented the club's pairing me with Tooley and after just a few minutes into my Cocoa Beach scuba class, I also found myself resenting the terms of the internationally-sanctioned certification course that appeared to be designed solely to benefit the dive shops that offered it. Despite having memorized the text books and despite having more diving experience than my instructor, I had to take time out of my vacation to attend the lectures and perform boring tasks in a swimming pool. In the end, though, I would be able to wave the treasured cert card at the next club meeting and proceed to pump as much air as I needed, as often as I needed.

Once Gloria and I were both fully recovered from our first day shocks, we quickly adjusted to the Florida vacationers' beachside lifestyle, or more accurately, the Ascension vacationer's version of beachside lifestyle. Although we had often listened to our fellow islanders boast of just how far they were going to go to blow off their three months of accumulated steam, most coworkers seemed to change their minds once they stepped onto the tarmac at Patrick Air Force Base. Relieved to be in the States, they exchanged their wild plans for a few weeks of somewhat milder fare—the simple pleasures that most US citizens have forgotten to treasure.

A vacation spent luxuriating in these simple pleasures would, by anyone else's standards, qualify for a trip to the travel agent's "Refunds" window. But our year of deprivation gave us a new appreciation for activities our condo neighbors would consider mundane: Who else but a barracks-dweller would have thought twice about the comfort afforded by a furnished three-bedroom apartment? Who else would have truly savored the sight, smell, and taste of supermarket-fresh food, unless they'd been on the receiving end of our infamous Hashpit warming trays for a year? For that matter, who else would have enjoyed a simple walk through the supermarket unless they had sampled the feebly-stocked micro-market in Georgetown?

Then, of course, there was the Merritt Square Mall. To see such a collection of stores and goods amassed under one roof was almost more than Gloria could bear; it even made me forget that I was a non-shopper.

We bought some new clothes and, although I'd always considered the Ascension laundry service to be one of our more appreciated benefits, it was a new feeling to pull out a pair of underwear that didn't have my name stenciled on it. Likewise, it was good to see a telephone book again, and to dial numbers longer than the three-digit barracks numbers.

Our evenings became the standard "dinner and a movie," and we made it a point to visit every ethnic restaurant in Brevard County and enjoy first-run movies with identifiable actors and audible soundtracks.

We did all this, and more, but our first thought each morning as we watched the sunrise through our two-story windows was the beach: How soon could we get out of the apartment and onto the sand? The stateside food, entertainment, and services were grand, but our front yard ocean-side real estate was grander still. Even the mall could wait.

One such morning, Gloria and I positioned our cooler and towels on the warm sand at the base of the dunes and walked down to the cool, wet, hard-packed strip at the water's edge. We strolled for a mile along the wide coastline, watching for signs of dolphins, rays, or other sea life curious enough to brave the shallow, turbid water. Whenever waves thrust themselves up to wash our ankles with cool, hissing water, we took the opportunity to kick up a spray of droplets and watched as the unfiltered sunshine transformed the airborne pattern into a shower of diamonds.

An excited bikini-clad two-year-old interrupted our walk, soliciting Gloria's opinion of her sand castle. The "castle" wasn't much more than a lumpy mound of compacted silt and it was already in danger of becoming a casualty to the incoming tide. Nevertheless, Gloria stooped for a closer inspection, possibly in search of some feature to justify the praise she began heaping upon the little architect.

I, meanwhile, noticed that a low, slow-moving shape out over the ocean was not a wave-skimming pelican, but a faraway airplane. This was a curiosity. While the skies above Cocoa Beach were always filled with traffic,

The Devil's Ashpit

the parade of vehicles thrumming overhead had thus far consisted of banner-towing biplanes and tourist-toting private planes. The shape in the distance, however, was different, obviously a much bigger plane. I wondered if the pilot was in distress, preparing to ditch his craft in the sea.

I felt Gloria returning to my side again and, after I pointed out the plane to her, we watched it for some minutes as it hugged the horizon, slowly winging its way north. Our perspective of the plane's outline gradually changed, and I realized it was turning. After another long minute, I saw that the plane had turned almost completely around and was getting bigger as it began to close the distance between us. I had just calculated that its new heading would take it somewhere south of our position when I was suddenly able to discern the distinctive shape of the airplane I should know better than any other.

I quickly recalled the day and estimated the time. Yes, everything clicked into place.

"Hey," I said, squeezing my wife's hand excitedly, "That's a C-141. It's the Thursday night flight from Ascension, heading for Patrick."

"Oh, no," Gloria replied. I heard the despair in her voice. A second later, I felt the same emotion attacking the pit of my stomach. No, this wasn't our plane; we still had two more weeks of vacation. But we had just been served a rude reminder that our carefree days of fun and sun were numbered. The effect took me back to my high school years, when the sound of the *Bonanza* theme song triggered the same subdued panic; as much as I enjoyed that Sunday evening television show, it was the signal that my weekend was over and, more often than not, a reminder that I hadn't done my homework.

The sight of the Starlifter served to dampen our spirits for most of the day, but we recuperated in time to attend a number of TGIF celebrations that evening. By the following week, we had forgotten the episode and before we knew it, we were in our final days of vacation. I had expected that the thought of our impending trip would have driven us to counseling during our last week. Instead, we were so busy that we had few opportunities to feel sorry for ourselves.

Our salvation lay in the shopping list our friends had given us before we left for vacation. This list was a part of the Ascension vacation ritual. Anyone taking a trip to the land of plenty was expected to spend part of their hard-earned time making special purchases for their friends across the sea.

The items that graced our list could be divided into two categories. First, there were those luxuries that couldn't be found in the dozens of mail-order catalogs that made their way to the island. A walk through a drugstore was usually sufficient to satisfy these requests.

The remainder of the desirables on the shopping list were much more of an imposition. These were generally big-ticket items, either impractical to order by long distance or too expensive to ship. The truck tires, the window-mounted air conditioning unit, and the room-sized carpet on our list fit into this category. Since the Air Force gave us a generous baggage allowance, these goods could accompany us on the plane but their purchasing and packaging took most of our time, energy, and good humor.

As frustrating as these bigger orders were to fulfill, our Ops buddy, Tom, had warned us that some of the drugstore purchases could be just as difficult. On one of his vacations, Tom had promised to buy some model cement as a favor to one of the other supervisors, whose hobby was building model ships.

Tom had cleaned out the store's display case, tossing a dozen tubes in his basket. The cashier, however, refused to ring up the sale. Instead, she had called the manager. Tom's explanation did not lower the manager's raised eyebrows. Buying for "a friend?" He lives on a little island, far away? Would you mind signing this form attesting to the fact that you are buying twelve tubes of glue?

The problem, of course, was that glue-sniffing had become a popular pastime for kids in the States. Still, I wouldn't have thought that Tom fit the description of a glue-pusher, although I had noticed that Ascension residents were generally less than traditional when it came to clothes and hairstyles. Nevertheless, even temporary fugitives from Ascension made an attempt to fit into society once they left the island. Since this episode had occurred at the end of Tom's vacation, he was probably relatively clean cut.

Gloria and I experienced no such problems in the drugstore, even when we bought another gross of condoms. I was glad to see that my overeager, hormone-inspired condom purchase of the year before had worked to our advantage, allowing us to remain on Ascension as long as we did without worrying about birth control. Of course, we could have asked one of our stateside friends to mail us a few dozen, but we were spared that awkward request.

Once we had our drugstore booty safely tucked away, we went out for one more big purchase, a motorcycle.

A motorcycle, it seemed to me, would suit our island travel needs perfectly and we would no longer have to rely on our wobbly, dangerous van, which seemed to lose a few more nuts and bolts with every revolution of the crankshaft. We would ride in style on a new 400cc Yamaha Enduro. The Enduro was a ruggedly built, lightweight version of a street bike.

When parked next to a true dirt bike, the Enduro lost some of its appeal, as its comparatively smooth and shiny styling made it look like a sissy bike. Sales personnel, however, had cleverly displayed the Enduros intermingled with the weighty, heavily ornamented street bikes. The

The Devil's Ashpit

contrast gave the crossbreed a fast and sporty look. It would be a pleasure to have such a sleek, reliable vehicle on the island; for once, Gloria and I could do a little joyriding, something we could never say we had done in the dangerous van.

With time running short, we crated up our export goods and, with the help of a few of our former shipmates, we trucked the boxes to Patrick Air Force Base. Gloria and I bid a sad farewell to the Sunrise Condominiums, returned our rental car, and before we knew it, we were standing on the tarmac outside Patrick's main hanger, waiting for the signal to begin boarding the C-141.

Suddenly, I felt a wave of depression washing over me. This wasn't too surprising; how many people look forward to going back to work after six-weeks of relaxation? But we weren't just leaving our vacation resort, we were leaving our home and returning to our island prison.

The circumstances surrounding this trip were very different from the last time I had stood on the Patrick runway; back then, all my thoughts had been devoted to reunion scenes with Gloria. Ascension, for the most part, had merely served to provide a nebulous backdrop for my daydreams.

This time, however, I knew what was waiting for me—boredom and sacrifice. In the past year, the stark attractiveness of our remote pile of rock and ash had worn thin, exposing the sores that festered beneath the surface. Gloria and I were going back to our tedious daily regimen. We'd be working with the same people and we'd be hearing the same complaints. We'd be eating the same bland food, watching the same second-rate movies, and avoiding the same habitual drunks as we had done six weeks before. And we were about to board a C-141 and endure a grueling thirteen-hour flight for the privilege.

This last thought reopened a mental wound inflicted only weeks before, when a Boeing 727 had collided in midair with a smaller plane near San Diego, California. A photographer had caught the plane in its out-of-control dive to the ground. Of course, every newspaper and news magazine splashed that horrifying picture on its cover, the first picture I'd ever seen of a disaster in the making. The resolution of the photo clearly showed the passenger windows, some glowing yellow-orange, reflecting the fire streaming from the plane's shattered wing. Mercifully, the photo was not good enough to show the faces of the people behind the windows. This, however, didn't stop me from imagining them.

With great trepidation, I boarded our carrier. We were not fortunate enough to get seats beside either of the two small windows, and for the first time, I experienced a terrible feeling of claustrophobia in an airplane.

Flying with the rotation of the earth, we quickly outdistanced what little sunlight the windows provided. The resulting lack of reference points triggered a near-constant attack of vertigo and I suffered the remainder of the trip, trying to ignore the sensation of falling.

Despite a smooth, uneventful flight, I found it hard to shake off my newly-acquired fear of flying. Gloria and I returned to the business of running a tracking station for seven more months before we garnered the courage to leave the island again. Then, within days of our arrival in Florida, another air disaster occurred. This one was in Chicago; a DC-10 crashed when one of its engines fell off during takeoff. Again, a photographer had captured the plane's final plunge on film. Again, the image was plastered on every newsstand.

For me, air travel would never be the same.

Chapter 10

Wake-up Call

By returning to Ascension for what would be our second year on the island, we could proudly count ourselves as members of a different caste within the American community. Understandably, a large part of our assessment of one another focused upon the amount of time each person had spent on the island.

At the bottom of the island hierarchy were those employees who had signed the customary contract committing themselves to a year of Ascension service but who had reneged on the promise. Of course, by the time we identified the people who fit into this category, they had already applied the requisite coats of paint to the Lizard and were within hours of changing their status to former Ascension residents.

The number of employees who broke their contracts was surprisingly small; generally, anyone recruited to make the trip was mature enough to stand by his decision. In my experience, the deserters were not the kind of people I enjoyed working with anyway. Bendix administrators may have realized this; rather than waving contracts at the unhappy workers, they quietly issued them return tickets to the States.

One technician to receive the early return ticket also holds the record for the fastest bailout. His change of heart occurred shortly after his C-141 landed at the airfield. While standing in the hatchway, the tech apparently didn't like what he saw; he returned to his seat and refused to leave. When the plane took off that night for its return trip to the States, the tech was still aboard. Obviously, the thought of two thirteen-hour trips in one day was more appealing than whatever he saw outside the hatch.

Another tech fared little better. He actually disembarked and went to work the next day. Afterwards, he did a little drinking. Then he decided to borrow one of the tracking station vans to do a little sightseeing. Unfortunately, the route chosen by his alcohol-muddled brain took him straight through a utility pole. When he took it out, he also took out the lines that carried our voice and telemetry data to the British satellite station. The next day found him back aboard a C-141 after having honored a grand total of three days out of his 365 day contract.

Next on the Ascension seniority ladder were those people intent on leaving immediately after fulfilling their one-year obligation. Again, although there were those who fretfully counted down their days to freedom, this percentage of the base population was not as large as one might expect. Overseas contractors had a little help in this area; the Internal Revenue Service had placed a hurdle in our path that was much more meaningful than any contract. This was the eighteen month rule.

Our overseas salary wasn't automatically exempted from federal income tax. If we wanted our net pay to equal our gross pay, we had to show that we had earned our money during an eighteen-month stretch at an IRS-approved site.

We had no trouble with IRS approval; Ascension was on the list. The eighteen months, however, proved to be quite an obstacle, particularly when the filer learned that he couldn't count just any eighteen month period; his overseas time had to begin and end within certain months in order for him to be eligible for the exemption.

Tax time never failed to devastate a few individuals who hadn't understood the tax laws, learning too late that some of their Ascension months didn't count towards the exemption. Those who did qualify for the tax break, however, reaped the satisfaction of what amounted to a twenty-five or thirty percent pay raise when compared to our stateside counterparts.

The eighteen-month barrier was a popular measure of success for Americans on Ascension and marked the date for many of our coworkers to return to civilization. By no means, however, did the completion of this magic interval mark the end of every employee's island tenure.

For most of us, our term could be defined by a simple formula; we balanced our greed against the inconvenience of our situation. As long as avarice continued to hold its thumb on the scales, we stayed. Like Fred C. Dobbs and the other prospectors in *Treasure of the Sierra Madre*, we had found our gold and had settled in to mine it for as long as we could stand the tedium. Eventually there would come a time when, just like the prospectors, our yearnings for a return to normalcy would outweigh the allure of the unmined treasure and we would abandon our claim.

At least, that was my view when I first arrived on Ascension. As time passed, however, I realized that money-grubbing couldn't account for everyone's presence. Some residents had celebrated five or more years on the island and gave no indication that they were considering pulling out. I had to reevaluate my theory; nobody could be that greedy.

One group of long-timers with obvious motives were the isolationists. These were all older men, none of whom had ever been married. They were featureless, colorless, and practically indistinguishable from each other; often, they were indistinguishable from the woodwork. None spoke more than the few sentences required to order an omelet or to answer a question about satellite telemetry signal strengths.

The isolationists didn't smoke, drink, womanize, throw parties, attend parties, swim, fish, or play sports. Their daily routine never varied and they never left their rooms except to go to work, to the mess hall, or to the movies.

Some of these men had come from the *Vanguard*, where they had led the same inconspicuous lifestyle. Whatever their phobia was, it seemed remarkably well-suited to hardship duty. They had cooks to prepare their meals, stewards to clean their rooms and launder their clothes, and chauffeurs to drive them to work. This no-frills, no-decision, monotonous lifestyle appeared to suit these introverts just fine. Where in the States could they find such a deal? Besides prison, that is.

That was certainly the question bothering one member of this group who saw his retirement approaching. While the company processed his termination papers, word spread around the island that the retiree was preparing for his departure in a somewhat unorthodox manner; he was giving away everything he owned, including his stateside possessions.

The inescapable conclusion was that the elderly gentleman was going to commit suicide. This thought gained even more credence when, on the day of his scheduled departure, he was nowhere to be found.

The retiree resurfaced only after his plane left. He'd been hiding in the rocks. The company brass belatedly recognized their employee's single-minded devotion and tore up his termination papers. He happily settled back into his rut.

The isolationists *wanted* to stay on Ascension. There was another group of workers, however, who felt they *had* to stay on the island. I called this group the "lifers."

The lifers were longtime employees who had been with the tracking station network since its heyday; at one time, the network they served had boasted as many as twenty stations around the world. While satisfying their wanderlust (and always looking for a better deal), these men had traveled most of the available continents and five or six of the seven seas. They had spent years living in some of the most attractive areas the earth had to offer.

In the process, these technicians accumulated much more money than someone with their education could normally expect to receive. They had the unfettered space program of the Sixties to thank for that. In those days, supervisors authorized overtime pay without question. Temporary duty assignments were common, and each employee received a generous *per diem* check along with not-so-subtle instructions to pad their expense reports to account for all funds dished out.

For assignments abroad, the IRS tossed in another incentive in the form of a no-limit exemption. Money earned overseas in that golden era was tax-free, period. In that respect, tracking stations on the lovely Canary Islands or swanky Bermuda were on equal footing with the facility on Ascension Island.

1969 saw the first returns of the country's investment in the expensive Apollo program and simultaneously marked the beginning of the end of the NASA gravy train. Nationwide, thousands of aerospace contractors lost their jobs. Unemployment hit the Cocoa Beach area especially hard; the most astonishing collection of technicians, engineers, and scientists the world had ever known was left without an industry. In a high-technology sequel to *The Grapes of Wrath*, families walked away from their mortgages, loaded their possessions into trailers and drove off in search of a new career.

The cutbacks extended their reach to the tracking stations. Some closed down immediately. Others remained in operation until the last Skylab crew splashed down in 1974. Then, with our astronaut force grounded and no manned spaceflights on the budgeted horizon, the necessity for a far-flung tracking station network disappeared. A few well-placed sites were all that were required to handle all of the unmanned spacecraft NASA still supported.

The overseas lifers were caught in a squeeze. They and their gradually acquired families had become used to the artificially high standard of living they had been enjoying. But no comparable positions existed in the States that could offer an equivalent salary. The lifers were looking at a move that would seriously crimp their lifestyle.

Furthermore, these workers had become specialists; they were tracking station technicians, accustomed to working on aging, often obsolete equipment. The lifers' years of experience had been accumulated at a heavy cost; their isolation from the mainstream had also sheltered them from the digital electronics boom that was occurring in private industry. Thus, in many cases, recent tech school graduates were better qualified to fill the available technical jobs. Where could the tracking station specialists apply their skills but at another tracking station?

Once the jobs and their perks began to disappear, these techs felt they had only one solution; they sent the wife and kids to the States and got themselves transferred to one of the non-family assignments, the only high-paying jobs left in the dwindling network.

It was my daily exposure to the lifers that resurrected a vague promise I had made to myself when I was in college, some five years before. On the day that I decided to forgo the seemingly insurmountable challenge of becoming an electrical engineer in favor of the simpler, shorter path inherent to becoming a technician, I told myself that the switch would be a temporary one; after getting my two-year degree, I would find a tech job and make some money for a few years before returning to school for the four-year degree.

Five years later, I was on the Rock and hadn't made a single move towards furthering my education. I looked at my forty, fifty, and sixty-year-old coworkers and wondered how many of them had made and broken the same promise. Undoubtedly, the ready money of the previous decades had clouded their judgment; people with secure, high-paying jobs don't generally storm the gates of academia.

But the future was anything but secure. Although the Space Shuttle was in the final stages of development, which would mean a renewed requirement for world-wide coverage, a new satellite system was also in the works. The goal of the Tracking Data Relay Satellite System (TDRSS) was to provide ground controllers with one-hundred percent coverage of earth-orbiting satellites. Unfortunately for network personnel, the ingenious TDRSS design would be able to meet that goal with only two tracking stations; one in New Mexico and the other in Guam. Development problems had resulted in a five-year postponement, but the TDRSS implementation was inevitable.

Unless we made some intelligent decisions, my coworkers and I were going to find our career paths taking some undesirable twists and turns. Not only were our tracking stations headed for oblivion, but there was some language in the want-ads of our week-old newspapers that made me realize that I was ill-prepared to interview for a technician job in the States.

My most marketable skill by far was my SCE experience, though at this point, I could only claim a total of two years on that equipment. In 1976, when Bendix had offered me the SCE position at the Quito station, I was thrilled to be receiving training on the most technologically advanced piece of hardware in the network's inventory. Where other systems relied on teletype-based operator interface, the SCE had the quiet keyboard and computer monitor that was becoming the new standard. Where other systems used paper tape punches and paper tape readers, the SCE had a pair of cassette tape drives.

The SCE's minicomputer, keyboard, monitor, and cassette drives all fit into a single 19-inch rack. By comparison, the station's main computer, built in 1963, was twice as wide, had half the memory, and in its original configuration, it was water-cooled! (The networks, though, installed the air-cooled option.)

The SCE, incidentally, was not without its problems. High on the list was a drawer called a Ground Verification Unit, or GVU. This unit's job was to ensure that the bits of the just-issued command to the spacecraft were identical to the bits that were leaving the S-band system. A solitary red LED on the GVU's front panel flagged any mis-compare and told the controllers that the just-issued command was suspect. But due to the GVU's notoriously complex circuitry, controllers relaxed their requirement for ground verification. Broken GVUs, therefore, tended to stay broken.

Each station had two GVUs but few of them worked. Ascension was an exception, though, and each time we reported to the Goddard controllers that we did have a GVU available for the upcoming support, we gave that confirmation with a bit of pride, albeit unearned—nobody on the Rock had ever fixed a GVU; we simply owned one that hadn't broken.

One slow month of midnight shifts after I had rung up a string of troubleshooting victories throughout the computer section, I decided to take the ultimate SCE test: I would fix our broken GVU. How hard could it be? My recent successes had me believing the I possessed a technological Midas touch. Another ace up my sleeve was the one working GVU, which gave me a tremendous troubleshooting advantage in that I could compare the signals between the two units.

I decided the best place to start was with the error light on the front panel; I would work backwards from the LED to find out what was turning it on. Then I'd keep working backwards until I found the root cause. Within five minutes, my heart sank as I made a horrifying discovery; the circuit card that drove the error circuitry on my "working" GVU was fried. I replaced the card and with every transmission of my test command, the error light beamed a solid red.

Astoundingly, the designers had created a circuit such that, if a component failed, the indication would be just the opposite—a permanent *non*-failure. I stared at the LED's bright red accusing message: *Why didn't you leave me alone?*

I hadn't broken the GVU, I'd just fixed the part of it that recognized failure, though I knew Goddard controllers were not going to see it that way. For years, they'd been recording, *Ascension GVU: Operational.* The very next spacecraft support summary would be different and would lump us in with all of the other stations' summaries and their implied message that Bendix techs were not smart enough to maintain a functional GVU.

Motivated by this perception of failure, I redoubled my efforts. My confidence had crumbled, though, as my discovery of the bad circuit card meant I could no longer follow my original troubleshooting plan of comparing the good unit with the bad one.

A week later, we were able to send Goddard some good news, as I was able to repair the second unit, the one I'd set out to fix in the first place. Ascension was back in the winner's circle. The GVU that had failed to annunciate its failures, though, had multiple problems that I just could not

The Devil's Ashpit

decipher. Still, the reputation of these monsters was such that the fact that I had repaired one secured my place in tracking station history.

Fixing a GVU was a personal triumph, but because Goddard had dropped the requirement for the units, my success didn't mean much to the station's day-to-day operations. On the other hand, the SCE's cassette drives were absolutely essential to support.

Unfortunately, these cassette tape drives were mechanical nightmares. This spelled trouble for each software load, which generally spelled trouble for each satellite support period on the schedule; in order to communicate with each spacecraft, the SCE required a unique configuration file and command list. These software loads failed more often than not and our only recourse was to remove and dismantle the shoebox-sized tape drive, clean the O-rings and tachometer contacts with alcohol, reassemble and cross our fingers. All SCE operators became adept at recognizing the correct sound of a cassette tape loading sequence: the *snick* as you slid the tape in edge-wise and the *ka-CHUNK* as you pushed the tape carrier down into its receiver. No *snick-ka-CHUNK*, no software load.

As these drives aged, the likelihood that we would not be able to issue commands to spacecraft increased. Our network designers tackled the problem and in 1978, they sent us a solution in the form of new cassette drives and—a first for the station—a hard drive.

Software loads became astonishingly trivial. We could copy all of our tapes to the hard drive and then put the cassettes on the shelf to collect dust. Once this bulk load was done, we only used the cassette drive if Goddard sent us a new tape. Furthermore, with the new-style cassette drive, loading the tape was quite literally a snap. You dropped the cassette into its holder and—*snap*—you closed the door. I soon lost my ability to identify a good *snick-ka-CHUNK* and took it off my résumé.

My SCE had once again increased its technological lead over the rest of the hardware at the station, but that didn't count for much. Inside the new cassette drive was a printed circuit board with the biggest integrated circuit chip I had ever seen. It turned out to be a microprocessor—and before its arrival, I didn't know a microprocessor from a food processor. If someone starting talking about "chips", my first thought was to look for dip. So if anything were to go wrong with my new hardware, I could have done little more than ask for a replacement.

I was better suited to help troubleshoot the main computer, a Sperry Univac 642B. The 642 was designed for the Navy and it was my belief the computer could shrug off a torpedo hit. The thing was *solid*. And heavy, with each of the three double-wide racks weighing in at 2,400 pounds. If the 642B had a memory issue, I broke out the socket set to retract the side connectors, then called for help to lift out one of the five memory drawers that held the hundreds of cards required to make up the 32K. These cards sucked up to 3,000 watts of power. (For comparison, today's notebook computers are thousands of times more powerful—no, make that millions of times—and might use 60 watts.)

I can't speak for the analog techs who ran the S-band antenna and its transmitters and receivers, but I know that my digital brethren in the Telemetry section were in the same boat. The telemetry techs were in charge of something named the Manned Space Flight Telemetry Pulse Code Modulation racks. By redefining P to serve as an acronym for PCM, NASA documentation referred to these racks as the MSFTPs. Site personnel referred to them as "misfits."

Like the 642B, the MSFTPs owed their design to 1963 technology; that is, before integrated circuits. The stations started out with five MSFTP-2 systems, totaling 1,600 cards. Then the MSFTP-3 came along, which managed to simplify the design and cut the card count in half. (As of this writing, there's a unit on the market that, despite being the size of a desktop computer, can perform the functions of 128 MSFTP-2 systems.)

We techs had all spent untold hours in school learning how to read schematics and operate the oscilloscopes and multimeters we would need to troubleshoot electrical systems. Systems like the MSFTPs and the 642B, however, highlighted a serious deficiency in our technical training. When faced with the prospect of spending untold hours painstakingly checking the test points on dozens of circuit cards with scopes and meters to find a problem, techs quickly learned that there was one tool their instructors had failed to wield; the first tool *we* grabbed from the box was a rubber mallet.

Our "hit it with a hammer" approach was not borne of the brute force mentality, but rather the simple fact that the circuit board-to-backplane connection had the highest likelihood of failure; the hundreds of circuit boards in a rack meant thousands of contact points to corrode or oxidize. Giving the board a whack often restored the connection. The purist might have scoffed at our methods and demanded that we use the more traditional tools of the trade, but the economist merely had to remind us that NASA was paying us to retrieve satellite data and not to fiddle with an O-scope.

I confess there are times when it felt good to hammer on my system. As I hammered, though, I felt my troubleshooting skills eroding. The arrival of the microprocessor-driven cassette drives drove that point home. I knew I wasn't going to solve any cassette drive issues with the mallet—and I knew I wasn't going to solve them with the O-scope, either. That first microprocessor served as my wake-up call. I swore that I would not share my coworkers' plight. When the tracking station jobs disappeared, I would be prepared.

My Ascension Island location made preparations somewhat difficult, but as we began our second tour of duty, I enrolled in a school that offered the only option available in those days before the Internet: Correspondence courses. Although I knew my plan was no substitute for classroom work, at least I would be keeping abreast of the microchip revolution. And not only was my conscience salved by my return to schoolwork, but my lessons added one more after-work diversion to the precious few available on the island.

Chapter 11

Back in the Trenches

Our schedule upon returning to the island had fortuitously placed us once again on the same shift as Cramer. We learned this on the evening of our first day back when Cramer himself showed up at our door to make the announcement and to generously offer to treat us to supper at the mess hall. This last, of course, told me that nothing had changed in our absence; base personnel were still eating for free and Cramer was still relying on stale jokes.

At the mess hall, we loaded our trays and, looking around the room, we spied a couple of Bendix Saints offering the empty seats at their table. One was Pat Harris, who, with his fair skin and blondish hair, I would have sworn to be a native Londoner. Pat worked in the communications center, which is where I had met him my first day at the site. At that greeting, he had introduced himself as "Paterris," or so it seemed to my ears that were still unaccustomed to Saintspeak.

Pat's companion in the mess hall was more Saintly in appearance; that is, he had darker skin and jet black hair. This was Donald "Duck" Joshua. He was our teletype repairman, which to me, meant he was some kind of mechanical wizard. I had seen the bucketful of tiny metal oddities that comprise a teletype and was convinced that anybody who could assemble one of these machines had a toolbox filled with phoenix feathers, unicorn hairs, and wands of all sizes.

"Hi, Duck," I said, placing my tray across from his. And then a thought occurred to me. I'd worked with Pat for a year and had never heard his nickname. "Patrick, do you have a nickname?"

"Of course," he replied. "All Saints have nicknames. The men, that is."

"Well?"

"Huh? Oh. Egg's me name, 'cause I was born with egg-white skin and egg-yoke hair."

"Really?" I asked. I looked from one Saint to the other. "Duck…and Egg? You two should never sit together!"

This little exchange opened the gates for a flood of other Saints' nicknames and their origins. Duck admitted that his namesake was Donald Duck. Sure, it wasn't very original or imaginative, but he actually felt rather fortunate; many nicknames were invented to commemorate something the new owner had the misfortune to say or do. A chap named Fart-Egg—no relation to Pat—was so christened when he loudly passed gas and simultaneously dropped the eggs he was carrying.

Duck's name, like many other Saints' names, dated back to his school days but there was no guarantee that he would carry the name to his grave. A Saint always had to be careful to walk the line or he might find himself with a newer, less attractive name.

I don't know how often that happened, though. Of all the Saint names I had heard, perhaps the least attractive (besides Fart-Egg) was Skunk, but he had earned his name simply by being born with a patch of snow-white in the midst of his thick shiny black hair. Another Saint got the name Globe by having hair curly enough to grow into a big, round afro. Names with more mysterious origins were Puddin', Piece-a-Cake, Sawdust, Skids, Brickdust, and Ramstones.

Some Saints I knew by their baptism name, some by nickname, and only a few by both. I generally called a person by the name that I heard others call him, or by the name he was introduced with. I wondered if some names were reserved for Saint-to-Saint communication, which, with its clipped, rapid chatter, British inflection, and odd turns of the phrase, I admit was at times still foreign to me. Maybe I *had* heard one of the Saints referring to Pat as Egg and I just didn't understand it at the time. This may certainly have been the case with a Bendix Saint called Bubba, a name that was the onomatopoeic approximation of his speech. The cruel joke at the site was, when you began to understand what Bubba was saying, it was time to think about leaving the island.

Then there were the Saints who picked up names according to their varying shades of skin color, which explained Blackie, Darkie, and Black-Cat. Seeing my surprise at the implied racism, both Duck and Egg smiled and assured me that, unlike much of the rest of the world, Saints did not associate skin color with social status.

Some of the Brits sure did, though. I thought Duck expressed his situation with a quiet dignity by saying, simply, "A few of the Brits…well, they have their ways." It's hard to gauge the number of Brits who felt themselves superior to the Saints, but perhaps one indication would be the utter absence of a Saint face in the by-invitation-only Exiles Club in Georgetown.

An even better example is the story of a Saint named Cheryl who, as a little girl, received an invitation from a Brit woman to swim at the Exiles pool. When they arrived, they saw the only two swimmers were another Brit woman and her dog. As soon as the woman in the pool realized that Cheryl was there to swim, she stopped playing with her dog long enough to call out, "You're not supposed to be here!"

Cheryl's sponsor soon set things right, but not until after the young, impressionable girl had gotten the loud and clear message that Saints ranked somewhere below Brit dogs.

While the Saints did not grade each other by skin color, that's not to say that all the Saints on Ascension were equal. Duck and Egg and every other Saint in the mess hall could be considered upper class when compared to the Saints who worked and lived in the two other settlements on the island. Saints stationed at the American base had better rooms, better food(!), and easy access to the Volcano Club and its nightly movies. They also enjoyed the same perks in the barracks as the Yanks did; that is, they had people clean their rooms, make their beds, and do their laundry. Furthermore, Saints on the base could take advantage of the terrific price savings at the Base eXchange and, with their "in care of Patrick AFB, Florida" address, they could order from US catalogs and not have to worry about overseas shipping costs.

On top of all that was the travel benefit. As employees of Pan American World Airways, the contractor for base operations throughout the Eastern Test Range, the Saints working on the American base were eligible to fly anywhere that PanAm flew at heavily discounted rates. And finally, PanAm gave a 10,000 mile bonus to Saints who put in ten years.

I was glad to learn that the Saints could travel the world so cheaply, but I wondered what they would do once they reached their destination. At a time when stateside minimum wage was a bit less than $3 per hour, the Brits controlled the Saints' pay and the number I heard, whether they worked on base or not, was on the order of 20 pence (or 35 cents) per hour. A piggy bank full of pence wasn't going to go too far in, for example, Cocoa Beach. On the bright side, it was 20 tax-free pence and even this paltry amount was a heady income for someone living on the base, where there were absolutely no expenses.

More importantly, it was good pay for St Helena, where jobs were hard to come by. The officials who recruited Saints for Ascension duty had an easy time of it, especially when the Royal Mail Ship (RMS) *St Helena*, the inter-island cargo/passenger ship made port and off-loaded the Ascension Saints. It was easy to tell an Ascension Saint—he was the one driving a car or motorcycle and smiling just a little more broadly.

Saints looking to mine some Ascension gold of their own registered at the recruiting office and were notified as jobs became available. There didn't appear to be much emphasis placed on skills or experience. For example, neither Duck nor Egg could type when they got their job offers to work at the NASA site. Evidently, the companies with the open requisitions planned on providing whatever training was needed.

The Saints accepted their offers by signing a twelve-month contract. Then, as their home had no airport, it was just a matter of waiting for a free cruise to Ascension on the *St Helena*, the island's only connection to the rest of the world.

I thought that the Saints' excitement over their new adventure surely must have waned a bit when they embarked and saw their sleeping quarters; for the trips between the two islands, the crew erected canvas walls on the main deck and furnished these "rooms" with cots for the Saints. The ship did have legitimate staterooms, but these were for the paying passengers who had boarded in Cape Town, South Africa. Duck and Egg, however, said they hadn't minded these accommodations at all. They treated the thirty-six hour sailing time between the islands as one long party.

I had only ever seen the *St Helena* anchored off Georgetown, but Duck told me that the *St Helena* had just recently begun servicing the islands. The *Southampton Castle* and the *Good Hope Castle*, much bigger ships, used to crisscross the ocean and each one reserved two hours in their schedules to pick up or drop off Saints, leading the Saints to refer to their transportation as the "two-hour boats." These ships had also erected canvas shelters on the deck to house the Saints.

For Duck's very first trip to Ascension, though, there was no on-deck canvas shelters or party; Duck had been fortunate enough to catch a ride on the USNS *Redstone*, the sister ship of the *Vanguard*. Since the RCA ship was between satellite tracking duties and had plenty of room below decks, these Saints got to ride in style. Thus Duck was not only leaving his island for the first time in his life, he was riding on a ship that was bristling with space-age antennas and was well-known among the Saints for its role in tracking the moon-walking Apollo astronauts.

Duck and Egg joined a Saint community on Ascension that had always been overwhelmingly male. This was undoubtedly the result of a longstanding need for manual laborers and the long-held tradition of sending men to do "men's" work. Saint women, on the other hand, had their own tradition of traveling to the United Kingdom to do "women's" work. They took jobs as maids, housekeepers, or *au pairs*.

Ascension's male-only tradition was reflected in the Saints' barracks-like accommodations with their common bathrooms. There were a few private rooms, though, and a few jobs that, in those days, were also undeniably female in nature (such as clerks, secretaries, and administrative assistants.) A fortunate few enterprising Saints were able to combine the two resources and send for their wives. Then as Ascension's value as a satellite tracking facility began to increase, so did the size of the base. New barracks sprang up designed with just two rooms sharing a bathroom. At the same time, the line between male/female jobs was beginning to blur and single Yank women began to make their appearance on the island, gradually followed by a few adventurous single Saint women. In 1978, however, Saint girls were still woefully scarce, especially at the base, where even our meager contingent of Bendix and RCA girls far outnumbered them.

I enjoyed our lesson on Saint history, but I was itching to jump back into Ascension's clear, inviting waters. We bid Duck and Egg goodbye and went back to our rooms so Cramer and I could pick up our snorkel gear. Then the three of us took the familiar stroll down the hill to Turtle Shell beach.

Although I had enjoyed our stay in Cocoa Beach, the silt and surf along the central Florida coast make the beach unsuitable for snorkeling. My lone underwater excursion outside of a swimming pool during those six weeks had been from a chartered dive boat out of Boynton Beach, a two-and-a-half hour drive south of our condo. There, I had joined a dozen other scuba divers hoping to receive their precious cert cards.

By the time I had arrived, my fellow students were all boarded and sitting shoulder-to-shoulder on the gunwale benches. I was surprised to see that nobody was smiling. Nor was anybody talking. Their looks of grim determination made me flash back to the newsreel footage of the soldiers packed into Higgins boats, preparing to brave the Normandy beaches. I had known nervous anticipation on my first dives, but these faces were positively glum. A *let's get this over with* mood clung to the boat.

Once we reached our dive spot and finally got in the water, I don't doubt that I wore that same look of grim determination. Sure, the sun was shining and the clear water allowed a great view of countless species of colorful coral, but as I had learned from my Ascension sorties, the main ingredient for underwater excitement is fish, and the waters off Boynton Beach were sadly lacking in that department. Without the constant motion of schools of fish, the scene was oddly two-dimensional—and hardly worth the five hours of driving I had to devote for the privilege. *Let's get this over with*, I thought, and stuck with my dive instructor while visions of Ascension grouper danced in my head. I breathed in, breathed out, and repeated the process for forty-five minutes. Back on the boat, my instructor signed my certification form.

At Turtle Shell, thanks to its comparative shallowness and the omnipresent hoards of blackfish, I actually saw more fish just by standing on the beach than I saw throughout my entire Boynton Beach dive. While Gloria watched from the shade of the covered picnic area, Cramer and I

The Devil's Ashpit

took a few steps into the water, put on our fins, cleared our masks, lowered ourselves, and pushed gently forward. I felt like a kid on the first day of summer vacation, taking his first dip in the community swimming pool. But my pool was infinitely more exciting.

Since I wasn't there to spear grouper, who generally preferred at least twenty feet of water above them, Cramer and I were content to play in the "shallow end" of our pool. Still, every lava outcropping and hole hosted its own aquarium that always seemed to include an eel of one species or another. Although I was still smarting from the bite I'd received when diving with Tooley (at least mentally), the morays at Turtle Shell this day remained true to their reputation for shyness and only peered at us from deep in their holes. I hardly minded them at all.

I spent more time under the water than on it, as I dove down to pick up starfish and bring them to the surface to see their true color, since even Turtle Shell's crystal clear water completely absorbs all red at the fifteen feet depth. When I did find a red starfish, I'd drop it from the surface and watch it gradually turn brown as it sank to the sand.

A half-hour later, as we walked back up the hill to the barracks, Cramer convinced me that no return to the Rock could be considered complete without a visit to the Volcano Club. Gloria demurred, deciding instead on a quiet evening. After a quick shower, Cramer and I met up again outside the barracks and walked across the street to the bar.

"The drinks are on me!" Cramer said brightly.

"Why Cramer! How generous!" I replied, playing along with the old gag. "But please let me know when the tab hits seventy-five cents—I have to work tomorrow, you know."

My three-drink stipulation was an actual limit I'd learned based upon my experience with any and all beers available on base. I don't know how the beer was stored, but I can't think of any other reason why a four-beer night would deliver a pounding headache the next day. I had experimented with this phenomenon a number of times and learned that the thirty-six ounce maximum was an absolute; three beers and just a swallow more served as an invitation to my cranial pile driver to rev up its engine the next day.

Cramer and I walked into the bar and, as was customary, our entrance caused most heads to instinctively turn in our direction. Their curiosity satisfied over the identity of the newcomers, the patrons then, to a man, swiveled their heads back to the dance floor where a young pretty girl with long chestnut hair was dancing up a storm with one of the Saints. The song on the jukebox ended just as we chose a table and, before we sat down, another Saint had already materialized in front of the girl to take his turn.

"That's Linda, the new girl," Cramer said needlessly.

"No shit."

Cramer smiled to acknowledge his superfluous remark before heading to the bar to buy our beers. He knew that when we landed that morning, exhausted as we were, we would still have picked up on the existence of a new girl, although I don't actually remember hearing anybody in specific talking about her. This was normal for Ascension. If a girl was delivered by submarine in complete secrecy and swam ashore in the dead of night and hid in the rocks, I'll wager that the next morning the island would be abuzz with questions about "the new girl." It was as though her presence had changed the very chemistry of the island.

Cramer didn't return until the jukebox ended its second song, probably because the Saint bartender was too busy watching Linda to take the time to tend to any customers—who were, of course, all watching Linda anyway. As the needle landed on the third record, however, Linda was making a "just a minute, please" gesture with her finger and walking to a table that held a napkin-wrapped can of Budweiser and a dozen more Saints, some sitting, some standing in line for the dance floor. Linda used her hands and a toss of her head to sweep her long hair back over her shoulders and, still standing, she picked up her beer to take a couple of swallows.

The Saints' awkward positions were comical, as each body contorted slightly in order to close the distance between them and the object of their desire, which I don't think was the Budweiser. It was as though Linda was a highly-charged magnet and the Saints were iron filings. Thirst quenched, Linda returned to the dance floor.

The song was a slow ballad and the Saint-in-waiting must have felt he'd won the lottery. When Linda held her arms up to him, he immediately dropped his hands to her hips. Linda never flinched but I saw her say something and the hands sprang from her hips as if they held hot coals.

"Did you catch what she said?" I asked Cramer.

"Yeah," he chuckled. "She said, 'If you ever want to dance with me again, you'll move your hands.'"

"I think she'll do all right here."

Linda was still a rookie in terms of Ascension experience, having arrived only three weeks before. She had been assigned to work in S-band with Cramer, so he was able to fill me in on a lot of her history. She was a 23-year-old from Baltimore who had been struggling to stay employed ever since graduating high school. Although she had followed what in the early '70s was the traditional path for young women, doing some waitressing and selling Avon, she had not shied away from any opportunity to bring in a paycheck. That included serving as an apprentice machinist—until union squabbles turned the factory into a war zone. She fled that job and went to work in the Baltimore shipyards where she described her job as bilge rat, squeezing between hulls to scrape muck into five-gallon buckets.

The Devil's Ashpit

Unfortunately, Linda had a knack for picking jobs with short expiration dates. The depressed economy and high unemployment rate combined with Linda's perpetual status as unskilled laborer conspired to make her number one on every lay-off list. The turnaround came when a boyfriend who worked at Goddard told her about the "easy money" to be had on Ascension and ultimately talked her into attending tech school.

"Linda told me she graduated first in her class," Cramer said, wrapping up his history lesson.

I flashed back to my own struggles with school. I'd done very well in my technical courses, but I wasn't the top performer.

"I'm impressed," I answered.

"Yeah, me too. Then she said, 'well, my one instructor *did* say we were the stupidest class he had ever seen.'"

The dozen or so girls we had on the base at any one time were generally young and single and had money-making philosophies that mirrored those of the men. That is, they came to stockpile cash to apply toward some goal. They made their money, made either their one-year commitment to Bendix or their eighteen month IRS requirement, and then made their weekly decision as to whether or not they would stay another seven days on the Rock.

In this respect, most of these girls, being electrical technicians, benefited from the attitudes that had begun to change where "women's work" was concerned. Ten years before, when I attended my freshmen engineering orientation at Penn State with a few hundred other hopefuls, I—and everyone else—couldn't help but notice the one girl in our midst. Similarly, when I'd switched to the technology classes a few years later, a glance around the classroom confirmed that a technician's job is real *man's* work; my fellow students were 100% male.

Sexual barriers began to fall, however, following the passing of the Equal Employment Opportunity Act of 1972. Two years later, I had Bendix to thank for being so quick to apply this enlightened attitude when it came to staffing its tracking network. How else would I have met Gloria on the *Vanguard* and how else would we have been able to work together on Ascension?

Not everyone was so welcoming. Many men resented these women in their workplace. The years of working in a male-only atmosphere had somehow resurrected the cave-man instinct, planting the notion that the equipment racks housed saber-toothed tigers and no female could even dream of acquiring the skills required to keep them at bay.

This deep-rooted superiority complex would get a severe test when the tiger-taming women appeared—and the tiger-taming women would be tested, as well. Linda told of the "practical jokes" her fellow machinists pulled on her; jokes that could have killed her if she had not given her machine a thorough inspection following each break. On Ascension, a telemetry tech hoped to set up his new coworker Pati for some ridicule by sticking a bad circuit board into one of her racks before leaving for the base. (Too bad for him; she quickly found it). An S-band tech was less subtle in choosing his brand of sexual harassment; he hacked the track computer to replace the message, "Syntax Error." with "Wrong, Nancy!"

These "jokes" weren't limited to the techs. The site's safety and training officer was a pretty, engaging 29-year-old named Emiline Jensen. Evidently, her inspections, attention to detail, master's degree, and gender irritated the men responsible for the site's facilities, who found ways to retaliate. One opportunity arose when Emiline scheduled a fire safety training class for some new techs. The hands-on portion of the class always took place on the grounds near a shallow trench lined with half-barrels into which a facilities tech would pour accelerant.

As Emiline had done many times before, she gave the signal for the tech to light the fire, then called for the first trainee to run up and douse it with a portable fire extinguisher. The first trainee (Pati, as luck would have it), gamely ran up to the fire but stopped short of the extinguisher's effective range. She had a good reason to stop—the tech had switched accelerants, making this fire much more intense than the ones Emiline was used to dealing with. It was, as he later bragged, "inextinguishable."

Emiline, standing behind Pati, did not feel the heat and pushed her trainee forward to what had always been the proper, safe distance to put out the fire. A second later she realized the stakes had changed and yanked Pati back, too late to save her from singed hair and first-degree burns. Some joke.

Back in the operations building, male techs not threatened by the thought of working side-by-side with females could still prove uncooperative based upon, of all things, the sexuality of the coworker. For example,

She: "What modulation index do I set for UK-5?"
He: Hmm. It's 0.3, but why should I help you if I ain't gettin' any?
He (aloud): "It's right there in the UK-5 Network Operation Plan. Look it up."

Life wasn't all bad for the female techs, though. I'm sure a lot of them had very cooperative coworkers, though perhaps not for the noblest of reasons. This was cooperation spurred by the notion, *maybe if I help you, you'll give me some!*

Not to be discounted in the workplace is the *you're so ugly, I got nuthin' to gain by helping you*, but I never saw that particular attitude on Ascension.

For the single girls, the thought must have occurred to them while signing their contracts that a year on Ascension offered, besides the big bucks, yet another important bonus—it should be an ideal place to find a mate.

At first glance, this would appear to be a smart move; there were hundreds of men and there was very little competition. But elimination of the socially retarded isolationists, the true-blue married men, and the confirmed alcoholics whittled the ranks. The Saints generally fell by the wayside, also. Even though some were lucky enough to enjoy a short-lived affair, cultural differences seemed to dictate that Yank girls return home with Yank boys. For that matter, unofficial island policies further stipulated that Bendix girls couple with Bendix boys, RCA girls with RCA boys, and so forth.

For the bachelors who remained in the potential dating pool, the girls then had to consider that a sex-starved guy might be less than honest, doing and saying whatever it took to keep a girlfriend on the island, but disappearing stateside when his contract was up. In the same vein, a girl entertaining a Saint suitor worried that his cupid's arrow might actually be aiming not for her heart, but for the States.

Once the girls had identified and discarded all the unacceptable prospects, that little fact of life called shift roulette could still spoil the game of love. The perfect match might never be made if the potential lovebirds only saw each other at the site during the daily changing of the guard.

No matter what a girl's motive was for coming to Ascension, the first thing she had to do upon arrival was learn to surf the overwhelming tide of testosterone that flooded the island. Nothing could truly prepare a girl for the experience.

Not surprisingly, the Ascension environment changed a girl, no matter how extroverted, self-confident, or poised she was, no matter how comfortable she was with her relationships with men. After initially enjoying her mass popularity, a new arrival would last only a matter of days or sometimes, hours, before becoming exhausted by the constant demands for her attention. She quickly learned that, for the remainder of her stay, there would be no such thing as a quiet drink at the bar, a solitary stroll on the beach, or even a restful evening in the barracks. Whether she liked it or not, each female who stepped off the plane found she had acquired an entourage, a collection of admirers who already had her barracks address and telephone number committed to memory.

The girls grew increasingly self-conscious of the constant stares from the love-starved populace and in a vain attempt to blend into the background, the young women learned to dress conservatively and unflatteringly. While girls in the States were following the trend towards tight and revealing clothes, their counterparts on Ascension tended to fill their wardrobes with baggy outfits that not only concealed flesh, but feminine curves as well.

Anyone who thought he was going to catch a glimpse of skin at a beach party was also disappointed. There, the very least a girl would wear was a T-shirt and cut-off jeans. Girls almost never went swimming during these affairs, but when they did, they kept their shirts on, covering their bathing suits.

A girl could either burrow into the volcanic rock to escape the attentions of all the men, or she could choose a lucky male and enter into a relationship. This pairing didn't protect her from the press of humanity at the bar or redirect the dozens of eyes that followed her every move, but it did serve to lessen the number of phone calls and unannounced visits to her room.

At least, that was my observation based upon my year on Ascension. Yet there in front of me on the Volcano Club dance floor, was Linda. After three weeks on the island she wasn't hiding in her room, nor was she wrapped in Amish dress. She was partying like she was still in the States. And again I thought, *she's going to do all right here.*

When I told her that years later, she laughed it off. "Sexual harassment on Ascension was nothing compared to what I'd been through in Baltimore. It started back in high school, where I got groped every time we changed classes."

Ah, so there *was* a training ground for women heading to Ascension.

The next morning, we settled back into our routine as if we'd never left; we had our breakfast, got into a van, and rode to the station. There, we talked to the midnight shifters to find out the spacecraft support schedule and reviewed the patch panels and the software loads. The relieved techs gradually filed out of the building and we settled in for the next eight hours. We didn't even think about the probability that this day would be the first of 365 straight days we would spend at work. This was a big part of settling back into our routine—the ability to flip that mental switch that suppresses the part of the brain that expects weekends, holidays, and vacations.

Our first day back at the site was different in one regard: since all mail was delivered to the station, not the barracks, our cubby holes were stuffed full of mail waiting for us. There wasn't much personal correspondence, since everybody we kept in touch with had known we would be on vacation. As expected, our credit card statement had arrived laden with vacation expenses but of course there were no mortgage, telephone, electric, gas, lawn service, or baby-sitter payments to make. I spied a new issue of *Skin Diver* magazine right away and Gloria and I both had a stack of advertisements and catalogs to pore over. Most people would have referred to this stack as a pile of "junk mail," but our overseas assignments had

The Devil's Ashpit

taught us to appreciate everything that the postal service delivered.

Mail call was mid-morning on the two days per week that the C-141 flew in, though the clerk, for fear of disrupting operations, always made sure that we weren't in the process of satellite tracking before making the announcement. The resulting scramble to the mail room was always accompanied by excited chatter and the sound of ripping envelopes. In just a few minutes, though, the only sounds were the equipment fans and the never-ending chatter of the Associated Press teletype as everyone pored over their mail, their link to the real world.

Just as predictable as the quiet time was the request over the internal communications loop that came an hour later.

"Anybody got any porn?"

This was the signal that Harley, an S-band tech, had finished studying whatever skin magazine he subscribed to and was ready to trade. I hasten to add, Harley didn't make this station-wide broadcast during the supervisor-filled day shift; he was discrete enough to confine his request to swings and mids, which was when, more often than not, the shift leads and operations managers joined the swap-meet.

After Gloria and I took our mailbox bounty back to our desks, I saw that Bob Frank had left a pile of newspapers for me. I had first heard Bob's name in Quito, as he was the first Ascensionite that Gloria had told me about in her letters, with good reason.

When Gloria had arrived on the island, it was just months into our marriage. She was still weak from her bout with dysentery, more than a little disoriented at being in such a different environment, and as she looked at the station roster, she didn't recognize a single name. She was sitting at the station feeling absolutely friendless when a tall, slim, older gentlemen with an unruly shock of gray hair came up to her.

"Gloria, are you related to John and Joan Kovalchik in State College?" he asked.

My wife's dumbfounded look said she was.

"Well, how about that! I used to work for Joanie's dad. I'm Bob Frank."

The "State College" Bob had referred to was State College, Pennsylvania, and is perhaps better known as the town across the street from Penn State. My brother John and I had attended school there—he for music education and me for electrical engineering. The engineering didn't want to stick, but music stuck with John just fine. Immediately after graduation, he started teaching in the State College school district and married Joanie, the girl who had supervised him while he fulfilled his student teaching requirement—the girl who gave him an "A." *Hmm.*

I was just as astonished as Gloria had been to find such a connection in such a remote place. I was glad, too, knowing that Bob's presence there essentially served as a family tie. And once I got to the Rock, I had another pleasant surprise; Bob shared his Sunday subscription to the *Centre Daily Times*, the State College newspaper. Thus even though I was nearly 6,000 miles away, I was able to keep regular tabs on the area that had made such an impact on my life and, because of my brother's continued presence, had become another synonym for "home."

I forced myself to put my stack of mail and newspapers aside so I could begin to reacquaint myself with my job. Although our duties in the computer center were largely repetitive, the satellite controllers in faraway Maryland occasionally sent us new software or modified our command uplink procedure. There was also the chance that our support would include a brand new satellite, although Gloria and I suspected this would not be the case; to our disappointment, we hadn't watched any rocket launches from the balcony of Sunrise Condominiums.

As I sifted through the box where we stored the SCE's software cassette tapes, though, I was in for a surprise. There was a new tape in the box. Evidently, the dayshift tech had forgotten to tell me about a new support requirement. The tape's label just contained a string of numbers and letters that made no sense to me, so I asked Ops if he knew what the tape was for. He confirmed my suspicion; we had a new support requirement—but not because there were any new satellites.

The new tape was for Skylab, the five-year-old project that had started my technical career and simultaneously marked the first time I was paid for what I had learned instead of what I could lift.

Prior to Skylab, my income had been pretty much based upon backbreaking labor. My first thirteen years or so were the easiest, as my salary consisted of the $2 per annum I received by merely surviving; every birthday, my grandmothers sent me a card and a dollar. This served as my *Mad* money, since, when pooled with my brother's $2, we were able to buy every month's issue of that twenty-five cent magazine.

My next jump in pay demanded a bit more exertion on my part, but with luck, I would rake in upwards of $20 each year. I earned this by clearing acres of hay and straw in summer, loading a five-ton truck with coal a few times a month in winter, and periodically shoveling tons of horse manure at the local mushroom houses. My big break came the summer I graduated high school and supplied masons with mortar, bricks, and concrete blocks six days per week for $2 *per hour*. That fall, I left for college with hundreds of dollars in the pockets of my new jeans and the feeling that I was going to be Rich Man On Campus. (The feeling lasted all the way up until I met my assigned roommate, who took me for a ride in his week-old Pontiac GTO.)

I graduated with a degree in electrical technology just a few months before the Skylab launch, and just when Bendix was in the process of reactivating a number of tracking stations that had been closed since the last

Apollo mission. When Bendix dangled their $3.50 per hour in front of me, I wasn't thinking that I'd probably be the lowest paid technician in America, I was thinking that circuit boards and soldering irons were nowhere near as heavy as bricks and mortar. I took the money and was glad.

Bendix didn't start me out as a computer tech; they sent me to a six-week school to learn how to operate and maintain a powerful transmitter that would be used to uplink commands to the orbiting space station. Then they sent me to Corpus Christi, where between Skylab support periods, I read the *Goddard News* and first learned of the existence of my wife-to-be, who was busy supporting Skylab onboard the *Vanguard*, off the coast of Argentina. Five years later, turning the Skylab command tape over in my hand, I felt that I would soon be talking to an old friend; the friend who had introduced me to Gloria.

The addition of Skylab support should not have surprised me. I had first heard of the project's possible reactivation when NASA announced that one of the yet-to-be-delivered Space Shuttle's first missions would be to boost the unmanned station to a higher orbit. And before Gloria and I left for vacation, we read in our network status reports that NASA engineers had begun communicating with Skylab via our fellow tracking stations in Bermuda, Spain, and Goldstone, California and had begun activating systems that had lain dormant since the last crew left in 1974.

In Florida, I had read an article that discussed some of the difficulties the engineers were experiencing and praised their solutions. I was most impressed with the procedure they developed to restore a set of batteries that had been designed to automatically disconnect from the charger if they had drained below a certain value. These batteries had been neglected so long that each was well below this threshold. Thus, every command to charge a battery met with failure.

The engineers studied the circuits and came to the conclusion that with every command they issued to connect the charger to a battery, the automatic disconnect did not occur until a few tenths of a second had elapsed. In theory, the battery was actually receiving a short-duration charge.

The solution was to write a program that would issue the charge instruction at a rate of 200 commands per minute. After issuing nearly 8,000 commands, the first of the batteries reached the design threshold and stayed online. Eventually, the engineers resuscitated fourteen batteries in this fashion.

I wasn't surprised at this success, having grown up watching reality television at its finest; that is, the minute-by-minute coverage of the thrilling NASA achievements of the 1960s and '70s. But the agency had appeared dormant for the three years since the manned Apollo-Soyuz Test Project splashdown. Yes, the Space Shuttle *Enterprise* had "flown" multiple times, but not to the accompaniment of thundering rockets; the shuttle had been carried aloft on a Boeing 747.

I wasn't surprised at the Skylab success, but I was delighted. This was partly because of my previous experience with the project and partly because I was in a better position to understand the engineering and partly because I relished the challenge of squeezing more life out of an abandoned project. I very much looked forward to my first Skylab support from Ascension.

After our six-week absence, however, we would have quite a challenge of our own to reacquire our Ascension legs. Thus it was probably for the best that the first satellite support that evening turned out to be one of our mainstays, UK-5.

I had just finished my pre-pass checks to ensure the SCE-to-S-band command link was patched correctly when I heard a string of obscenities from Dean, the tech in the telemetry section. Then the internal comm loop came to life.

"Ops, TLM. I can't get any of the misfits to lock up on the sim data." Dean paused to retrieve his cigarette from the ashtray and took a long drag. "I think the simulator's okay. I just don't see any data getting to the misfits."

When Gloria and I had reported to work that morning, we were happy to see that Tom, my Question of Arrows trivia partner, was our operations supervisor. He knew better than to ask for details. Dean's time would be better spent troubleshooting the problem, and with the UK-5 clock running, he needed to get back to work.

"Okay, TLM," Tom answered. "Keep me posted."

Dean's racks of MSFTPs were directly opposite my computer racks and I watched as he fiddled with pushbuttons, patch cords, switches, and dials. There was nothing I could do to help him, as my knowledge of the telemetry techs' job ended with their in-house announcement, "Telemetry has lock." Unfortunately for Dean, that knowledge put me on a par with Homer, his telemetry section coworker and one of the zeroes Bendix kept on the payroll. Homer helpfully furrowed his brow for a few minutes until even that effort became too taxing. He gave up and went back to reading his mail.

Homer could have at least offered to hold Dean's cigarette. For some reason, Dean left it burning in the ashtray a few steps behind him while he worked on his racks. Every thirty seconds or so, he would rush back and grab his cigarette for a full five-second drag before carefully returning it to the ashtray and spinning back to resume troubleshooting.

I had known Dean for a few years, having worked with him on the

The Devil's Ashpit

Vanguard. Even in that environment, where smoking was practically a requirement, Dean's devotion to the habit was above and beyond any that I had ever seen. Tobacco completely defined Dean; nobody could describe him without making some reference to cigarettes, smoke, or ash. I found it hard to talk to Dean because he was so nervous and jumpy—and also because he smelled like an ashtray even when we stood on deck with a twenty-knot ocean wind at my back. Although we had sailed for months in the tropics, Dean had a grayish pallor that, when combined with the sight of his dull, wrinkled clothes, forced me to conclude that Dean's complexion was the result of layers of ash.

After a few more minutes struggling with his MSFTPs, Dean decided to call Norm, his supervisor. What followed was the most amazing display of nicotine addiction I had ever witnessed. On the phone, Dean nervously nodded his head, uttering *uh-huh* sounds as he followed Norm's troubleshooting path. Then it was time for action.

"Okay, Norm, I'll try that. Hold on."

Dean placed the phone on the table and, clock ticking, he picked up his cigarette for another long pull. He set it back in the ashtray and rushed to try out the troubleshooting step Norm had suggested. He paused to check the results and then rushed back to…his cigarette. Another long drag. Ironically, Dean sucked in that smoke as if his life depended on it. Again he carefully returned the cigarette to the ashtray and then picked up the phone to give Norm the results and restart the cycle.

Fortunately, the oddly-choreographed troubleshooting technique worked. Dean let out a smoky sigh of relief and lighted a fresh cigarette from the butt of the old one. Minutes later, Homer earned his paycheck.

"Telemetry has lock."

I never smoked except for a few nausea-inducing experiments, but like anyone else raised in the '50s and '60s, I grew up around smokers—smokers who thought about as much about second-hand smoke as they did about their car's emissions in those days before unleaded gasoline. My dad picked up his habit in World War II when the American tobacco companies, eager to do their part to help win the war, provided cigarettes free-of-charge to servicemen. The companies recouped their patriotic investment many times over as these men continued to smoke long after their discharge. Dad smoked while working on the house and while working in the house, hunched over his workbench fixing television sets. He smoked after eating and while watching TV. He smoked with his wife and seven kids in the car and most notably, he smoked while sitting on the one toilet in our house, reading the newspaper. I tried *not* to be next in line.

Outside the bathroom, we rarely considered Dad's smoking. If anything, we were rather grateful that he smoked because that made gift-giving easy.

We bought him ashtrays, lighters, and would have even bought him the smokes had we been old enough, because the various media taught us that smoking was absolutely normal—even desirable. We watched actors casually smoking on many of the popular television shows. Often, the show itself was sponsored by a tobacco company, so we watched commercials of rugged, athletic men and lovely young women living life to the fullest with their brand of choice.

We didn't always have to break away from the show to get the message. Variety shows, for example, trotted out dancing cigarette packs between acts. The musicians for the number-one-rated *Beverly Hillbillies* modified their famous theme song to tack on a plug for the sponsor. The ad-men didn't stop there, though—they blatantly injected commercials right in the middle of Jed Clampett's Beverly Hills mansion; in one episode, Jed convinces Granny that their sponsor's cigarettes would serve her better than the corncob pipe she's carving.

The same cigarette company sponsored the popular animated kids' show, the *Flintstones*, where advertisers searching for a new low stooped to paying the cartoonists to draw up vignettes of Fred, Barney, and Wilma pulling cigarettes from their sponsor's pack. This was no simple product placement, as the smoking cartoon characters sat back and between puffs, threw superlatives the sponsor's way.

Celebrities from all walks of life had been paid to pitch smokes for years. A very few of the Who's Who preceding Jed and Fred were Ted Williams, Joe DiMaggio, Jackie Robinson, Ronald Reagan, and John Wayne. After this line-up, anybody who still had an ounce of resistance was met with the steely gaze and frank, appealing words of Steve McQueen. Who's going to argue with the King of Cool?

In the middle of this media bombardment, I remember coming home from school and seeing a lone, half-smoked cigarette in the kitchen ashtray. This was a rare enough occurrence that I had to ask about it.

"Mom, is that your cigarette?"

She gave me a look that I had seldom seen on her, a look of shame and disappointment.

"Yes," she admitted sadly. "I keep trying to smoke, but I just don't like it. It makes me sick."

A few years later, Pennsylvania levied another tax on cigarettes, bringing their price up to a whopping fifty cents per pack and giving Dad an incentive to quit, although I never heard him make that declaration. And even though I'd been living in Dad's cloud of smoke for some fifteen years, I didn't even notice my new smoke-free environment until a month later when Dad boasted that his abstinence had bought a pair of winter treads for the car. Each day since the price hike, he had been setting a dollar aside as a tangible reminder of the money he was saving by breaking his two-pack-a-day habit. The financial reward system worked for him, as he never smoked again.

Meanwhile, the smoking culture continued. People smoked in bars, restaurants, planes, buses, and trains. My classmates lit up in my college classrooms. The phrase, "Mind if I smoke?" was simply a conversation starter. The expected response was, "May I join you?" or better yet, "Here, have one of mine." Nobody seriously believed that anyone would deny them their right to smoke.

Then I got my job at the tracking stations and learned to breathe smoke in the workplace, too. When Gloria and I went to Quito, we found that South Americans smoked even *more*. One Ecuadorian explained that he, like my mother, got sick from cigarettes, but he had to keep smoking as a sign of affluence. That affluence showed itself in the nine-passenger van that took me to work and back every day, as seven of my coworkers smoked during the ninety minute ride. Every time I came home to Gloria's loving embrace, she gave me as brief a hug as possible and sent me to the shower. I was a non-smoker who was starting to look and smell like Dean!

By the late '70s, though, the movement for non-smokers' rights was gaining momentum; so much so, that the tobacco companies mounted a new ad campaign extolling the virtues of "freedom of choice," as in, the freedom for non-smokers to choose to continue being non-smokers and the freedom for smokers to choose to continue lighting up in bars, restaurants, planes, buses and trains.

Ironically, it was the sudden appearance of these ads that alerted me to the ongoing controversy and started me thinking that maybe I did have the right to breathe smoke-free air, especially in restaurants and closed-in situations. I contemplated my response to the next conversation starter.

"Mind of I smoke?"

I'd smile and, lifting one cheek, I'd ask, "Mind if I fart?"

After living twenty-eight years in a smoking culture, however, I didn't *really* think there were going to be any big changes. I assumed that tobacco taxes would continue to increase and the number of places that tobacco companies were allowed to advertise would continue to decrease. Meanwhile, I would continue to make whatever choices I could to lessen my exposure to smoke; choices like avoiding the Volcano Club and riding the (unofficial) non-smoking van to and from work.

At work, though, I knew I had no choice. For as long as I could remember, where there were techs, there were multimeters, oscilloscopes, and cigarettes, so I didn't really begrudge them their smokes. Except for Homer and Sam, that is.

Sam was my computer coworker at the time; he nursed the 642B while I cared for the SCE. Sam was a good soul, intelligent, conscientious, and considerate in all matters but one: Both he and Telemetry-has-lock-Homer were the kind of smokers who took one drag from their fresh cigarette and then laid it on the ashtray to burn itself out. They might take another hit or two before the glowing coal hit the filter, but that was all. The rest of the time, their cigarettes lay there emitting a thin plume of smoke that rose just a few feet before hitting the station's air circulation system that whisked most of it in my direction.

Dean completed the trio of coworkers surrounding me, but Dean was a chain-puffer as well as a chain-smoker. He sent as much smoke my way as Sam and Homer did, but at least he was getting what he paid for. The Sam and Homer style of smoking made as much sense to me as someone who takes the first drink from a can of beer and then lays it on its side to drain in case he might want to grab another swallow before it empties.

I shared my complaints with Gloria during one smoky evening at work. As the conversation progressed, we began to name all of the non-smoking techs who were in the same predicament. To my great surprise, we were able to piece together a completely smoke-free shift. Just as soon as we dreamed up the roster, though, we knew it would never be implemented; for one thing, it would be impractical to jerk people away from their natural shift progression. Worse, though, was the force of plain old inertia. Tracking stations were not known for their forward thinking or their rapid implementation of new ideas. Especially the Ascension station. This might have been a side-effect of that mental switch we all flipped to enter "Ascension Mode." Our non-smoking Dream Team would remain just that—a dream.

One of the techs who made the team that never materialized was Alvin, who worked in S-band. Alvin, like us, had been on the island for about a year, but aside from my admiration for his non-smoking status, I didn't know much about him. Alvin did not make a favorable first impression, which is why I pretty much dismissed him until our little Dream Team session. One glance had told me Alvin's rightful place was on the cover of *Nerdweek* magazine. He had a soft, white, marshmallow body and judging from the still-erupting acne on his face, he may have been following a marshmallow diet, as well. Alvin's thick, black-rimmed glasses and unruly mass of oily black hair accentuated his pale skin.

I never went out of my way to avoid Alvin, but neither did I ever go knocking on his door. One evening at work, however, Gloria and I had found ourselves sharing a Hashpit table with him.

While we stabbed ineffectually at our thrice-reheated food, Alvin showed off his new programmable calculator, punching in numbers, pressing function keys, and storing his program on little magnetic cards that zipped through a slot on the side of the case.

I was impressed and dismayed at the same time. This was 1978 and

Alvin's half-pound toy, powered by a nine-volt battery, was ounce-for-ounce the most powerful machine at the station. By comparison, the formidable racks that comprised the mighty NASA tracking station computer section housed fifteen-year-old equipment that drew more current than an arc-welder. And since the tracking station network was slated to be replaced by the Tracking Data Relay Satellite System, I knew I would not be seeing any major equipment upgrades or replacements for the remaining life of the network.

The calculator wasn't the only thing that won my respect that evening; Alvin impressed me, too, with his quick, sure keystrokes and articulate, confident, explanations. Here was a young man, I thought, who was wasting his talents. He needed to ditch the antenna job and move into the computer section. Ancient as our machines were, they were still computers, and if Alvin attacked them with the same zeal that he directed towards his calculator, both he and the station would benefit.

Thus, when Coach announced that Alvin had indeed approached him about transferring, I was ready to welcome him with open arms.

"Yes," said Coach, his nose gleaming with a fresh coat of sunburn, "All we need is Wilmer's okay and Alvin will be ours."

Now there was a problem. Since John Lacewell's departure, Wilmer was the head man at the station (more about that later.) Wilmer's looks fit the role, as he was cut from the same mold that all dictators seem to share. On an island whose inhabitants got haircuts about as often as they got birthday cards, Wilmer kept his hair trimmed "high and tight," the military way. He was also tall and lean and had a set of steely blue eyes that seemed to be fixed in a permanent glare. Above all, Wilmer possessed an in-your-face demeanor that seemed to shout, "I'm talking to *you*, mister!"

That message came through loud and clear, even though Wilmer's actual pronunciation was closer to, "'M awging a you, ngster!" This subtle shift in speech pattern was the result of Wilmer's barely decipherable backwoods Southern accent being further transmogrified by a cheekful of Beechnut.

Nevertheless, even this speech was a model of clarity compared to the gibberish Wilmer spouted whenever his emotions got the best of him, which was often. Helpless recipients of this unintelligible, tobacco juice-laden invective could only stand straight-faced and take their comeuppance. Wilmer, after all, had a reputation for throwing things; not little things, like pencils, but big things, like chairs.

Alvin's transfer was in jeopardy because of Wilmer's apparent need to flex his leadership muscles; he very often exercised his option to say "no." A request that would have had managers at other stations shrugging, "Sure, why not?" sent Wilmer into a cud-chewing, head-shaking frown and no one disagreed with Wilmer; not twice, anyway.

Thus I was amazed when, the next day, Coach asked me to start training

Alvin on SCE operations; Wilmer had not objected.

"How'd you manage to get Wilmer to agree?" I asked. "He's never agreed to anything I've asked for. In fact, I honestly don't believe I've ever heard the man use the word *yes*."

Coach smiled knowingly. "Me neither. So you just turn that to your advantage. I didn't ask Wilmer if Alvin could transfer. I asked, 'You don't mind if Alvin transfers to computers, do you, Wilmer?'"

"A-ha! So he still gets to say *no*!"

"Yes!"

As common as station-to-station transfers were throughout the network, a section-to-section transfer was actually rather extraordinary. We Ascension technicians were especially notorious for our reluctance to leave the equipment on which we had originally trained. After spending a year working in the same area, the job was as familiar as an old shirt and few techs were willing to try another job on for size and risk a bad fit. Although our most common complaint about the island was the lack of variety in our lives, we declined to take advantage of the obvious opportunity presented by our workplace.

Therefore, knowing that Alvin had initiated his intra-station transfer further bolstered my already high opinion of him. Within days, however, my delight with our new recruit began to wane. Within weeks, I would have traded him for any three chain-smokers on the island.

My first indication that Alvin was harboring a few character flaws came within minutes of teaching him our job. In Alvin's book, anything he didn't already know wasn't important; at least, that was the impression he gave. Alvin's reaction upon hearing something new was to purse his lips and shrug, a visible "so what" maneuver. Then, whenever I mentioned something that my pupil already knew or might have guessed, he dropped the aloof posture in favor of an impatient, "stop patronizing me" attitude.

Admittedly and ironically, it didn't take a rocket scientist to set up our equipment for satellite support; most anyone could have performed the chore after watching the operation a couple of times. But learning a task by rote doesn't prepare someone for the little surprises that have a way of popping up.

It had also been my experience that people, not machines, were usually the cause of these little surprises. Whenever anything went wrong during our satellite support (for example, if we weren't receiving the satellite's telemetry), the quickest way to discover the problem was to assume one of the techs hadn't pushed the right button or plugged a patch cord in the right place.

Again, that was my experience. I'm sure, however, that the folks at Goddard Operations had a completely different point of view. This was because of the Bendix/NASA contractual agreement that created a mountain of difference between the two possible reasons for loss of spacecraft support: The Operator Error and the Equipment Malfunction. Per the contract, EMs were regrettable but forgivable problems. OEs, though, were the result of poor training, bad management, or just plain inferior technicians, all indicators that NASA was not getting its money's worth. OEs were therefore deemed absolutely *un*forgivable and resulted in a significant bite out of the Bendix profit.

Thus, committing an OE at a tracking station pretty much branded the responsible party a felon and blackened his soul with a mortal sin. The obvious solution was to find a way to blame any data loss on a piece of equipment instead of an operator and throughout the worldwide network of tracking stations, that blame came to fall on the patch cord.

The patch cord was an obvious, easy target. It was ubiquitous, appearing in every tracking station subsystem, and although it was a short sturdy cable terminated with big durable phone jacks, it was subjected to the wear and tear of thousands of plug-ins and pull-outs every year.

We blamed the poor patch cord for so many problems that I pictured a whole department of people at Goddard whose job was to file all of our "bad patch cord" reports. Every day that I leaned over the teletype that hammered out the AP news, I expected to read that a government committee had been formed to investigate the fraud being perpetrated by the patch cord manufacturers.

Since Bendix had hired Alvin and me in the same month, we both had the same five years of dealing with spacecraft support preparations and their pitfalls. He had to know that the job called for a little self-doubt: "Did I load the right program? Did I type the right command? Did I, uh, turn on the power?" It happened to everybody. But it was plain to see that if anything out of the ordinary happened while Alvin was at the controls, his ego was going to overrule any suggestions that he had made a mistake.

And that's exactly what happened. After I watched Alvin successfully load the SCE for a dozen or so satellite support periods or "passes," as we called them, I left him alone so I could concentrate on my own work. On the very next pass, I heard the SAS-3 spacecraft controller's voice over the loudspeaker, complaining that our SCE didn't send him a verification for the command he had just transmitted. I looked between our racks to check a little push-button patch panel in the Telemetry section. None of its lights were lit. Dean had forgotten to set it up.

Dean quickly pressed the appropriate switch and the SCE's verification messages finally had a path back to Goddard..

"SAS, Ascension, we had a bad patch cord," our Ops reported.

"Roger, Ascension, we're seeing those verifications now."

The spacecraft controller was happy. I wasn't. While training Alvin, I had made a point of checking Dean's panel before every pass. I knew Alvin had been listening to my setup lecture because his annoying body language made it very apparent that he thought I had fallen back into the "patronizing" mode. Then, the first time I gave him the opportunity to bring up his system alone, he had ignored my checklist. I confronted him.

"What are you talking to me for?" he demanded. "Dean made the mistake. It's not my fault."

It's not my fault. I didn't realize it at the time, but this would be the first of many times that I would hear that phrase. General MacArthur famously said *I shall return*. President Truman was known for *The buck stops here*. All Alvin could come up with was *It's not my fault*.

"Alvin, I'm talking to you because Dean's patch panel is on our checklist," I replied.

"WRONG!" he shouted in his most obnoxious voice, "Dean's patch panel is on *your* checklist. I went by the checklist in the book, and it says the Telemetry tech is responsible for that panel, not me."

Alvin's childish defense made me want to strangle him. My second impulse was to walk away, as had always been my custom when faced with unpleasant situations provoked by unpleasant people. But tempting as both thoughts were, I had to reconsider; in my year on the island I had risen to the position of shift leader for the computer section and had even served as the acting computer supervisor in Coach's absence. It was my duty to help ensure that our tracking station provided the proper support for the multi-million dollar hardware orbiting overhead. We had also come dangerously close to earning NASA's ultimate demerit—an Operator Error. Technically, the OE would be on Dean's record but in reality, the blame would fall on the site; one way or another, we would all suffer.

Knowing that I would get nowhere if my words betrayed even a hint of accusation, I changed direction.

"Look, Alvin," I whispered conspiratorially, "As you know, very few of the techs on our shift are as good as we are. And although it's not our job to baby-sit people like Dean, I've always felt it was my job to make sure that everybody gives the SCE what it needs."

Alvin's glasses had slid down his nose and he lowered his head to peer at me over the frames. His look told me that I could add "you're lying" to his repertoire of facial expressions. Then he nodded his head, just barely. I was on the right track.

"Now, the SCE needs that patch panel to be set up right," I continued, "You are the SCE man, and I need your help to watch Dean and the others so they don't screw us up."

"You're right," Alvin admitted, "They are a pitiful bunch, aren't they." Slowly, a smile came across his face. "Don't worry, Dan, I can handle it."

The Devil's Ashpit

Handle it he did. Alvin took to watching Dean's patch panel like a hawk. Every time he saw that Dean had set the panel correctly, Alvin died a little. On the occasions when he didn't punch the buttons, though, Alvin could barely contain his glee. Even so, he wouldn't tell anyone about the problem until seconds before we needed the patch. Then he'd make a big show of "helping" Dean, making sure the whole station knew the Telemetry section had fallen down on the job. I didn't approve of his methods, but we never had another problem with that patch panel.

Dealing with Alvin's daily eight-hour dose of arrogance was an unappealing part of my job and quite a bitter pill to swallow. What was *not* part of my job, however, was any requirement to associate with Alvin outside of work. I took that job interpretation quite literally, meaning I chose to avoid my nemesis unless we were within the confines of the operations building.

Fortunately, when we weren't working, the circumstances that kept me from meeting Alvin during our entire first year on the island were still in place—we continued to run in vastly different circles. The only time Gloria and I saw Alvin on base was in the chow hall. Even then, we were in no danger of being forced to sit with him; there were always more than enough tables to accommodate the diners.

Of course, to be really serious about squeezing as much non-Alvin time out of my day, I had to consider the van rides to and from the station.

In Alvin's world, the people who drove the nine-passenger vans were not taking a subservient "chauffeur" role, but the take-charge, leadership position implied by the word "driver." Alvin wanted to be in the driver's seat. That was fine with me; I just waited to see which van Alvin was taking, then I'd take a different one.

During one afternoon shift change, Gloria and I left the operations building together and saw that Alvin had already commandeered his preferred van. We were making our way to the next empty vehicle when I saw Cramer sitting alone in the back seat of Alvin's van, motioning for us to join him. I shook my head no, but he shook his head emphatically, *yes*. I decided to make an exception to my no-Alvin policy just to see what Cramer was up to. Gloria and I climbed aboard.

Cramer shushed us, then secretively showed us what was so important. It was a simple push-button switch, attached to a pair of wires that led to the side of the van and disappeared behind the plastic molding. I couldn't imagine what the switch was connected to.

"Just wait," Cramer whispered.

When a full complement of passengers had finally settled in and filled the seats in front of us, Alvin started the engine and began to back out of the parking space. I saw Cramer flex his thumb, putting pressure on the button. Simultaneously, our van's horn emitted a short blast.

Alvin slammed on the brakes, snapping everyone's heads backwards. The vanload of techs demanded an explanation for the rude stop.

"It's not my fault!" Alvin instinctively yelled over the din. He stared dumbly at his horn button. He gave it a tentative tap. When it didn't work, he pounded on it a few times. The horn still didn't work; Cramer had obviously disconnected it.

Confident that the horn had just emitted its dying gasp, Alvin eased off the brake and started backwards again. Again Cramer tapped his button and again we heard the blast of the horn. Alvin repeated his previous performance, hitting the brakes, denying responsibility, and pounding on the horn button. When he calmed down a bit, he began to methodically check the rest of the vehicle's electronics, checking to see if the headlights, turn signals, fan, windshield wipers, and dome light all worked.

While Alvin diagnosed the problem, the other passengers began to really dish out the abuse. The worst came from his former colleagues, the S-band antenna techs. Apparently, I wasn't the only one whom Alvin had antagonized during his time on the island. I began to wonder if perhaps Alvin's transfer to the computer section had been inspired not so much by a keen desire to learn as by a keen desire to escape from a group of people who so obviously didn't appreciate his talents.

While Alvin was puzzling over his problem, I noticed Wilmer leaving the building. As a member of the station's higher echelon, Wilmer had been allocated a car and a gasoline allowance for his personal use. Our leader enjoyed this little symbol of his position and drove himself to and from the station every day. This was just as convenient for the rest of the station's personnel as it was for Wilmer; he was universally unadmired. It was the sight of Wilmer's lone silhouette in his car that had once prompted a coworker to observe, "There goes Wilmer and all his friends."

Cramer's horn prank had been amusing, but as I watched Wilmer ease his car out of the parking lot and head slowly down the hill in front of us, I began to think we were going to pay too high a price for our entertainment. Wilmer drove the island roads at a leisurely pace. The animosity he so easily cultivated at the station was nothing compared to the antagonism he generated in a van full of techs impatient to get to the Volcano Club. Having to share the road with another vehicle was bad enough; now the rugged terrain would force us to crawl behind a car traveling at least ten miles-per-hour slower than our normal speed.

Wilmer's departure in the midst of Alvin's crisis had not gone unnoticed; our fellow passengers began to berate Alvin unmercifully for letting Wilmer get ahead of us. I could see Alvin's cool, haughty exterior begin to crumble. To silence his verbal assailants, he abandoned his investigation of the wayward horn, hurriedly put the van in gear, and lurched out of the parking lot.

The Devil's Ashpit

Alvin should have known that his burst of speed would only serve to make matters worse. We were trapped behind Wilmer and would be forced to tailgate him down the winding mountain road, all the way to Donkey Flats. Sure enough, we caught up with Wilmer within a minute of leaving the station and Alvin began braking to keep from mating bumpers. Cramer sat rigidly beside me, his thumb poised over the horn switch. He was leaning slightly, cocking his head in order to get a clear view of our approach. Cramer's eyes narrowed. He looked like a fighter pilot ready to put a burst of cannon shells into an unwary enemy.

He hit the button, twice; two long blasts. Alvin, to his credit, didn't steer us off the mountainside, but did increase the pressure he was already applying to the brakes. Thanks to his parking lot experience with the horn, he actually reacted rather calmly to its renewed blaring.

Wilmer, too, seemed to take the rude interruption in stride, merely looking up into his rear-view mirror. I could see his jaw moving but he may have only been working his chaw, as I saw his cheek bulging with a fistful of tobacco.

Cramer was more surprised than anybody. Disappointed that he hadn't gotten the reaction he desired, he began to lay into the horn with a vengeance. Alvin quickly realized the awkward position he was in and applied the brakes in earnest, putting a hundred feet of asphalt between the two vehicles. Before we fell back, however, I saw Wilmer's jaw really moving, and his head kept flicking up to look at us in the mirror.

As soon as Alvin dropped back, Cramer stopped beeping the horn. We continued to trail Wilmer from a distance, but our manager's over-cautious driving and the steep mountain slope conspired to bring us within a few car lengths. When Cramer felt we wouldn't be getting any closer, he hit the horn again and we repeated the chain of events.

In this fashion we continued down Green Mountain. I couldn't tell what effect Cramer's joke was having on Wilmer, but the techs in the van were having a great time riding Alvin. Alvin, perhaps not realizing the potential severity of the situation, shrugged off the remarks of his coworkers and periodically punched the non-working horn button to confirm his innocence.

At last our little caravan left the mountain road's twisting turns and emerged on the straight-away at Donkey Flats, where Alvin stepped on the gas to finally pass Wilmer. Cramer, as I might have expected, showed no mercy. He hit the horn long, hard, and often, like a New York City cab driver at rush hour.

Wilmer had had enough. He accelerated, cut us off, and stuck his hand out the window, motioning for Alvin to pull off the road. As we rolled to a stop, the raucous laughter that had started at the station parking lot suddenly ceased. Wilmer was already out of his car, his eyes fixed on Alvin and his jaw working furiously on his tobacco. As he strode purposefully to Alvin's window, the silence in the van was such that I could clearly hear the crunch of Wilmer's steps on the cinders.

Alvin had stuck his head out the window, but reading the rage on Wilmer's face, he pulled himself back in. That didn't slow down Wilmer. He was tall enough to stick his own head and shoulders through the window, and in a flash, Wilmer was screaming at Alvin like a drill instructor reaming a fresh recruit.

Alvin, ashen-faced, offered no intelligible words in reply, but then, he was at a severe disadvantage; no living being could have deciphered Wilmer's tirade. Instead, Alvin wisely began beating on his horn switch, demonstrating that it was out of order. Cramer, thankfully, kept his thumb off the button all this time.

The significance of the silent horn finally dawned on Wilmer and he jerked himself back out of the window and appeared to ponder the new information. Alvin finally spoke. I barely heard his words.

"It's not my fault."

It was almost a sob. All trace of arrogance was gone from the cowering, terrified form behind the wheel.

Wilmer gave Alvin a suspicious look and spat out the juice that hadn't already sprayed the inside of the van. He growled something that might have been an observation that something was "goddamned suspicious" and marched back towards his car.

Cramer was ready. He gave his button a quick tap and the horn bleated a single mocking note. Wilmer staggered as if he'd been shot. I wondered if Cramer had gone too far, but Wilmer leaned on his car to steady himself, then appeared to recover enough to get in and drive away.

I put my hands together as if in prayer and held them up to Cramer. He looked at me questioningly and I gave my head a barely perceptible shake. He grinned and tucked the switch between the seats. Meanwhile, Alvin sat stone still, watching Wilmer's car. From our vantage point, we could see the base about two miles away. Alvin didn't pull back onto the road until everyone agreed that Wilmer had indeed pulled into the base parking lot.

That night, fearing Wilmer might order the van dismantled to verify Alvin's claims, Cramer surreptitiously removed his accessory. Afterwards, I bought him a beer. Not only had his prank provided us all with some welcome excitement, but it had also afforded me a perfect response to Alvin's tiresome "not my fault" excuse. Like an unforgiving parent, I'd respond, "Yes, Alvin. Just like the horn wasn't your fault. Tell it to Wilmer."

Chapter 12

Things That Go Bump

As I began my second year on Ascension, I harbored a deep, disturbing secret; my fascination with the island's underwater life had begun to dissolve. I still went skin diving at least three times a week, but I began hoisting my dive bag more out of a sense of obligation to my lifelong dreams than to any overwhelming urge to explore another submerged rock or to swim through another crowd of blackfish. I would have been the last to admit it, but diving had becoming a boring chore.

Our Cocoa Beach vacation had rejuvenated me somewhat, in that I had begun to miss Ascension's deep, clear water and its free fish dinners. Even more satisfying than the taste of a fresh-caught grouper fillet, however, was the happiness I felt when the mail brought my diving certification card, my reward for devoting two weeks of my vacation to the classwork required to pass the course. At last I could use the Ascension Divers' air compressor without sucking up to the Tooleys who ran the club.

Nevertheless, another month of underwater exploring went by with no indication that a coral reef was about to spring up around the island. Neither had there been any sign that a pod of Sea World-trained performing dolphins had taken up residence off Turtle Shell beach. My enthusiasm for diving had just about bottomed out when Gloria bought me an underwater camera.

It was a perfect gift, with perfect timing. The camera allowed me to view every underwater sight from a fresh angle and challenged me to transform the dull blues and grays of Ascension's deep into dramatic portraits. The flash attachment provided another dimension, painting fish with Day-Glo brilliance and finding splotches of colorful algae on rocks that had appeared drab and lifeless to the unaided eye.

With Gloria's gift came an unexpected bonus. Once news of my camera spread around the base, diving partners began coming out of the woodwork. I had plenty of models, all very eager to pose in scuba tanks.

Some of my subjects sent their pictures out in the next mail, alerting the folks back home of their eat-your-heart-out escapades. Others carefully arranged their glossies in their own photo albums, happy to possess yet another view of a unique island that only a select few can have the opportunity to visit.

Without exception, my diving companions complimented me on my Kodak moments. I realized, of course, that this may have been a ploy to get free copies. If this was their game, it worked; I never charged my dive buddies for photos. After all, modeling can be a tedious, frustrating job under the best of conditions. In the water, the photo subjects had even more pressing concerns, like breathing. In between breaths, they had to contend with shy fish, changing currents, curious morays, and a confusing bombardment of hand signals from their photographer. My models earned their pictures.

I don't know whether it was my generosity or my photographic skill that convinced Cheryl, a lovely eighteen-year-old Saint girl, to accompany Cramer and me on a trip to English Bay.

Cheryl's figure and her pretty, island-girl-next-door looks would have made her popular in any stateside setting. Thus, on girl-hungry Ascension, she was deified. Had she chosen to, Cheryl could have capitalized on her situation, garnishing the wages of each adoring Yank in exchange for a mere smile.

I told myself that my interest in photographing Cheryl was purely professional, but when Cramer and I drove to her barracks and saw her standing outside, I found myself gaping at her in perfect imitation of the stereotypical sex-starved Ascension male.

The afternoon sun had become a bit too much for Cheryl and she had gathered her long black hair in her hands and lifted it off her neck. She stood with her legs slightly scissored and her back arched, and I imagined her "Ascension Me Come From" T-shirt and her short-short cutoffs melting away, replaced by some of Frederick's of Hollywood's more risqué lingerie. I couldn't wait to get to the beach and watch her strip down to her swimming suit.

Cheryl, Cramer, and I drove to English Bay, pulled out our gear and began going through the ritual inspection, assembly, and checkout of our scuba equipment. I made a show of examining every O-ring and fitting on my regulator, but all the while, I was distracted by the anticipation of Cheryl's disrobing. I wondered if I'd be able to concentrate on my camera settings with Cheryl's lithe, young, near-naked body floating in front of me.

Finally, the moment of truth arrived. Cheryl pulled off her T-shirt. No wonder she'd been hot; she was wearing a wetsuit top. Kicking off her shorts uncovered the bottom half. My disappointment was complete. The

The Devil's Ashpit

much-anticipated unveiling had failed to reveal even one extra square-inch of flesh.

We took our dive and I took my pictures. They were nothing spectacular, although there remains the chance that they could be a collector's item some day; if pictures of Ascension girls are rare, pictures of Ascension girls under water are rarer still.

After the dive, I deposited Cheryl back at her barracks and Cramer and I stopped in the Volcano Club; we had to have some beer to wash out the dry, metallic aftertaste left by the mixture of saltwater and cold, compressed air. Cramer discussed the fish habits and habitats we had seen during the dive and I described all my photo opportunities.

As usual, our conversation strayed to football, school, and a dozen other subjects before we lapsed into silence, drinking our beer and staring at the wall. Then, without changing expression or moving his gaze, Cramer spoke.

"I was really looking forward to seeing Cheryl in a bikini."

He said it quietly, wistfully, and not at all in character. I was glad to hear that I wasn't the only one affected by Cheryl's charms, but although I had known Cramer for over a year and had spent more time with him than many people spend with family members, I had seldom heard him speak his feelings. Certainly, he had never spoken so solemnly where a girl was concerned.

So even the mighty Cramer had been smitten by our resident enchantress. I wondered if the Rock was taking its toll on my happy-go-lucky buddy.

Cramer and I continued to dive at every opportunity and I ran through my film at the previously unheard-of rate of thirty-six pictures per dive. Of these, a good roll would net me two or three shots that I felt captured the right combination of lighting, focus, subject, and interest.

At that pace, I would have thought that the almost limitless supply of creatures in the sea would have provided me with a lifetime of photographic entertainment. Instead, I was as frustrated as a *National Geographic* photographer who had been relegated to shooting passport pictures. As interesting as the sea-dwellers were, I felt my scenery was lacking.

Part of the problem was that I knew what I was missing; my experiences in the South Pacific had introduced me to majestic underwater castles of coral, each emitting an impossibly kaleidoscopic array of colors. On Ascension, I had seen nothing but blemished rocks. I wanted to change my backdrop.

When Cramer heard my griping, he told me about a hard-to-reach little sanctuary on the northeast shore called Hummock Point. Cramer had explored the area during his first trip to the island and had been surprised to see some rock-hugging coral growths developing. These few polyps, he hastened to add, would certainly not overwhelm the color capabilities of my film, but they might be enough to provide a splash of color to the otherwise monotonous background.

I was immediately interested; our next dive had to be Hummock Point. Cramer again cautioned me about the arduous trek, explaining that we would have to negotiate Ascension's rocky coastline for about a mile to get to the spot. I brushed off his warning. I'd go anywhere to find some coral.

Cramer's warning was not to be taken lightly, however. Since I wanted to take pictures, a simple mask and fins excursion was out of the question. Serious underwater picture-taking requires plenty of bottom-time, allowing the photographer to stabilize against the currents and to gradually float towards the skittish subject. Serious underwater picture-taking, therefore, is well-nigh impossible without a scuba tank. This meant that we would be toting a load of diving gear over a patch of rock, ash, and sand that would be a challenge even to the unencumbered hiker.

The tanks were our heaviest burden, of course, but since we could strap them to our backs, they weren't all that hard to carry. We also wore our weight belts buckled around our waists.

The dive bags were a different matter. They were bulky and weighty, containing our masks, fins, buoyancy compensators, regulators, knives, and miscellaneous extras in case of loss or breakage. I also stuffed all my camera gear in my bag and managed to fit in a gallon of water, besides. This last I included partly in anticipation of thirst, but I was actually more concerned about quickly rinsing the saltwater off the camera after our dive—at least, that's how I felt prior to our first trip to Hummock Point.

Our new dive spot was near North East Bay, a great sandy semi-circle cut into the reddish rocks at the base of Bears Back slope. The underwater life in the bay was marginally better than what could be found at Turtle Shell or South West Bay bordering the American base, but its comparative isolation kept us from visiting it as often as the other dive spots around the island. Nevertheless, when the unpredictable giant waves or "rollers" pounded all our west coast beaches, the comparatively calm waters in North East Bay were a welcome sight.

Still, I always found it odd to load up our van with dive gear and then head inland; unlike most islands I've visited, Ascension had no road or path around its perimeter. Of course, the cross-island route we had to take took us to our destination faster than any coastal road would, but it also took us through a volcano-studded area that was one of the few places on the island where a person could not see the ocean.

The half-way point of our trip was marked by Two Boats, a tiny village of two dozen boxy houses built on asphalt streets and cinder lawns located in the exact center of the island. The town's odd name came from its first man-made structure; the Royal Marines had propped up two longboats to serve as a shady rest stop for the Georgetown ox-cart driver on his way to the water tanks at the top of Green Mountain.

At Two Boats, we veered left and passed the absolutely lifeless slopes of Butt Crater and Street Crater. The road then followed the low ground between the red ash of Upper Valley Crater and Bears Back before skirting Lower Valley Crater. There, we finally emerged from the volcano field and were rewarded with our first sight of the ocean since leaving the base.

The road forked at the foot of Lower Valley Crater. On my previous expeditions, I had turned left and coasted down to North East Bay. This time, however, I took the right-hand path and followed it to the north and east a few hundred yards before it emptied into a cul-de-sac of hard-packed ashes a hundred feet above the surf.

This was where we slipped on our tanks and weight belts and hefted our bags, throwing them across our shoulders. A circuitous path led us down the cliff to the rough, pitted lava flows that stopped at the edge of the water. Cramer and I negotiated a dozen of these expanses, each one bounded by a giant outcropping of rough, craggy lava rock that had erupted out of the earth and cooled to form a dividing wall between the semi-flat stretches.

Surprisingly, the worst part of the mile trek was not the rocks, but a two-hundred yard loose sand beach that seemed to suck each foot into its own ready-made sinkhole, forcing us to expend twice as much energy for every half step we took. We plodded across the sparkling sand like Eskimos plowing through snowdrifts. I found myself apologizing to the island gods for complaining about the lava rock we had just crossed. The twisted formations, though treacherous, at least had provided solid footing.

At the end of the beach we crossed one last dividing outcropping and found what we were looking for; a tiny sand beach not twenty paces wide. It lay nestled under a protective and impassable slab of stone that arose from the sand and thrust itself fifty feet upward and out into the water.

Since the beach was situated between the outcropping behind us and the miniature Rock of Gibraltar before us, I would have expected the sandy shore to have benefited from this protective embrace. Instead, a near-constant three-foot wall of white surf crashed between the rocks, each wave manufacturing another handful of sand from the remnants of the seashells that rimmed the tiny inlet.

The surf had nowhere near the force of the whitewater cataclysm that I had hurled myself into when diving with Tooley, but I couldn't imagine the spot yielding anything more than a cloudy, dirty-water dive. I hid my disappointment as I suited up.

To avoid the clumsy, ridiculous duckwalk forced by the swim fins, I usually carried my flippers into the water with me, then pulled them on when I was in water deep enough for the air in my vest to support me. These waves were so rough, however, that I worried that I might lose my grip on the fins, or even worse, drop my camera. I slipped the fin straps over my heels and walked tentatively backwards into the water, holding my camera ensemble against my chest for protection.

Although I never relished the feeling of diving blind, I wanted to get below the battering waves as soon as possible. Sure enough, the view below the surface gave the impression that I was swimming through carbonated milk, as the sun glistened off billions of molecules of air trapped in the frenzied water.

Suddenly, I could see. In a split-second, the blinding white light was replaced by an amazingly clear, blue panoramic view of sunlit ocean. My eyes followed one of the shafts of dancing sunlight downward and I was astonished at the clarity with which I could see the sandy seabed almost fifty feet below. The coastline we had crossed on our way to Hummock Point had been deceiving, hiding a progressively deeper drop-off and keeping the washing-machine action of the waves from supporting the sand particles culled from the beaches.

Cramer led me towards the base of our Gibraltar. As we descended, I saw that the smooth, sheer wall that had marked the end of the beach was distinctly different underwater, riddled with great holes, ledges, and shallow caves, each of which hosted swarms of fish. I didn't see any new species represented, but these familiar dive companions were ten times more abundant than I had seen on any of my previous Ascension dives.

These fish were also braver than their west coast cousins, who tended to scatter at a diver's approach. As we glided by the holes and swam through great arches, our hosts moved aside, then closed in behind us. A thousand fish maintained an almost perfect arms-reach distance from our bodies, as though we were pushing them away with some unseen force field.

Watching the clouds of fish hovering around us, I again had to marvel at the crystal clear water; the fish floated as if on cushions of air, and they banked, weaved, and darted about like sparrows. It was easy to imagine that the soaring fish were maneuvering not in competition for some floating tidbit, but in celebration of the absolute freedom provided by the medium. Their unfettered antics also served to make me self-conscious of the unwieldy equipment I had to strap to my body in order to visit their world. My clumsy kicks, my leaking mask, and my trail of bubbles all reminded me that I was strictly a temporary visitor to this alien environment.

For the most part, each of Gibraltar's cavities held a different underwater species; one hole teemed with red and white mottled squirrelfish, another served an army of crimson soldierfish, and so on. I was reminded of the segregated pockets of a big city, with its neighborhoods separated by race, creed, and color.

The Devil's Ashpit

I was so enthralled by the marvelous collection of fish and their sparklingly clean habitats that I almost overlooked the coral. Cramer had been right—Hummock Point was no coral jungle. There were no clusters of elkhorn or stag coral reaching out to graze our legs, and no elegant fan corals waving in the currents. Nevertheless, patches of the rocks at the foot of the wall were adorned with coverings of a soft lime green star coral resembling a rock-hugging honeycomb. The edges of each eye in the honeycomb looked rigid and calcified until I waved a hand at it, and watched as every eye winked shut.

I quickly ran through half my film before Cramer beckoned me to follow him along a rock ridge leading away from the wall. As we swam above the ridge I saw that each crevice held a miniature copy of the fish life we had just seen in the wall. It was breeding time, and families of baby angelfish, triggerfish, and even tiny grouper swam to and fro in their natural aquariums, emboldened by their impenetrable sanctuary.

This domestic scene, however, was not the reason Cramer had pulled me away from the wall. At the end of the ridge, sharply outlined against the sand, rested one of the large sea turtles. I had long since conquered my fear that one of these giants might be inclined to mate with the diver of its choice. On the contrary, I found them to be extremely shy—frustratingly so, as I had yet to get a good, close picture of Ascension's most famous visitor.

I kicked my fins furiously, racing to close the distance before the turtle woke up, but I was still too slow. He saw or heard me, and with a deceptively easy flick of his flippers, he launched himself from his resting place. In an instant, the huge turtle had doubled the distance between us, gliding effortlessly above the sand and heading towards the deep sea. I watched him in awe as his shape slowly dissolved, mixing with the blue light and shadows in the distance.

I had just begun a slow turn to head back to the wall when something, more of a notion than a recognition, made me look back to where the turtle had disappeared.

There, at the limit of visibility, something flitted in and out of sight. I watched for a few more seconds before I realized that I wasn't looking at just one thing; I was looking at a lot of things. With a sudden chill I identified the flickering shapes. The sun was glinting off a dozen or more dorsal fins.

In perhaps two hundred Ascension diving excursions, I had never seen a shark, but of course, that didn't mean they weren't out there. I was always on the lookout for intruders and the sight of these dreaded dorsals made me catch my breath. In a second, however, our paths brought us close enough to make out the difference in the profiles.

They weren't sharks, they were bottlenose dolphins. Sixteen, I counted.

Moving as one, they changed their course and swam leisurely in our direction. Suddenly, one pair pulled away and circled us, not ten feet away. Cramer and I hung suspended in the water, slowing revolving to watch these two beautiful creatures when, to our surprise, they slid silently past another duo circling in the other direction. Looking left, right, up, and down, I saw that we were surrounded by pairs and trios of dolphins, each swimming a different orbit around us.

If the dolphins made any sounds, they were drowned out by the noise of the bubbles I was forcing out as fast as I could breathe. These were the biggest underwater creatures I had ever shared the sea with. Even though dolphins had been heavily anthropomorphized throughout my life via such vehicles as television episodes of *Flipper* and numerous theme park shows, I was still leery; these were wild animals and our awkward ungainly strokes and noisy breathing showed we were definitely outsiders. The presence of three calves among the group was further cause for worry, as they brought to mind the legendary maternal instincts of bears and their often-fatal effects on unwary hikers.

The dolphins' show continued for some minutes and I took pictures as fast as I could frame them and shoot. Then, the animals regrouped as suddenly as they had disbanded and, as if taking a bow, the dolphins made a slow, sweeping upside-down U-turn and resumed their original course.

This encounter constituted the most exciting, memorable, five minutes I'd ever spent, either underwater or topside, and by the time I pulled myself out of the surf, I had completely forgotten my fears. All I could think of was how soon I could develop my film and how soon I could return for a repeat performance. Thus, despite the difficult hike across the island's northeast topography, Hummock Point became my preferred dive spot.

Apparently, though, the dolphins weren't as impressed with Hummock Point as I was. I made the next hundred or so scuba dives there without a sign of a dolphin escort. Then, just as I was beginning to give up hope, my perseverance was rewarded. Another pod of dolphins appeared and put on a show that was almost the exact duplicate of the first one. Absolutely thrilling.

A month after our first dolphin encounter, Cramer decided that he was ready to expand his underwater horizons; he was ready to try some night diving.

Up until then, I had never considered the possibility of diving after dark, at least, not in Ascension waters. True, I counted an underwater flashlight as a part of my dive gear, but to me the light was strictly a daytime tool; I used it to shine into some of the deeper rock holes. A pair of tiny, glowing, ruby red eyes in the depths would tell me I had found a lobster. A mouthful of wicked white teeth would tell me I'd found a moray eel. Guess which creature was in the majority.

Night diving? How could I bring myself to swim in the deep dark ocean with nothing but a narrow beam of light to show the way when, for all my experience, I still cursed diving masks for blocking my peripheral vision? Navigating the ocean depths is a three-dimensional art form that comes naturally to oh, let's say large, wide-jawed predators, for instance. I doubted that any of these hunters would be so sporting as to take my vision handicap into consideration and confine themselves to head-on attacks. Sure, I had yet to see a shark on Ascension, but perhaps that was because Ascension sharks only came out at night. Yes, I had considerable qualms about night diving.

But Cramer insisted. He had only one argument, but it was a good one: he reminded me that I was the one who always complained about the lack of diversity. A night dive, Cramer pointed out, would be a sure-fire boredom-killer. I nodded my head, but still I only went so far as to agree that a night dive would be a sure-fire killer. One day though, after an especially laborious trip to and from Hummock Point and an incredibly mediocre dive off nearby Turtle Shell, Cramer raised the topic once more. I caved.

"Okay, okay!" I said as I drove us back to the barracks, "Let's do it!"

"Do it?" he said, his eyebrows arched in mock surprise, "You mean you and me, here and now? What will Gloria say? No, never mind that, pull over!"

I had known Cramer would deliberately misconstrue my sentence; his delight at comebacks like this one was way out of proportion to the amount of wit or originality contained in the supposed *bon mot*. But since it required such a small effort on my part to generate such delight, I took (almost) every opportunity to set myself up.

Cramer, for his part, was no dummy; he accepted my little gifts for what they were and I was not obliged to laugh uproariously at his responses. Good thing, too.

"No," I replied, "I mean let's do a night dive. Tonight, maybe?" Having taken the plunge, I didn't want to have too much time to think about what I'd gotten myself into.

"Great," Cramer said, "No wait, Maggie's taking me to the Georgetown movie tonight."

"Tomorrow then," I said with only the slightest disappointment. "I'll fill the tanks and aim for what, nine o'clock?"

"Tomorrow's fine, but forget the tanks; we'll just snorkel. And don't worry, you won't live to regret it."

I gave Cramer a hard look.

"What'd I say?" He paused and reflected. "Oh. I meant, 'you won't regret it.' What do they call that, a Freudian slip?"

"I hope not," I replied, "Because that would mean that deep down inside, that's what you really meant. But you didn't really mean it, right?"

"Course not."

"Okay," I said. But it wasn't okay. I was already regretting my decision.

The next evening found me working on a very severe attack of the butterflies. I had just about decided this attack was the worst I'd ever experienced when Cramer's knock came at the door. Suddenly, the butterflies were gone, replaced by vampire bats.

Cramer, though, had brought a surprise, a calming influence in the form of Michael Benjamin, a young Saint we knew from work.

Michael's surname seemed to be one of only a half-dozen or so that the Saints all shared. Benjamin, Thomas, Moyce, and Fowler are as common on St Helena as Smith, Jones, Hernández, and Nguyen are in the States. On the other hand, Michael's Saint name of Newpence certainly set him apart. He acquired his nickname soon after Britain decimalized the pound in 1971. At that time, Michael was pumping gas on St Helena and he much preferred the math involved in 100 "new" pence to the pound over the old scheme of 240 pence per pound. A customer attempting to pay his bill in old pence would be met with a double handclap and a, "New pence, please. New pence!" For some reason, the Newpence name didn't catch on with the Yanks. We called him "Michael B" or simply, "Mike."

As one of the most energetic Saints, Mike was a standout; he was always digging for answers and trying to augment his education. He hadn't left St Helena just to bide his time on the Rock; his goal was to build up his résumé and list of references in order to find a job in Great Britain or in the States.

I hadn't done any diving with Mike but I was very happy that Cramer had brought him. Who better than an island boy to help us get through our first night dive?

I stuffed my mask, snorkel, fins, and a six-pack into my catch bag, shouldered the bulky bag, and moved towards the door. Gloria had already announced that she wasn't going with us; we were all crazy and she wasn't going to be sitting on the beach where she could hear our screams. My attempts to reassure her rang hollow. I gave her a goodbye kiss, hoping as I did so that it wasn't a farewell kiss.

The night was pitch black; a layer of clouds blocked even the starlight. As Mike, Cramer, and I walked down the steep, winding road to Turtle Shell, we had to use our lights periodically to keep from stepping off the edge and tumbling down the cliff.

Mike, meanwhile, spoke eagerly of the joys of night diving. Prepare to be amazed, he said. The sea itself was much calmer at night and the fish we were used to seeing would be sleeping. By the same token, those fish on

The Devil's Ashpit

night shift would come out of hiding; lobsters, which I had never before seen outside of their deep dens, would be out exploring the neighborhood. Even our underwater lights were going to make a big difference since their beams would paint the rocks and fish with more color than we had seen with the sun's sea-filtered rays. And speaking of lights, Mike added, since we each had our own, we were better off than many of the Saints who went night diving; they usually didn't have enough lights to go around and ended up sharing. Jumping in the ocean at night without your own light? I didn't believe it, but I later found out that Mike had spoken the truth.

Finally, we stood at the water's edge on Turtle Shell beach. As dark as it was, we could still make out the shining white surf as it materialized noisily in front of us. These waves had beckoned us in daylight with a friendly, sunlit, "play with me." On this night, they seemed to be hissing, "go back." I tried to tap courage from Mike and Cramer, although Cramer had been extremely quiet during the last ten minutes. I wondered if we really would have come this far if it hadn't been for Mike and his excited play-by-play of what we could expect to see.

"Ready?" asked Mike. Without waiting for an answer, he plunged forward. Cramer and I quickly followed; there would be no danger of us falling behind.

I began to shiver as soon as I hit the water. This was going to be a very uncomfortable hour, I thought. I also seemed to be having trouble swimming. Try as I might, I couldn't bring myself to pull away from Mike, and we bumped shoulders and legs as we slowly kicked our way into the deeper water. The beams from our lights were disconcertingly narrow, and we flailed them about like searchlights at a Hollywood premier.

Mike hadn't warned us about the cold, but he was right about everything else. The surf that appeared to be so ominous from the beach was actually much milder than it had been on practically any other day. And sure enough, the clouds of fish that had always accompanied us on our other dives had disappeared, even the blackfish. Instead, the sleeping fish had wedged themselves into all the nooks and crannies of the lava rock, where their colorful scales glittered like gemstones under the beams of our lights.

It was all very interesting, but so far, it was something I could have lived without experiencing firsthand. I had every intention of finishing this dive, hanging up my light, and sending for a "Night Diver" patch I'd seen advertised in a scuba magazine. I was bitterly cold and not at all pleased at the extremely narrow field of view afforded by our dive lights. I felt I was living in some cheap thriller movie, where one of the expendable actors is searching an unlit house for villains and finds a circuit breaker just in time to illuminate the flash of the killer's knife. Not only did I expect to see a shark's gaping mouth with every sweep of my flashlight, but I expected to hear the clashing chord of the studio orchestra.

Then I saw the lobster; the beams from our three lights hit the creature simultaneously. His eyes glowed like red coals and his carapace gleamed a creamy yellow under sharply defined brown mottling, a far cry from the dull color to which we'd become accustomed in the daylight. The bug was on the sand, ten feet from the closest rock, casually picking the spines from a sea urchin and stuffing bits of its flesh into its mouth.

The lobster never had a chance. The three of us dove as one, catching and bagging the bug before he had a chance to drop the urchin. After we swam a while further, I realized that after this first bit of action, I wasn't bumping into Mike anymore.

I even became so bold as to fall behind my dive buddies after spying a lobster that they had missed. I caught the bug, but it wasn't a clean catch; I needed both hands to hold the struggling creature. With my fingers tangled and intertwined in the bug's legs and antennae, the lobster naturally pushed and pulled his appendages while flapping his tail furiously.

Click.

The light switch had given way. I was in utter darkness. I didn't even have the beams of my dive buddies to orient me; they had turned an underwater corner and were hidden from view. There I hovered, feeling like a floating bait bucket. Neither of the two lobsters in my catch bag or the one in my hands had been injured, but I had read stories about the phenomenal abilities of sharks. My lobsters' capture and subsequent attempts to escape certainly could have been picked up by some cruising brute who was closing in on me that very minute.

I wanted to panic. I wanted to open my hands and fling the lobster away from me, rip the catch bag string from my belt loop and swim furiously for shore. Of course, by tossing my lobster away I would also be throwing my light away. That wouldn't make me feel any better. Neither did I have much of an idea of where the shore was. I knew where I was when the light went out, but not which direction I was facing. At best, I was facing a two-hundred yard swim in the dark, but only if I had my bearings right.

I had something in my favor; I hadn't moved my hands. I forced myself to remember on which finger I'd felt the light switch pressure. I pushed that finger, hoping the light would come back on, but dreading what I would see.

It worked. The light came on and showed me an empty ocean, nothing more. Greatly relieved, I carefully guided my catch tail-first into the bag. Then, with a little more speed than was really required, I swam around the rocks that had separated me from my dive buddies and quickly located them by the wavering beams of their lights.

We caught two more lobsters before the cold and the excitement drained us of our energy. Back on shore, as we stowed our snorkeling gear and hoisted a celebratory beer, Mike made a rather surprising toast in praise

The Devil's Ashpit

of the three divers who had just earned their night diver patches. Three divers? Sensing that Cramer and I had not really been comfortable with the idea of jumping into a pitch black ocean, Mike had lied about his experience; the tips and clues he had given us had been gleaned from the night diving stories the other Saints had told him.

Mike's lie didn't spoil our celebration. Despite the physical and emotional drain I had suffered, I was elated to have found another activity on Ascension, especially one so unexpectedly rewarding. Once I got over my initial fear of the unknown, I enjoyed the new scenery. Our lights had forced us to concentrate on relatively narrow slices of the ocean, distorting our landmarks enough to remove any sense of familiarity we had gained in our hundreds of sunlit excursions.

The only drawback of our dive had been the chill I had suffered. I remedied that, or so I thought at the time, by buying a mail-order wetsuit. However, when I still found myself shivering under my forty dollar investment, I had to conclude that my problem wasn't being caused by the cool waters of the evening tide. Obviously, despite my rational self-assurances to the contrary, I was quaking with fear.

Nevertheless, I was reluctant to forgo my newly-discovered diversion. Neither did I want to give up my lobster diet. Instead, I told myself I wasn't shivering from the cold, or even from the fear. I was shivering from the excitement.

After that first night dive, Michael B became a welcome addition to our diving parties, both day and night. A bona fide island boy, Mike's considerable store of knowledge nicely augmented the lessons that Cramer and I had already learned about the Mid-Atlantic waters.

Mike's first order of business was to finally cure me of my last vestiges of fear of moray eels. He accomplished this quite easily by demonstrating that the vicious-looking creatures weren't bulletproof, or in our case, spearproof. Mike's demonstration didn't end there, though. He brought the writhing four-foot mass of mean ashore, then cleaned it and cooked it on the beach. I was hesitant to taste a portion of my mortal enemy, but Mike had cut the strips of meat to look just like the grouper fillets I was used to seeing. I took a bite and couldn't believe my taste buds; appearance was where the similarity ended—the eel's flavor was far, far superior to the grouper's. I was dumbfounded. The eel meat must have been one of Ascension's best kept secrets.

I immediately informed Mike that I would henceforth be leaving the grouper alone; all my future seafood dinners would be eel meals. That's when I learned the rest of the story. Ascension's moray eels apparently had the capability of carrying a deadly toxin in their meat. Eating Ascension eel was thus a bit like playing Russian roulette. Mike didn't know the odds, but guessed they might be in the neighborhood of a thousand to one, which of course weren't bad odds—unless you were the One. I sampled only one other eel during my time on the island.

It was ironic then that instead of eating eels, Mike and I began feeding them. Eel-feeding (by hand) had recently become a favorite photo subject in the skin diving magazines, and while we weren't ready to risk putting our fingers too close to those horrid rows of teeth, we weren't averse to spearing a blackfish and offering it from the safety of the other end of a six-foot pole. The moray would eye the fish warily for a few seconds before the smell of blood caused it to throw caution to the tides and snap at the fish's head. After a fierce tug-of-war, the eel would free the fish from the spear's barbs and, just like a snake, the eel would expand its jaws to astonishing lengths and accommodate even the largest fish, finally swallowing it whole.

While I was becoming more and more comfortable with moray eels, however, I was becoming more and more apprehensive about sharks, even though a full year had passed without a sighting. The dangerous predators were out there, as evidenced by many island stories, and surely it was only a matter of time before I'd have my own story to tell, if I was alive to tell it.

Knowing that Michael B would have all the up-to-date information on such matters, I asked him for his advice. What should I do when I see sharks? I wasn't satisfied with his answer.

"Don't mess with them," he replied.

"I don't intend to, Mike. But what if they want to mess with me? What should I do?"

"I don't know. I haven't seen too many sharks. The ones I did see just swam past me a couple of times and then disappeared."

I had seen too many movies and read too many adventure novels to think that sharks would continue to leave me alone. I knew the clumsy, low frequency beating of my flippers would sound like a dinner bell to some cruising brute.

The available diving literature was not particularly helpful, either. One magazine article that caught my eye was entitled, "Diving With Sharks." In it, readers were told not to worry about sharks because...they would probably never see one! Not a word of the article was dedicated to the wisest course of action a diver should take upon realizing he was "Diving with Sharks." I compared the writer's approach to that of a flight attendant handling the in-flight safety demonstration by asking, "Anybody want to know what to do in case of an emergency? Here it is: Don't worry. Statistics show most airplanes don't crash. Now, who needs a drink? Wow! That many?"

My two-hundred-some shark-free dives did little to convince me of my invulnerability. After all, I knew something about statistics, too, and I knew that people who weren't on an airplane at the time of a crash had a markedly better chance of survival than people who were. Similarly, I knew that the only way to guarantee immunity from sharks was to stay on the beach. But I wasn't about to make that sacrifice.

Luckily, when the inevitable finally happened, it was in such an amusing way that I found myself chuckling through my snorkel.

One sunny afternoon at the bottom of the ocean, Mike and I had just performed some of our eel-feeding charity work and were speeding for the surface and a breath of air when we saw a shark watching us. This wasn't the shark of my nightmares, however, but a small sleek silver-white specimen, hardly two feet long.

The comical aspect of the encounter was in the shark's choice of companionship. Swimming in the midst of our ever-present blackfish escort, the shark looked somewhat like a big white bulldog puppy trying to blend in with a pack of Chihuahuas. The similarity to a happy little dog was so strong that I pictured myself teaching the shark a few tricks, using a rap on the head with my pole spear as a substitute for a jerk on the leash.

How cute, I thought. The critter was hardly the vicious killing machine portrayed in the documentaries. Little did I know that the appearance of my little pet that day was a warning sign; for whatever reason, whether due to breeding cycles, tides, or just bad karma, my remaining two years in Ascension waters found me spending at least two out of three dives in the company of sharks. Real sharks. Sharks four or five times bigger than our little bulldog playmate.

These sharks never made a grand entrance, but like prowlers, kept their distance, gliding in and out of the gloomy limit of our visibility. Occasionally, one would gradually close to within ten feet or so, circling us for a few heart-pounding moments before it casually steered for deeper water, its curiosity apparently satisfied.

These brief appearances by the undisputed underwater King of the Beasts terrified me. My mask flooded as my facial contortions made a watertight seal impossible, and the air I wasted clearing the mask and panting in fear took ten minutes off my bottom time. Still, my heart palpitations weren't enough to send me racing for shore. After all, although the potential for disaster was real enough, I hadn't witnessed any outright aggression. And at the rate the sharks were showing up, my diving log would begin to show an embarrassing number of five minute dives if I had to leave the water every time I spotted a shark.

I decided that, if I wanted to keep diving, I'd have to learn to share the ocean. I'd keep an eye on our escort and go on with the business of the dive.

Of course, this didn't mean I started taking buckets of chum with me. Nor did it mean I flaunted my catch bag in front of the potentially vicious visitors if I had been spear fishing. I still preferred the shark-free dive. If a shark arrived while I was spear fishing, I left the water. I wanted to share the ocean, not my appendages.

For the longest time, the members of the Jaws Society voted to hide their numbers, only allowing me to see one, two, or on rare occasions, three of their members. One memorable evening, this number changed dramatically.

Mike and I had suited up in our scuba gear to explore the underwater world off Saint's Hut, the shelter built up against the cliffs south of Turtle Shell. The rocks past the hut contained a ledge that served as a flat, easy access to the ocean, and the area's thirty-foot depth meant we wouldn't have to waste precious air swimming through the shallows.

We jumped into the cool water, cleared our masks, and headed away from the wall, beginning a gradual descent to the ocean floor. As I expected from the low sun and overcast sky, the water, although clear, was dark and shadowy. That's why I became so confused when, without warning, the light went from gray to black.

It had happened like the flip of the switch. I was completely blind, not able to see my own hands. After a small eternity, I adjusted to the dimness and saw the reason for the blackout. Mike and I were surrounded by hundreds of thousands of small fish, a variety of herring known locally as "fry".

I had heard about the fry. Once or twice a year, the Georgetown Brits would spread the word, "The fry are running!" Soon, everybody with a basket would be on the beach, where they would simply take a few steps into the water and scoop up the fish. Further offshore, the water boiled with activity as jacks, tuna, dolphins, and sharks gathered to feast.

With that feeding frenzy image in my mind, it suddenly dawned on me that Mike and I were swimming *against* the fry; meaning we were swimming directly into the jaws of whatever was chasing the massive school. We instinctively headed for the bottom.

There, we were trapped. The ledge we had jumped from was an easy entrance, but a near impossible exit. Our dive plan had been to swim past two hundred yards of rock wall to get to the beach. It was a route we'd followed dozens of times, but on this day, our strategy would expose us to whatever was causing this frantic migration. At thirty feet below the surface and only ten feet under the fry, I watched the wondrous river of fish and thought, They're running from jacks, tuna, and dolphins. Not sharks…dolphins. Please let it be dolphins.

It was sharks. Only sharks. A hundred reef sharks, bull sharks, and who-knows-what sharks.

Back-to-back, Mike and I waited on the bottom as we watched this magnificent but terrifying parade. The sharks, intent only on grabbing mouthfuls of fry, ignored us completely. Ten minutes later, however, after the last of the fry had gone by, sharks were still emerging from the now-murky water, attracted by all the activity. I knew that these sharks would be the ones to fear—they were following a one-hundred foot wide chum line and had no visual clues as to what was on the menu. A few of these came within a few feet of us, gave us the once-over, then continued down the chum line.

Through it all, Mike and I remained frozen, our terror-induced hyperventilation generating a great pillar of bubbles to mark our spot. As with my first full-sized shark sighting, my mask couldn't conform to the contour of my wide-eyed face and I wasted even more air in my efforts to clear my vision.

The sharks gradually thinned out, but never entirely disappeared. Thinking these stragglers just might be angry enough at missing the dinner bell to take a random bite out of anything in the vicinity, we abandoned our post and swam cautiously back to the ledge. From there, we followed the rock wall until it ended two-hundred yards later. We were on the beach.

This episode was enough to ruin my sleep for three nights. But if I hadn't had a year's experience learning we could peacefully coexist with sharks, I probably would have died of fright, or at least whipped up a good panic. Although I remained wary of sharks and preferred to swim exclusively with fishes whose mouths are smaller than mine, I knew that was impossible. As an Ascension Diver, I had to continue to share the ocean.

Chapter 13

That's Entertainment, Too

The motorcycle I had bought during our last week in Florida turned out to be a mistake. Even though Gloria and I had ridden together many times, both in Florida and in many of the countries we'd visited while with the *Vanguard*, my wife just couldn't get comfortable riding on Ascension. The island's twisting, winding roads were to blame, with each blind corner holding too many surprises. Worse, the cinders and ragged rocks that lined either side of the pavement were unforgiving. Gloria didn't want to be adding our names to those that had suffered "death by misadventure," British officialese for traffic accident fatalities.

Of course, we still had our van. But while I wasn't convinced that the unique handling characteristics of the van weren't going to launch us off the road and into the scenery, I had to admit that if it did, our corpses would be in much better shape than if we took the same flight path on the motorcycle. Disappointed, I agreed to sell my new toy.

The buyer just happened to show up on the next plane. To my surprise and delight, it was Ralph, a fellow computer technician in his mid-twenties who was responsible for the few good memories I carried of my stay in Quito, Ecuador. I had had black friendships before, but none of those came close to the rapport I felt with Ralph. Our shared hardships as strangers in a strange land had certainly played a role in putting us together, but it was Ralph's delightful personality that made me urge Gloria to plan on double-dating with Ralph and his wife Penney as often as our schedule would allow.

Although Ralph spoke very softly, it paid to listen to him; his mutterings were filled with hilarious jokes and asides. He was a bit mild-mannered, but also friendly, easy-going, and generous; in Quito, when Ralph had found out that I was a motorcycle lover, he had shared his bike with me.

While Ralph brought me up to date on all the happenings at the Quito

The Devil's Ashpit

station, I wondered how I could have missed the news of his transfer. One step in the normal chain of events required to move a tech from one station to another was to notify the new station of the transferee's arrival. Coach, my computer supervisor, was always good about sharing correspondence that affected our group. How come he hadn't told me about Ralph?

Because he didn't know, that's why. Ralph's transfer was decidedly outside the bounds of what we considered normal. Ralph was a fugitive.

Just a few days before his arrival, everything had been rosy for Ralph and his family, or at least, as rosy as things could be for a gringo living in Ecuador. The pre-Lent Carnival festivities had begun. Unlike the famous Rio de Janeiro celebrations with samba schools parading in all of their finery, Quito's celebration takes a different tack. In Quito, Carnival month generally marks the end of the wet season and with dry months fast approaching, the citizens of the city in the mountains celebrate the temporary abundance of water by literally showering each other on the streets, either by dumping water from above or by throwing water balloons.

While walking home from the market, Ralph's wife caught a water balloon in the crotch. Hurt and embarrassed, she grabbed a can of juice from her grocery bag and hurled it in return. The young man on the receiving end lost his celebratory mood. He grabbed Penney and roughed her up.

Penney broke away, turned the corner, and was home, shrieking the details of the attack to her husband. Then my mild-mannered friend, apparently thinking a man's got to do what a man's got to do, put a .45 in his waistband and tore out after his quarry. Sure enough, the balloonist was still on his street corner. A chase ensued. Ultimately, the only fatality was somebody's front door that Ralph kicked open, but the owner of that door turned out to be a Somebody. The irate politico set the police on Ralph's trail.

Ralph beat feet out of the country. Bendix, to their immense credit, didn't fire him for abandoning his assignment, but sent him to us on a temporary basis until they could straighten out the mess he left in Quito.

I was astonished at this turn of events, but when Ralph sheepishly admitted that it was all true, we got a good laugh out of it, especially when I reminded Ralph of a statement he had made when we were both in Quito, discussing our futures.

"Me go to Ascension? No way. The only way they'd get me there was if I had to join a witness protection program."

Before leaving for work, I fished my motorcycle key out of my pocket and tossed it to Ralph. As long as he didn't use my bike to go storming up the hill to the island administrator's office, I told him, he could use it for as long as he wished.

Ralph stayed longer than he wanted and ended up buying the bike, but in the meantime, Gloria got a lead that a Brit couple in Two Boats was considering returning to their home in England. We called the couple, and sure enough, they not only had made their decision to leave Ascension, but were in the process of writing up a list of items they were going to sell, which included their car. They named a price, we accepted it, and a week later, Gloria and I parked our canary yellow, three-year-old Mercury Capri outside our barracks. We had the best vehicle on the base.

With the acquisition of some safe, reliable transportation, I could no longer postpone a trip to the farm atop Green Mountain. Gloria had been suggesting that we tour the farm ever since I had arrived on the island; promising that I would think I was in a different world.

I didn't believe her. Although Green Mountain was the biggest volcano on the island and served as its most easily recognizable landmark, I wasn't impressed with the vegetation that covered the top third of its ragged profile. We couldn't see the mountain from the base, but from Georgetown, I could easily cover the whole thing by holding my thumb a few inches from my eyes. Nevertheless, one morning after a midnight shift, we packed a picnic lunch and pointed our car towards the mountain.

It was a strenuous drive. The road from Two Boats, elevation 900 feet, took us up Green Mountain's northwest slope to the tune of 1,600 feet in the space of a mile. The Brits referred to this back-and-forth road as the Ramps and like everything else on the island, it was steeped in history. The Royal Marines had forged the road to ease their trips to the tiny water supply that dribbled out of one of the mountain's clefts.

My hands flew around the steering wheel, maneuvering through the hairpin turns while trying to keep up our speed. I shuddered to think what I would do on this road if I stalled the engine and had to deal with the clutch pedal. Despite my exercise, I noticed the air getting cooler and realized that the burning sun was gradually being blocked by a thickening canopy of overhanging trees. It was an Ascension first for me—I was actually in the shade of a tree.

At the 2,500 foot mark, we passed through the gates of Shangri-La.

The transformation wrought by the island's topography was astounding, and the Brits had taken full advantage of it. There really was a gate, and a series of moss-covered stone walls led us past large, well-tended gardens and a plush, honest-to-goodness green, green lawn. The watchtower of the Red Lion, a hundred-year-old building built to house a complement of Royal Marines, stood high above a hillside choked with tropical plants. I saw great clumps of bananas and bulbous mangoes ripening in the sun.

Further up the road was an array of greenhouses and a grand old house with a front porch that was built right out to the top of a cliff, giving its

The Devil's Ashpit

tenants a commanding view of the tiny oasis we had just passed. The house was known as Rock Cottage, and Gloria informed me that we could rent it for four dollars a night.

"Do it," I immediately replied.

The mountain road took us through yet another turn and deposited us on an even higher level. When we broke through the trees that shaded the bend, I actually gasped aloud. I stopped the car and jumped out, never taking my eyes off the horizon. Rock Cottage, the Red Lion, and their shining emerald carpets lay immediately below us. Beyond, a line of coconut palms towered over the edge of the escarpment. In stark, utter contrast to this tropical wonderland lay the rest of the island, dead mounds of rust-red, brown, and black cinders sprinkled amidst the flat wastelands. The wretched land below us even overpowered the hundreds of square miles of sparkling blue water that seemingly reached right into the sky.

The proximity of the sharply contrasting colors—the ruinous canvas of detritus between the two brilliant odes to life—gave me pause. For the first time since my arrival, I wondered at the extraordinary events that had led to the island's colonization. Simultaneously, I pitied the poor contingent of Royal Marines who had pulled duty on what must have been the most miserable assignment ever handed out by the Lords of the Admiralty.

As we stared at our little corner of the world, a small breeze washed over us, carrying a scent that brought back memories of my youth. I smelled trees, plants, dirt, and...pigs! Sure enough, a row of sties occupied the hillside directly behind us, their occupants oblivious to what had to be the most magnificent view the island had to offer.

The sties themselves were quite impressive structures, more like stone-walled barracks than the shanties I had seen as a kid. It turned out that the sties predated the Red Lion as the soldiers' barracks. The pigs not only lived on what might be considered Ascension's best plot of land, they were honored with the seal of the Royal Marines above their doorways.

Gloria and I left the car behind and continued our journey on foot. The road, which began to look more like a tractor path, took us up to the great mountain's spine.

This area held its own surprise, its ragged, richly carpeted contours reminding me of a farm we had seen in Tahiti. Sure-footed cows dotted the mountain's steep slopes, and we gazed in wonder at yet another legacy of the Royal Marines; a pair of huge stone catch-basins hugging the mountainside. These acres of masonry caught the moisture of the trade winds as their rapid ascent to the cooler temperatures at the mountaintop caused the water to condense on the flat rocks and drip down to the basins.

As I tried to digest this utterly unexpected aspect of what I had considered to be a rather one-dimensional island, I saw a familiar face.

"Maui!" Gloria and I cried in unison.

The huge, pot-bellied donkey walking towards us broke into a trot at the sound of his name. He nudged his way between the two of us and lowered his head for a rub.

We had first met Maui as a youngster when Bear (the tech whom Goddard had labeled a jack-off) had found the little donkey standing in the middle of the road. The animal was no more than a month old and no other donkeys were in sight.

Bear guessed that the baby's parents had been the victims of the local constabulary's latest thinning of the ranks. Although the donkeys had been imported in the 1800s to carry the Marines' water barrels between Green Mountain and Georgetown, that noble service was no longer required and the growing numbers of the island-roaming herds periodically became a nuisance.

Bear had bundled the orphan into the back of his jeep and let him loose on the tracking station grounds. The energetic burro was an immediate hit, frolicking around the station like a carefree colt and stamping impatiently outside the Hashpit door, waiting for techs to emerge with carrot and celery treats. Anyone returning to work with empty hands received a playful push on the back of the knee, a little reminder that a high-energy youngster needed all the handouts he could get.

As Maui grew, however, his nudges reached higher and higher and he learned that a shot between the legs would get a much better response. A few months more, and the donkey could easily rest his muzzle on my shoulder. I heard that he had begun biting the techs who refused to bring him a treat.

Despite this little strong-arm stunt, no one suggested that Maui be relocated. It wasn't until the second of two mishaps occurred that Maui had to go. First was an outdoor circuit breaker that brought down the electronics that drove the huge S-band antenna, causing us to lose some satellite data. I didn't believe that a donkey could have switched off the circuit breaker, but the S-band techs assured me that it was not only possible, but the likely cause. The circuit breaker was actually in the form of a big safety bar; Maui could have leaned against it, perhaps to scratch his butt.

The incident that sent Maui packing, however, was more suspect. The building that housed the station's generators had some outdoor plumbing that included a valve to drain water and other impurities from the bottom of the diesel fuel tanks. One night, a thousand gallons poured out of the fuel tanks and sank into the cinders at the edge of the Devil's Ashpit. The diesel mechanics quickly blamed Maui, but it would be a little harder to pin this deed on the donkey. Leaning against a circuit-killing safety bar was one thing, but twisting a valve a few turns was something else. Our supervisor,

The Devil's Ashpit

Wilmer, irately insisted that someone had obviously opened the valve to drain the water and had forgotten to close it. The mechanics stuck to their story.

Wilmer couldn't prove otherwise, but decided to remove the convenient scapegoat and banished Maui from the station. Bear, who had brought the foundling up the mountain in the back seat of his jeep, now put a rope around the donkey's thick neck and walked him back down the mountain to the aptly-named Donkey Flats. There, he could mix with his own kind.

Maui didn't mix for long. He sniffed out the closest gathering of people, which turned out to be at the clubhouse of the One Boat Golf Club, and began taking advantage of the club's open windows to beg the patrons for treats. Of course, the sight of Maui's big head sticking through the wall was highly comical and too good of a gag to pass up. A common joke was to squint drunkenly at the donkey and cry out in mock recognition,

"Wilmer! Is that you? C'mon in and have a beer."

The natural extension of this joke was to actually pour a beer for the animal. Maui took so willingly to the brew that his benefactors began feeding him straight from the beer can. The antics that followed were even more entertaining, as Maui, a thick froth forming around his muzzle, bobbed his head drunkenly and blew suds over the closest tables. This, of course, won him another beer.

Despite his popularity at the club, Maui managed to wear out his welcome, this time by biting the members who refused to buy him a drink. Bear was once again called upon to relocate his adopted offspring, or as he later explained, "They told me it was time I hauled my drunken ass up to the Green Mountain farm."

By the looks of Maui's pot belly, it was evident that life on the farm agreed with him. It was also evident that he enjoyed our attention as he cocked his head and leaned into us as we scratched his ears. Still, I wasn't sure whether our old friend was going to be satisfied with just a head rub. Was he still a biter? I put a little more vigor into my rub and sent Gloria to retrieve our picnic lunch from the car. She wisely kept the cans of beer out of sight while she fished around for an apple. Apparently, our offering was sufficient. Maui chowed down on the apple, bobbed his head as if to say thanks, then turned away and walked across the field.

After that first trip to the farm, Gloria and I made a point of braving the Ramps every six weeks or so and some months later, we even sacrificed a precious double-time day in exchange for a mini-vacation in Rock Cottage. The little sanctuary on the mountaintop was no five-star resort, but it was the exact opposite of everything the base was, and except for its distance from the ocean, it was my idea of what island life was supposed to be.

About the time that Gloria and I were falling in love with Green Mountain, history was being made down at the base. Television had come to the island. It was introduced by some enterprising veterans of the Eastern Test Range who had managed to maintain a number of contacts at the various tracking stations. Familiar with the range's entertainment shortage, the entrepreneurs took advantage of the new Video Cassette Recorder (or VCR) technology and went into business for themselves by persuading the sites' recreation committees to purchase televisions and VCRs.

The new "business" was simply a video taping service. Every week, down-range subscribers received a bootleg recording of up to six hours of commercial programming. Every other week, the site managers returned these tapes so they could be used again.

Gloria and I first learned of our new diversion following a movie at the Beachcomber Theater before a remarkably small audience. The flick earned its mediocre, two-star rating, especially when delivered with our pitiful, no-star sound system. But that was our typical fare, so why the poor attendance?

The reason was perched on a shelf in the Volcano Club. Gloria and I found this out when we stopped by for an after-movie beer, but couldn't squeeze our way through to the bar. Ascension had television—one television—and the women, cars, and wild antics of "them Duke boys" had the crowd mesmerized.

The introduction of television meant we could finally keep abreast of all the shows we'd been reading about or sampling during our vacations. Besides the *Dukes of Hazzard*, our tapes usually contained episodes of *The Misadventures of Sheriff Lobo*, *Three's Company*, *B.J. and the Bear*, and *Charlie's Angels*.

These were all prime time shows in 1979, but even Mr. A. C. Nielsen would have to admit that, in spite of their popularity, these series were hardly representative of TV's finer moments. Nevertheless, gauging from the crowd's response, one would have thought that each tape held nothing but Emmy award contenders.

Gloria and I, though, thought the shows were a complete waste of time. And because boredom is bad television's greatest ally, we watched every minute of every tape just to make sure our judgment was sound.

Six weeks later, the system's slipshod management accomplished what bad programming could not; we gave up on TV.

The first sign that the recording business was losing some of its luster was when the tape's program list went from a type-written label to a hastily scribbled message no more descriptive than "football" or "movie". Eventually, the label bore no clue whatsoever as to the contents of the tape.

This omission would have meant nothing were it not for our supplier's

The Devil's Ashpit

second shortcut; they decided that it was too much trouble to completely rewind the recycled tapes before recording over them. As a result, we began receiving tapes that contained segments of as many as a dozen programs before we came to the main attraction. Of course, without a label, we didn't know what that main attraction was, so we never knew which shows we were going to see in their entirety.

Gloria and I eventually became so frustrated that we left this supposed entertainment to the Saints, who were so enthralled by the technology that they would have watched a test pattern, and to those Yanks drunk enough not to care.

Once we weaned ourselves off the television, we had a few more hours each week to try to entertain ourselves within the bounds of Ascension's limited resources. I decided to try once again to get Gloria excited about the ocean.

"I'm not saying you need to get a scuba-diving certification," I told her. "It's just that snorkeling could be another thing we could do together. Besides, I feel guilty leaving you here every day while I go to the beach."

"Oh, I've told you before not to worry about that," she replied. "I'm just happy that you're doing something you love."

"But you're missing out on the fantastic undersea life! Don't you want a little more adventure?" I persisted.

For an answer, Gloria put her hand up to my head and ran a finger across the scar the eel bite had left on my temple. I guess *adventure* had been the wrong word to use under the circumstances. I tried one last gambit.

"Listen, how about Comfortless? You know, it's just sand, sand, sand. No rocks for eels to hide in."

Knowing that Comfortless Cove housed the calmest water on the island, she reluctantly agreed to give it a try.

Although Gloria and I had long enjoyed Comfortless, the cove had a sad history. It was first known as Sydney Cove and kept that name until the mid-1800s when a ship brought in victims of yellow fever to convalesce. The locals gradually began referring to the place as Comfort Cove, but as the infection took its toll, islanders felt that the name had become too ironic and even mocking to those victims buried in the graveyard that sprang up behind the beach. Comfortless was the natural choice.

No matter what it was called, the place was unbelievably inviting; it looked like it had been intentionally carved out of the lava to accommodate swimmers and sunbathers. The cove was a south-facing horseshoe of an inlet, which offered protection from the prevailing winds and waves. The view from the surrounding rocks was quite impressive, looking over the wide, white sands of Long Beach and the Georgetown forts and other buildings and behind all of that, the volcanic cones. Climb down the thirty or so steps, however, and you found yourself in a world apart, the cove having a perfectly smooth beach leading down to what I considered my very own Olympic-sized swimming pool nestled between the lava cliffs. The open end of the horseshoe was nothing but sea and sky, as the cliffs blocked out any other sight of land.

Here I helped Gloria adjust the straps of the mask I'd bought her the year before and fixed the angle of the snorkel for a comfortable fit. I took everything slow and easy; we knelt in waist-deep water until Gloria got used to breathing with her face submerged. When she agreed that she was ready to try swimming, we pulled our inflatable life vests over our heads, pulled our fins on, and eased into a horizontal position.

I wasn't kidding when I had said sand, sand, sand. I quickly became bored. I stood, spat out my snorkel, and touched my wife's shoulder.

"Hey, let's go over to the wall and look at the little fishies. It's like an aquarium over there."

She lifted her head and pulled out her own snorkel.

"No, this is nice. I like it right here," she said, and returned to looking underwater at the sunlit, featureless, do-nothing sand.

I relented and joined her for a few more minutes, but a sand dive has some way to go before it can be as exciting as watching paint dry. I got Gloria's attention again and assured her that we would stay in the sand, far from the rocks, but couldn't we at least get off the beach and into some deeper water? The islanders had strung a thick hawser across the cove, well before the entrance and Gloria agreed to my suggestion that we swim to the rope and back.

As we headed out, I offered my hand, but she shook her head and I saw under the water that both of her hands were occupied, clutching her life vest. I smiled to myself, causing my mask to leak a bit. Well, never mind the hand-in-hand; I was content to be side-by-side. We idly kicked and watched the sand slope gently away beneath us, the reflected light diminishing ever-so-slightly.

Suddenly a fish came into view. Life! Action! It was what we called a tile fish, with a slender white body that was about a foot-and-a-half long. It hovered just a few inches above the sand that was fifteen feet below us, eyeing our silhouettes.

I swiveled my head so I could catch Gloria's eye and point out the fish to her, but all I saw were her fins. She was kicking straight for shore as fast as she could manage.

I caught up with her and pulled her up to find out what was wrong.

"I saw something!" she said a little loudly, a little shakily. "It looked dangerous! I thought it was going to bite us!"

I assured my wife that I had seen the same thing and it was a harmless tile fish. Then I announced that we had practiced enough for one day, though I knew Gloria was feeling that we had practiced enough for a lifetime. I also knew that this would be our last snorkel together. Gloria's fear of Ascension waters ran too deep.

Gloria had been so scared I chose not to ask the burning question, *if you thought it was going to bite us—that's "us" mind you—then why didn't you warn me?*

Time not spent on the beach meant time spent in our rooms—which, more often than not, meant time spent reading. In order to read, though, we had to spend a lot of time perusing mail-order bookstore catalogs. I am still mystified that the base didn't provide an actual library.

I ordered a number of the giant "Complete Works of ..." volumes, which ostensibly afforded me the opportunity to, for example, read every word written by Charles Dickens and follow every clue discovered by Sherlock Holmes. For more contemporary reading, I bought every Steven King novel as soon as it was published, thus continuing the trend that Ralph had begun in Quito when he introduced me to *Carrie*. Following a random paperback purchase at the tiny Georgetown store, I happily added author Wilbur Smith and his exciting sagas of African gold, ivory, and diamond seekers to my must-read list.

On the days when I needed a quick fix, I turned to the short story anthologies, my favorite genre being the murder mystery. My mother may have helped to influence this choice, as she devoted any free time to either a Nero Wolfe novel or one of the dozen mystery magazines she kept with her knitting. I was probably the only kid in first grade who hurried through the *Fun with Dick and Jane* primer so I could pick up the new issue of *Alfred Hitchcock's Mystery Magazine*.

The more I read short stories, the more I longed to see my name in a magazine's table of contents. I had a few ideas for storylines, but every time I tried to commit them to paper, I'd get bogged down after just a few paragraphs. I needed guidance.

Once again, the US Mail came to my rescue. Since I was already enjoying the correspondence course I had enrolled in to keep abreast of the burgeoning integrated circuit revolution, I decided to plunk a couple of hundred dollars down on a course in short story writing.

My materials quickly arrived. The package held two loose-leaf binders, one containing the lessons and the other filled with short stories to use as examples. I raced through the first chapter and its assignment: *Provide three synopses of short stories you would like to write*. A week later, a C-141 brought me my instructor's glowing words, his constructive criticism, and his permission to proceed with chapter two. And I did. I studied chapter two as I had never studied anything before. I pictured O. Henry's heirs writing me to admit that ol' Henry was a hack compared to my fascinating, character-rich, intricately wound short stories. Finally, I finished the chapter and read assignment two: *Choose one of your chapter one synopses and turn it into a short story*.

Huh? This was the chapter *two* assignment? Did my loose-leaf pages get jumbled up? I checked, but the page numbers were all in order. I stared at the assignment for a few more minutes and then closed the binder and put it on the shelf, thus bringing an end to my short story writing career.

Gloria loved to play cards, but the only card games I had ever played at home were Klondike Solitaire, Old Maid, and War. Oh, and I played 52-Pickup—once. In college, I had tried a few hands of poker, but my math course in combinations, permutations, and probability had used a lot of poker hands for examples and when my mid-term came back with my lowest-ever grade of 28%, I realized that all I really knew about this fascinating branch of mathematics was that the probability of supplementing my income with poker winnings was going to be zero.

Gloria's card game of choice was Hearts, and we also played checkers and Scrabble. This was when I learned how differently we approached our games. I wanted quick games. I often threw down a card, moved a checker, or played a word just to keep the game moving and see what would happen next. What happened next was Gloria taking her time to play the right card or jump two of my checkers or land on the triple word score and beat the pants off of me.

I didn't mind losing; I did mind waiting, especially for checkers. I got bored watching Gloria study the board. I thought my problems were solved when I found a mail-order house selling the Fidelity Checker Challenger. The Checker Challenger would allow Gloria to play checkers by herself, or more accurately, against her computerized opponent.

As a computer game, the Challenger was extremely rudimentary; it consisted of a calculator-like keypad built into the corner of an actual checker board. Each checker square had a number on it. To make a move, you keyed the appropriate location numbers into the From and To displays, then moved your checker. When the computer displayed its own numbers, you relocated the computer's checker as indicated and then planned your next move.

Gloria was excited by the new technology and by the knowledge that her new opponent would not grouse about playing checkers with her or complain that she was taking too long. But then there was a problem.

"Shit!" she exclaimed.

"Huh?" I asked, looking up from my magazine in surprise.

"I led the computer into a double-jump trap, but it says it's an illegal move. It says I don't have a checker on square fifteen."

"Well, there's a lot of button-pushing involved. Maybe you punched the wrong number in?" I suggested.

She agreed. That lasted an hour.

"Shit!"

"Again?"

"Yes!" she said, pulling the plug and returning the game to its box. "And this time I *know* I did everything correctly."

"What was the difficulty level set to?" I asked helpfully, "Maybe you get to a certain level and the computer's allowed to cheat?"

Gloria's glare answered my question. And that's the last I saw of the Fidelity Checker Challenger.

In between reading and playing games, there was plenty of time for talking—or to be more accurate, for bitching. I was also beginning to notice a lot of nastiness among the Bendix troops. It often commenced just a few seconds after stepping into the van for the drive to the station and only ended after work when we stepped into our rooms and closed the doors behind us. Something about Ascension seemed to attract people with personality disorders, or perhaps the island just had a way of drawing out a latent disorder. It's even possible that Ascension skewed the eye of the beholder into *thinking* that a personality disorder was at work. In the end, though, all that mattered was that Ascension had a way of bringing out your inner bitch.

Furthermore, the morale of the Bendix troops had been in a steady decline since the departure of our NASA overseer, Steve Stompf, and the arrival of his replacement, Zach. Gloria and I were well acquainted with Zach, as he had been around the tracking network as much as we had. Work-wise, I couldn't vouch for Zach or, for that matter, any of the NASA station directors; we peons never attended their meetings with Bendix station managers. On the other hand, there were plenty of opportunities to socialize.

And when I socialized with Zach, I found his affability seemed a bit forced. Granted, this observation may have been founded somewhat on the resentment I felt when, as I was leaving for my last *Vanguard* cruise, I had mentioned my hope that at the end of the assignment, I would be able to transfer to Ascension to join Gloria. Zach had laughed as if I had just uttered the most ridiculous nonsense he had ever heard. That had stung me deeply since, at that time, I had no way of knowing if Bendix management in Maryland was laughing just as loudly at my transfer request.

Our top Bendix manager at the site at the time, John Lacewell, may have felt the same way about Zach; when Steve left and the NASA house that he and John shared had passed to Zach, John declined his new coworker's offer to stay. John moved back to a room in the barracks and only a short time later, he left the island for good.

Our British hosts may have felt the same way about Zach; the new NASA representative received far fewer invites to Brit functions than Steve and John had enjoyed. Thus it was time for Zach to harbor a little resentment of his own. I had the privilege of witnessing it first hand in the Volcano Club one night when Zach and I shared a table.

"I met the island administrator for lunch today," he said. "He asked if I was the chap who'd moved into Lacewell's house."

I waited for Zach to continue, wondering if his statement was the setup for a punch line or the beginning of a laundry list of his activities for the day, or maybe just a boast that he had met the island's top Brit. But he just sat there chewing his lip and looking around the club.

"Lacewell's house," he finally muttered. And then he turned to me and yelled. "It's *my* house, damn it!"

I made a few half-hearted attempts to soothe his ego, reminding him that John had been a fixture on the island for years and was the Brits' favorite Yank. Inwardly, though, I was delighted to know that Zach had been wounded by this failure to recognize his self-styled status as the high-and-mighty lord of the Devil's Ashpit Tracking Station.

I don't believe his lordship had much to do with Bendix policy, but he may have been an important link in the chain of events that led to John's departure—and the subsequent rise of Wilmer to station manager. Bitching among the Bendix troops increased three-fold.

I hadn't tried to categorize Wilmer prior to his promotion, but as I pondered life under our new boss, I realized that I had never ever seen him anywhere except the site or the road to the site. Even at the site, he never ate in the Devil's Hashpit; he must have had a Saint bring him a tray. For that matter, rather than eating that reheated tripe, he may have driven himself back to the base for lunch. I never saw him at the movies or the cafeteria or the club or the beach. Other than the sightings at One Boat, which on closer inspection always turned out to be Maui, we never saw him anywhere.

Wilmer ignored situations that screamed for his attention, as in the case of the supervisor who subjected her direct reports to her own megalomaniacal style and massive mood swings. While she was making an already difficult situation into an impossible one, Wilmer was busy micromanaging trivial issues, where he had so many more opportunities to exercise his veto or at least express his disapproval.

One morning at the site, Wilmer came over to the computer section to talk. He motioned for me to join him.

"I heard you helped Riley to his room yesterday," he said.

By this time, I was getting pretty good at translating Wilmer's speech to English, but I could hardly believe my ears. He sounded as if he was preparing to thank me for my humanitarian act. The evening before, Gloria and I had returned from the beach to see two very drunk Bendix Saints, Skids and Mongo, sitting in the cinders with a dead-drunk Riley sprawled nearby. Mongo (named after the *Blazing Saddles* character) waved.

"Dan," he called, "We're trying to take Riley to his room but nobody will help us."

Of course they wouldn't. Riley was universally reviled. Time has softened my sour memories of him, thus elevating him in my mind to the category of sneering, arrogant, asshole. Not only had everyone refused to help Riley, but I saw a bootprint on his T-shirt where someone had innocently mistaken him for a patio stone. I briefly wondered why Skids and Mongo had chosen Riley for a drinking partner, but decided that they, too, were willing to try anything to alleviate the boredom.

I told the two Saints that I'd take care of Riley, then I watched as they staggered off, comically leaning against each other. I was surprised that the much drunker Skids was able to support the much larger Mongo. When I was satisfied that they would be able to take care of themselves, I lifted Riley over my shoulders in a fireman's carry and took him to his room. There, I dropped him on his bed, rolled him on his side, and thoughtfully placed a trashcan on the floor near his head. In short, I did for him what I had done for my brother (and he had done for me) more than a few times on those special college football weekends.

At the site, I answered Wilmer's question with a modest "yes" and prepared for my pat on the back.

"Do you know what happens when people pass out from drinking too much?" he said, his voice undergoing a gradual crescendo. "They throw up, they choke on their own vomit and they *die*! Maybe you'll think of that next time!"

With that situation handled, Wilmer stalked off, no doubt looking to deliver a similar morale boost to another deserving employee.

No matter how much reading material we squirreled away or how many games we had at our disposal, cabin fever could still send us outside, looking for the path of least wind resistance. We got back into our old habit of walking down to the beach, an activity we'd put aside during our brief flirtation with television. We usually passed Turtle Shell in favor of the long crescent of Pan Am Beach. There, we'd check the subtle changes in the direction of the tide, calculate the bit of shore line that would provide the best view of ocean spray, and seat ourselves in the sand to watch a thousand or so waves smash into the rocks. It was the visual equivalent of a drum roll and a crash of cymbals. The resulting spray shimmered like a diamond shower, backlit by the setting sun. The sun's rays also shone through the curl of each wave, giving it a translucent emerald glow and perfectly outlining the silhouettes of a chain of the ubiquitous blackfish.

On one of our first visits, something in the sand stirred and drew our attention away from the ocean's spectacle. A baby turtle was making its first appearance after clawing its way up through two feet of sand. A second later, four more babies popped out of the same hole. These pathfinders must have opened the floodgates, for in the next minute, the sand boiled as the entire clutch of a hundred or more baby turtles emerged and scrabbled frantically, inefficiently towards the water.

All the newborns had to do, though, was to get close to the shoreline, as the breaking waves sent rushes of water up the beach to engulf the struggling turtles, pulling them into the medium for which they were born. Once in the water, they flitted quickly and effortlessly from rock to rock, until, just a few feet from shore, we could follow them no more.

Gloria and I helped a few of the stragglers, getting them off the beach before they became too dehydrated to continue, or before they became a snack for the "wideawake" terns that nested in the nearby rocks. The ten feet that we carried the youngsters to the water's edge paled in comparison to the journey they were embarking on; Ascension turtles travel nearly 1,400 miles to the coast of Brazil before returning home to the beach where they were hatched, ready to renew the cycle.

Witnessing the birth and departure of baby turtles, however, was the exception rather than the rule. For the vast majority of our ocean-side evenings, there was nothing to distract us as we sat watching the waves and listening to their accompanying roar as they collapsed on the beach. Nothing, that is, until the sun's red-orange disk began to dip below the horizon. At that point, any conversation ceased, and we strained to keep from blinking as we tracked the orb's slow subsidence. By silent mutual consent, we were on "flash watch".

One of the pages out of my island boy catalog of wishes was the hope that I would join the ranks of those privileged to view the green flash, a phenomenon I had read about at the age of sixteen and had yet to witness, even after my two years on the *Vanguard*.

Some people claimed to have seen the apparition twice or thrice weekly, but by strange coincidence, these people also seemed to be the heaviest drinkers on the island. I was convinced that these party animals were confusing green flashes with green flushes, referring to the green deodorizer cakes in the Volcano Club urinals.

After watching a hundred sunsets with no discernible hint of a change in colors, I decided that the flash was pure myth. At best, the effect was a residual retinal image, the spectral opposite that anyone would get by staring fixedly at a red object for a length of time. Yes, the flash was a myth. But I had heard so much about the phenomenon that the thought occurred to me that maybe one of George Orwell's assertions might apply here: "Myths which are believed in tend to become true."

If this myth did become true, I was determined to be at my post when it did. This glimmer of hope kept me gazing westward every evening.

The Devil's Ashpit

We often had four-legged company for our beach walks. Snoopy, the aging Black Labrador mix, would occasionally forsake the Chief and his sodden collection of sea stories, songs, and coughing fits, and join us. Snoopy was an old-timer, maybe twelve years old, and the painful way he struggled to his feet every time he awoke from a nap told me that he wouldn't be around much longer. When Snoopy first volunteered to accompany us on a beach walk, his slow, stiff-legged gait told me that our one-mile walk down to Turtle Shell and back would be his last. I didn't want the death of the site mascot on my conscience.

"Snoopy, go home," I commanded. "Go get the Chief. Chow-time, Snoopy. Chow."

"Ride, Snoopy," Gloria chimed in, "Chief will give you a ride."

We continued to search our knowledge of Snoopy's vocabulary to find the word that would turn him back to the base. At the moment, though, the only word he cared about was the one he overheard in our hallway. Beach. Snoopy lifted his big gray head, gave us a mocking smile, and continued to plod down the steep road to Turtle Shell.

There, a different dog leaped across the sand, streaking toward the ocean. The gray hair was the same, but the old tired joints and stiff-legged walk were gone. Snoopy threw himself into the surf, dove under a wave and came up with a blackfish in his mouth. He spat the luckless fish onto the dry sand above the tide mark and for the next fifteen minutes, proceeded to bark at it, roll over it, and finally, crush it with his jaws. Then he dove back into the water to catch another.

An uninformed witness to these beachside blackfish massacres might have been surprised that the old dog harbored such a hellacious mean streak. I, however, had already heard stories of the old rogue's checkered past, including some jail time he had served as a sheep-killer.

Ascension sheep are pitifully ugly creatures; the swirling volcanic ash that sweeps the island's plains has permanently discolored the animals' matted coats. Their drab, dreary wool hangs in tatters, torn by the rocks and cactus. The sheep's ubiquitous presence serves as an additional impediment to the greening of Ascension; the untended animals wander the island at will, competing with the donkeys for the tidbits of cactus and straw-like greasy-grass that dot the plains. I had become so accustomed to the sheep's scraggly appearance that one night on base I was leafing through a magazine and happened upon a picture showing a herd of animals with what seemed to be enormously thick, impossibly white coats…and I had to read the caption to find out that they were sheep.

Unfortunately for Snoopy, the Brits consider the sheep to be another living tribute to the Royal Marines' strenuous efforts to farm the Rock a hundred years before. The Georgetown police took an especially dim view of the young dog's energetic efforts to cull the herds and actually tossed him in the clink, where he remained until the Yanks paid his fine.

Snoopy's advancing years ultimately saved the sheep (or more probably, Snoopy himself) from extinction, but the blackfish enjoyed no such immunity, nor did they swim under police protection. Thus, it was these fish that bore the brunt of Snoopy's killer lust.

When he was done terrorizing the blackfish, Snoopy chased crabs around the rocks for awhile, then settled into a tidal pool. The uneven lava floes that skirted the island's border hosted myriad depressions that captured the high tide waters and warmed them to hot-tub temperatures. These pools were the highlight of Snoopy's beach appearance and their therapeutic effects were his only ocean-side concession to his age. Snoopy dog-paddled around the pool for a full half-hour, allowing the hot water to penetrate his old muscles and joints.

Afterwards, the refreshed dog would return to our room with us and walk into our shower to wash off the salt. Then, with a wag of his tail, Snoopy would bid us good-bye, disappearing down the hallway. We knew he had other mascot duties to perform, visiting other techs at the base or hitching a ride to pull a shift at the site. We may have been the only tracking station in the world that allowed a dog to roam freely between the equipment racks.

We Bendix workers sometimes referred to the pooch as our Silver Snoopy, a pun that played on the dog's hoary appearance and the name of a coveted NASA award. Designed by the astronaut corps, the Silver Snoopy had been created to acknowledge the space industry's most conscientious performers. Each Silver Snoopy award honoree received a framed citation and a silver lapel pin of the astronauts' official mascot—a space-helmeted rendition of Charlie Brown's adventurous dog. Considering our distance from the NASA mainstream, we knew that our aged, panting comrade was as close to a Silver Snoopy as we were going to get.

We rather made sure of that one evening in 1979, a day after I had asked Coach if I could come to work an hour late. My reason? I wanted to go to a pig roast on the beach. It could be argued that this excuse was a bit flimsy, but in my two years on the island, I had yet to attend a pig roast. Every time someone organized one, they somehow managed to ruin both the pig's day and mine as well, since they scheduled the roast to coincide with my work shift. And although I'd attended countless cookouts where we grilled fish fresh from the ocean, another of those activities I'd always associated with idyllic island life was the beachside pig roast.

It was worth the wait. While I savored the tasty, succulent pork, I had another rare treat; I got into a conversation with fellow computer tech Daryl Dabbs. Daryl and I had been on different shifts our entire time on the island, so our meetings were pretty much limited to the site, when he relieved me on the SCE at shift change. Daryl had started with Bendix in

The Devil's Ashpit

1972, the same year I did, but unlike me, he had gone straight into the computer section. This experience coupled with his natural intelligence meant Daryl was easily the sharpest computer tech on the island and perhaps in the entire network. He was also a lot of fun to talk to, as was his girlfriend, Emiline, the site's safety supervisor.

Gloria and I tried to hang out as much as possible with this couple—as much as shift roulette would allow us, anyway, for not only did I enjoy Daryl's company and Gloria enjoy Emiline's, but we were good cross-over friends as well.

Unfortunately, my one-on-one conversation with Daryl was once again short-lived as Cliff strolled up to join us. At the site, Cliff proved himself a sharp technician, but he was no member of my Dream Team; he began each of our daily meetings at the site by lighting a fresh cigarette and blowing the smoke in my face. Behind this cloud he described all of the horrific technical issues that had occurred under his watch and were subsequently mine to deal with. He then followed this with a "Just kidding!" before giving me the actual equipment status. I didn't find Cliff's "joke" amusing in the least, but even after 365 consecutive days, the delighted chuckle that punctuated his wit never tapered off. For my part, I just thought *to each his own...especially on Ascension.*

At least on the beach I was able to step upwind of Cliff as the three of us talked shop. We'd only been standing together for a few minutes before Emiline arrived and walked up to us with a big smile on her face.

"Now here's something you don't see every day," she announced. "All three SCE techs talking on the beach!"

The importance of Emiline's words hit us at once as evidenced by three jaws dropping in unison. *Who's watching the store?*

No sooner was that thought completed when the telephone mounted on the beach shack wall started to ring. Someone picked it up and hollered that Coach needed me at the site.

It was already too late. Apparently, during the shift change that I had missed, either Coach had forgotten to ask Cliff to stay another hour, or more likely, Cliff was looking forward to the pig roast as much as I was and just jumped into the first van to take him down the hill. Thus when our satellite support time arrived, the computer section consisted only of Coach and a wet-behind-the-ears tech named Gene Weiand. Ordinarily, this would not have been a problem, but Coach had focused on the site's 642B computer operations for so long that his SCE skills were rusty. So even though Coach loaded the SCE correctly, as I saw by the printed log, he had enough self-doubt that he allowed Gene to convince him otherwise. Unfortunately, following Gene's instructions caused Coach to wipe out the command table. Every time he tried to send a command, the SCE complained that there was no command to send.

I was incredulous that Coach had listened to Gene, whose only SCE experience was in the middle of the orientation briefing I'd given him on his first day at work, a few weeks before. He'd been working the 642B under Coach's guidance ever since. Furthermore, Gene was fresh out of tech school and as seemed to be the new trend, he did not have the advantage of attending any of the classes taught at the training facility near Goddard.

Gene was *so* green that for a while, it was difficult for me to talk to him because I'd forgotten how much jargon had worked its way into my normal speech. For example, after our introductions our first conversation went like this:

"Okay, Gene, throughout the network, we always use GMT, so anytime you hear someone talk about the time, you'll know they're giving it to you in GMT. And that's one advantage of working on Ascension; we're already on GMT, so we don't have to worry about converting."

"What's GMT?"

I had already made a mental note to precede every acronym with an explanation, but GMT to us was no different from anybody else saying AM or PM. This exchange told me not to overwhelm him with too much information, so after explaining Greenwich Mean Time, I did my best to explain the station's operations in the most basic of terms. In the process, I showed Gene how I prepped the SCE for support. Because my commentary slowed me down, the Ops got antsy.

"SCE, OPS," he called. "You ready for support?"

I picked up the handset and confirmed that we were. I noticed Gene had a puzzled look on his face.

"He said, 'SCE, OPS.' Why didn't he say, 'OPS to SCE?' You know, like 'Kirk to Enterprise.'"

I smiled as I recalled my own confusion when I was first learning communications protocol. Rather than plumb those depths, I just explained that it made more sense to place the other person's name first so you have their attention from the start. I also pointed out that even though we may have known these people for years in many cases, we still used the call-signs, like OPS or SCE or Recorders instead of Tom or Dan or Gloria. On one hand, it sounded a bit stilted, but on the other, I thought we sounded very professional.

Gene had done well in his few weeks, despite his neophyte status. He was conscientious, eager to learn, and cooperative. He also had the trait that was perhaps most treasured in an Ascension coworker—an agreeable personality. I felt bad that he was going to have to bear the stigma of NASA's mortal sin, the Operator Error.

The OE may just as well have been called an OS for "Oh Shit" since these words often heralded the arrival of each new OE. A neverending source of controversy was the "oh shit" to "attaboy" ratio, as in, *how many attaboys do you need to make up for one oh shit?* The discussion was essentially moot, since Bendix never actually handed out any attaboys.

I hope Gene's memory of his Ascension service leans more towards his Skylab support and not to his OE. Following the foul-up, Coach assigned Gene to follow me full time. Simultaneously, Goddard began to throw a lot more Skylab passes our way. I found this ironic because NASA had learned some months before that their efforts to restore the space station to its former glory were destined to fail. Increased solar activity had increased the drag on the massive satellite. NASA engineers had successfully commanded Skylab into a path-of-least-resistance orientation, but at that time they were still counting on the new Space Shuttle to save the day.

Unfortunately, the massive Shuttle project was still hitting numerous snags, one of which was how to get its heat insulation tiles to stay in place. As my father uncharitably described the problem in one of his letters, "NASA hasn't discovered Elmer's Glue yet."

Shortly after the announcement that Skylab's reentry was imminent, I saw Harley ("got any porn?") sitting at his antenna console wearing a hardhat. From the computer section, I could see that he'd doctored the hardhat to some degree, but all I could make out was S...P...D.... My curiosity piqued, I closed the gap until I could read the tiny letters. Harley had made himself a Skylab Protection Device.

The SPD was good for a laugh, but in our media-poor environment, it took us a couple of weeks to learn that a Skylab-reentry frenzy had gone international. With good reason, I'd say. One source projected up to 25 tons of metal debris landing in 500 pieces over an area 4,000 miles long and 1,000 miles wide.

Even if we had remained oblivious to the media coverage, I still would have felt myself lucky to be working during the predicted reentry orbit. I'd tracked a few brand-new satellites in my short career (Skylab being the first) and I was on the *Vanguard* for the manned Apollo-Soyuz capsule reentries, but I'd never tracked a satellite to its absolute end.

I got my chance on July 11, 1979. I badly wanted to take charge of the SCE during Skylab's final orbit, but I couldn't bring myself to push my pupil aside. So just like I had done all week, I stood beside Gene while he prepped the computer, tested its link to S-band, and (correctly) announced, "OPS, SCE. We're go for commanding."

And I was standing beside him at 16:01:31 when he sent the very last command that Skylab would ever receive. The command turned on the doomed spacecraft's Attitude and Pointing Control System so that the onboard computer would transmit rate-of-tumble information, helpful in predicting where on earth the mission would come to an end.

Attaboy, Gene!

Chapter 14

Movin' On

I was approaching my three year anniversary on Ascension when I began to seriously consider putting the Rock behind us. My string of one-thousand days on the island, unbroken except for the two short vacations we had taken, was synonymous with one-thousand work days, and I could tell that the strain of mining Ascension gold was beginning to show.

One of the main symptoms of "too much Rock" was a growing impatience with my fellow workers, particularly those in the computer section. It was as though Alvin's transfer to my domain had opened the doors for a number of other losers, each hosting his own particular brand of personality flaw. What was worse, our regular supervisor, Coach, had begun a series of training courses, vacations, and temporary assignments to other sections, leaving me as the person directly responsible for these techs.

The least offensive of the new arrivals was a young man who called himself Stick. Stick looked like he had just stepped out of a '60s flower-power poster, and following a brief conversation with him, I deduced that his nickname must have been an abbreviation of Thai Stick, the name of one of the more respected members of the marijuana family.

Stick's problem was his utter devotion to marijuana, which I'm sure had contributed to at least one other problem; years of whispered conversations about the subject of his passion had apparently left him with the inability to raise his voice. Thus, the question, "What?" became a familiar punctuation mark in the computer section, as we strained to hear Stick over the din of the equipment's cooling fans.

It was always a good bet that the repeated sentence would bear a reference to dope. First and foremost was the subject of smoking dope. From what I could hear, Stick didn't stop there, but also spoke softly about his favorite dope, the cheapest dope, the most dope, and how to roll dope, cook dope, and brew dope. Then he whispered about dope songs with dope lyrics, dope laws, dope parties, dope-sniffing dogs, doped-up dogs, dope albums, dope movies, and dope posters. For a change of pace, he compared and graded bongs, roach clips, pipes, and hookahs, and finally, I caught a few words about his own invention, a stash box that looked like a jewelry box but contained compartments for papers, pipes, incense, and of course, dope. Stick was going to mass produce his stash box and sell it via an advertisement in the anti-establishment magazine, *High Times*.

Stick, furthermore, was a bit of a dim bulb—fittingly, I watched as he misdiagnosed a burned-out light bulb—and his constant smokes did nothing to enhance his IQ. I counted myself fortunate when, after an eight-hour shift, Stick's contribution to the section was zero; more often, his blunders put us behind.

When I suspected that my flower child was enjoying the occasional mid-shift mellow session, I resolved to give him a talk on the need to stay sober on the job. Admittedly, I felt a little silly; here I was lecturing someone for taking a hit or two from a roach while many of the other techs, supervisors, and even operations supervisors were known to have blood-alcohol levels that would pickle an egg.

Stick listened to me, then gave me his hushed reply. Whether he agreed with me or told me to go to hell, I'll never know; I couldn't hear him.

Some weeks after Stick's arrival, I looked up from my computer terminal to find Wilmer standing beside me with a sullen-looking young man in tow. Wilmer introduced the new guy as Walter, another technician for the computer section. On this first meeting, Walter did not return my welcoming smile, nor did he move to accept a handshake until long after my own hand had been extended. When I took my new trainee on a tour of the station, he acted aloof and bored.

I assumed Walter was overwhelmed by the surroundings. I had seen that before. It was one thing to be introduced to a brand new job, new company, new policies, and new equipment somewhere in the States. It was quite another thing to be introduced to all these changes while trying to cope with Ascension's unique circumstances, as well.

I guessed that Walter needed some time alone. I cut the tour short and led my new recruit to Coach's desk, where Wilmer had left some forms for him to fill out. Hoping to guide Walter through some of the paperwork, I sat down beside him and noticed that he had printed "John" and "Philip" for first and middle names on his savings bond enrollment form.

"Hey," I said, pointing to the mistake, "Did you mix up your 'applicant' with your 'beneficiary'?"

Walter jerked his head up and stared at me for a full ten seconds. Then he spoke.

"That's my name."

He said it slowly and evenly and tightly, as if through clenched teeth.

I was taken aback by the vehemence of his reply. Completely flustered. I tried to remember which of Wilmer's mangled words had fooled me into thinking he was saying "Walter." Apparently, I had over-estimated my ability to understand Wilmer's speech. No wonder the guy was pissed off; I had just introduced my new tech as "Walter" to twenty people around the station.

I could only stammer the obvious.

"I... I thought your name was Walter."

"Walter's my nickname," he said. This time, his voice told me that he was trying to figure out who was the bigger fool; me for not knowing his given name was John Philip, or me for being the only person in the English-speaking world who didn't know that Chuck was a nickname for Charles, Tony was short for Anthony, and Walter was a derivation of John Philip.

This little exchange turned out to be the high point of our relationship. Later, I would think back to Walter's first day and wonder how he had managed to act so well-mannered. On his good days, he was testy, peevish, and argumentative. On his bad days, I was thankful that firearms weren't allowed on the island.

The third in the string of new hires was Barry. Barry's arrival was not the surprise that his two predecessor's had been; this time, Wilmer gave me a day's warning. He also surprised me by letting me review Barry's résumé.

The résumé was thick with the list of computers and peripheral equipment (meaning tape drives, disk drives, printers, and so forth) that Barry had worked on. In every instance, however, Barry had written "computors" instead of computers, and "periphials" instead of peripherals. He also made it plain that he did not know that the word "modem" was constructed from "MOdulator/DEModulator" because he referred to these devices as "modums."

Furthermore, Barry claimed to have completed two-thirds of the courses required for an engineering degree from "John Hopkins University." I had to wonder, was this another careless misspelling, or were students allowed to drop an 's' from that venerable institution founded by Johns Hopkins?

These miscues triggered a synapse shower of warning flares in my mind; Barry's application went against everything I had ever learned about applying for a job. But different people, I told myself, placed a different emphasis on various aspects of life; just because a person filled his writing with casual spelling didn't mean he couldn't do a good job.

When Barry showed up, I gave him the standard tour of the station and its people. Ominously, Barry's apparent indifference was strikingly similar to Walter's. When I demonstrated how we loaded our computer programs, for example, I looked up to see that Barry wasn't even watching. Was my little demonstration too elementary for a John Hopkins lad? Perhaps Barry was waiting for an introduction to orbital mechanics. I led him to our huge wall-mounted world map to point out how our little tracking station fit into the big scheme of the worldwide network.

Barry suddenly snapped out of the spell that had held him. He spanned the map's mileage key with his thumb and pinkie. Then, placing his thumb on Ascension, he walked his hand up the map, crossing Africa, the Mediterranean, and Europe before his pinkie came to rest on Moscow.

"It's just as I suspected," he shook his head glumly, "We'll be atomized in the first strike."

This left-field departure from my tour of the computer section left me speechless for a moment. I countered with a comment to the effect that I didn't think the USSR would waste a nuke on our tiny outpost, but that remark caused Barry to recoil as if he'd just watched me eat a bug, and he began to lecture me on how World War III would be fought.

Barry appeared to be a know-it-all, but only about abstract subjects. The more abstract or obscure the topic, the more he knew, and the more he knew the more he talked. Unfortunately for Barry, the more he talked, the more we realized that he didn't know what he was talking about. I put up with the lectures for a while, as Barry was obviously seeking attention. Later, however, it became obvious that what he should have been seeking was *psychiatric* attention.

Barry's problems became most evident during one strange week in April, 1980. The first of a series of unconventional events that week occurred while Gloria and I were enjoying our after-dinner walk to Turtle Shell; we heard an odd sound overhead. Now, there aren't too many sounds that can come from above, especially man-made sounds, which this one certainly was. But the strangely familiar *whump-whump-whump* was, nevertheless, completely alien to Ascension. Many seconds passed before my brain allowed the obvious answer to surface—there were helicopters flying in from the ocean.

At least I recovered my senses quickly enough to deduce that the choppers must have come from a ship, and indeed they had. We could see a number of sleek, hazy-gray silhouettes, just barely visible on the horizon. This subtle change to the majestic mural of the South Atlantic, which had remained unblemished by a human presence during our three years on the island, was quite an exciting development. Soon, the whole island was abuzz with news of our visitors. We had no way of knowing that this task force was on its way to the Indian Ocean to launch the tragically unsuccessful Iran hostage rescue attempt.

The next day at work, Barry warned me that he was pretty tired; he had been up most of the night. With that, he began a yawning, stretching, and moaning session that I knew would not cease until I asked him the reason for his late night.

"All right, I'll bite," I said. "Did you get laid, or what?"

"Oh, nothing like that," Barry replied, pretending to sort some computer tapes, "But I had a great meal. The admiral's cook is top notch."

Now I was impressed. With so few visitors to the island, we pounced on any yacht crews, Goddard temporaries, and even C-141 crewmembers and treated them like royalty. Since word had spread that one of the off-shore ships was a carrier, it looked like Barry had been in the right place at the right time to score a major coup. I guessed that the cook had been one of the chopper passengers; Barry must have met him at the airfield and struck up a friendship with him that had culminated in an impromptu dinner at one of the island's facilities.

I congratulated Barry on his accomplishment and made a little small talk with him. And regretted it. Barry said he never met the cook. He just ate the meal the cook had prepared for the admiral.

"Then after we ate, the admiral gave me a tour of the ship."

"You had dinner on the carrier...with the admiral." I said. I looked carefully at Barry.

"No, not dinner. It was more like midnight chow."

"And just how did you get to the ship? I saw you at the movie long after we heard the last of the choppers take off."

Barry didn't even blink.

"Rubber boat. The admiral sent my old commando squad to get me. They picked me up an hour after the movie was over."

At this point, I was thinking rubber room, not rubber boat. I continued to joust with Barry, pointing out inconsistencies in his story, but he never wavered. Nor did he even hesitate; when he produced a photograph as proof of his Navy connection, I saw that the unflattering portrait showed a young recruit wearing a patch with crossed keys on his shoulder.

I didn't know much about the Navy, but I knew that patch. My dad wore it during World War II.

"Barry, you said you were an ensign. Since when does an ensign's uniform bear the insignia of a storekeeper?"

Again, no hesitation.

"This picture was taken the day before we sailed," he replied while stuffing the photograph back into his wallet. "In port, we always switched uniforms and insignia. That was the admiral's way of confounding the enemy."

I surrendered. Listening to Barry's outrageous whoppers had been entertaining for a while, but I preferred my fiction to be committed to page and endorsed by a major publisher. I resolved, right then and there, that our future conversations would be limited to the business of tracking stations.

The Devil's Ashpit

Another supervisor might have continued to try to reach out to Barry, but another supervisor might not have had the handicap of working on Ascension Island and worrying just a tad about his own sanity, either.

My coworkers and I agreed that the arrival of these three oddballs lent credence to our assertion that Bendix recruiters cared little about the caliber of people they sent to overseas hardship positions. I'll admit the recruiters had a tough job; the Rock would be a hard sell under the best of conditions. But Bendix made it even harder on themselves by relying on a poorly conceived booklet called the *Ascension Island Story*, purported to contain "some useful facts and figures for personnel proceeding to the...station at Ascension Island." The dull, stodgy prose seemed to hint that the life of an Ascension Islander was only slightly more appealing than that of a concentration camp worker. Dull, stodgy, underdeveloped black and white pictures perfectly complemented the dry text.

The rare bird who did express an interest in Ascension filled out an application, took a test in his area of expertise, took a physical, and got his plane ticket. I suspect many an applicant "got his plane ticket" prior to anybody reading his application or test results.

In the rush to get the new-hire down range, there just could not have been any time to do anything resembling a background check, as was confirmed by one newbie fortunate enough to sit beside a young attractive female tech on the C-141. An hour into the flight, he confided that he was heading to the Rock to escape rape charges. Whether his story was true or just a perverse attempt at a pick-up line, it provided a window into a soul that few would want to explore. He then attempted to feel her up.

Ascension wasn't the only tracking station to employ workers of dubious qualifications and/or backgrounds. When I first reported to the tracking station at Corpus Christi, Texas, six years before, my coworkers on the transmitter/antenna equipment that would send commands to Skylab were Art and our lead tech, Karl.

Two months later, it was just Art and me. Karl had stopped coming to work; he was too busy mailing me bomb threats and then spreading the word among my coworkers that he was reconsidering...because "it just might be simpler to shoot that bastard."

My management naturally bubbled this issue up the chain to the Bendix headquarters management in Maryland, but we were unprepared for the astonishing response, "Can't you get Karl to come back to work?"

It's hard to apply any logic to that request other than financial; Bendix knew that if Karl wouldn't come back to work, their Texas station would have only two techs to cover the 24/7 requirements of Skylab support. They were in danger of exceeding their budget for overtime pay.

I'm going to give my manager the benefit of the doubt and assume that he neglected to contact Karl. Instead, he placed Art and me on the sliding eight-hour shifts that would keep us in sync with Skylab. Then he filled out Karl's termination notice. Karl acknowledged his termination notice by stepping up his letter campaign.

I had no clue what I had done to send Karl over the edge; I didn't even know we were on bad terms! One of the other lead techs finally told me that Karl had once come to him and said, "What am I going to do with that Dan? I tell him to do something and he ignores me."

Well, that was easily explained: Karl was a mutterer, and he was a long-winded mutterer at that. As we sat in the trailer that shook from the noise of the fans in the transmitter, the console, the giant wall-unit air conditioner, and twenty other miscellaneous pieces of hardware, Karl told long pointless stories of...well, I don't know. A person can only say, "What?", "What's that?", "What'd you say?", etc. so many times before switching to a head-nodding, "Uh-huh."

Apparently, Karl was ending his stories with a work assignment, something along the lines of:

"... and sure, that theater's an extra twenty mile trip, but you can save five cents on popcorn. You need to replace that console switch."

"Uh-huh."

I received a second clue a month after Karl got fired. It was a peaceful 4:00 AM and we were between Skylab passes so I was sitting in the trailer, reading. The phone rang and it was Karl.

Ever since Karl's last day at work, he had talked to my coworkers, but never to me—all I got were the terse, strangely worded threatening letters. Suddenly, there he was on the phone making polite chit-chat, which I returned in kind. Then Karl switched gears.

"Dan, remember that last night at work? I saw you at the parts counter in the hanger."

"Yep, I remember. I was getting a new resistor and power transistor to replace the ones that burned out." The problem only cropped up near the end of the shift. Otherwise I would have replaced them myself.

"So you gave me the parts to replace."

" ...Yes," I said slowly, having no idea where he was going with this.

"Dan, I took those parts to the trailer where *you* left the 10 kilowatt transmitter running."

I said nothing. I didn't know how to respond to that. It's common practice to troubleshoot with equipment powered up. It's just as common to power it off prior to replacing parts. And, there was no mistaking the roar of the fans and the array of lights on the transmitter panel as soon as

The Devil's Ashpit

you opened the trailer door. You had to be deaf and blind to miss it. Or crazy, I guess. Karl didn't really wait for a response.

"You tried to kill me, Dan, and now I'm going to kill you."

"Karl?"

But he had hung up. Up to that point, we had been handling the issue with our own small security force. The station was fenced in and visitors had to stop at a guarded gate. But after the phone call, the security folks told me to take my collection of bomb threats and my coworkers' affidavits and hand them over to the police. So this 22-year-old, just a few months removed from the quiet hills of Western Pennsylvania, strode into the Corpus Christi Police Department to demand justice.

The police captain shuffled my papers with a frown.

"You work at the NASA tracking station? Out on that old naval air station property?" he asked.

"Yes."

"Well, that's federal property," he responded. "And that's federal jurisdiction. You need to take these to the FBI." And he handed me back my package.

So this 22-year-old, just a few months removed from the quiet hills of Western Pennsylvania, strode into the Corpus Christi branch of the Federal Bureau of Investigation to demand justice.

Whatever the FBI did, it did not include locking up Karl. I suppose they were satisfied when the threats to federal property ceased. For my part, being an ordinary citizen and not federal property, I was advised to take my case to a justice of the peace and initiate a "peace bond" against Karl. From what I understood, Karl had to hand $1,000 to the city of Corpus Christi. He could have it back at the end of a year, but only if he had refrained from killing me in those twelve months. Sweet justice.

Luckily, our fellow workers could only work their little drive-you-crazy magic during our shift at the site. Afterwards, night or day, Gloria and I would take advantage of our proximity to the best therapy in the world—Pan Am beach. We'd walk there and sit a few feet above the high water mark left by the crashing waves. We found ourselves there again the evening after hearing that the task force had sailed (leaving Barry behind, unfortunately). We scanned the horizon, looking in vain for any disturbances that would indicate the presence of a straggler. There were none. Our brief, tenuous reminder of the real world had vanished, leaving no evidence that the ships had ever existed.

The sun dipped lower during our search, and treated us to another variation of the brilliant Ascension sunsets we had become so accustomed to watching. This time, the sphere passed through a low band of clouds that completely bisected the glowing orb and altered the course and tint of each ray. The changing light bestowed a full range of special effects on each cloud, slowly shifting from back-lit incandescence to softly tinted reflection.

Duty-bound, we began our "flash-watch," but my mind wandered. The sudden arrival and departure of the fleet had changed the way I looked at the ocean, giving me an almost palpable feeling of distance, loneliness and isolation as I surveyed the unbroken expanse.

I had always thought of myself as a bit of an adventurer, having circled the globe with the *Vanguard* and having worked jobs in South America and the Mid-Atlantic. But what kind of adventurer was I, feeling stranded while living on an island that boasted regular jet service and space age communications? How would I have reacted had I been a part of William Dampier's crew, who, forced to abandon their leaking ship, had come to Ascension's shore in 1701? Ascension's forbidding rock had never been a regular stop for ocean travelers; how long would the crew have to wait before they could be rescued? For that matter, how long would the crew have to wait before they would even be declared missing? With each sunset, the fading light must have taken with it another grain of the sailors' determination to survive.

Dampier's ordeal lasted a mere six weeks before he and his crew were rescued by a passing ship. Forty-two days didn't sound like much, but then, the sailors hadn't known what that magic number was going to be. It just as easily could have been a hundred and forty-two, or a thousand and forty-two. There was just no way of knowing that deliverance was at hand.

From our perch on the deserted beach, gazing over the empty ocean, I thought of the phrase, "stranded on a desert isle." In previous contexts, the phrase had always been used rather blithely, as when some interviewer asked the cliché question, "If you were stranded on a desert isle, what book would you want to read?" The stock answers were titles such as *Moby Dick*, or *Huckleberry Finn*, which seemed like satisfactory answers at the time. With my newfound appreciation of the phrase, though, I knew my answer would be *How to Build Your Own Boat Out Of... Anything!* by Angus MacGyver.

Perhaps Gloria was thinking similar thoughts of abandonment and rescue. Just after the sun disappeared with, of course, no discernible flash, she turned to me, pulled some strands of wind-blown hair aside, and spoke.

"Maybe it's time we thought about leaving."

I knew she wasn't talking about leaving the beach; she was talking about leaving the island. And since most everyone's thoughts during their waking hours were in some way connected to leaving the island, I knew that what my wife really meant was, it was time we actually *did* something about leaving Ascension.

Grumbling about the job, the people, and the general hardship was as much a part of Ascension life as wind, cinders, and drunken donkeys.

The Devil's Ashpit

Employees' threats to "paint that fuckin' Lizard and catch the next flight out" flowed as freely as drinks at the Volcano Club. But while everyone discussed what their first purchase would be upon hitting the States, almost no one mentioned what their next job was going to be.

What little career talk I did hear centered around transfers to the other tracking stations, especially to those in Bermuda, Hawaii, and Florida. But I knew that openings at these attractive sites were few and far between and the competition for these slots was stiff.

Besides, there was the threat of the Tracking Data Relay Satellite System (TDRSS) looming on the horizon. This new system promised to give ground controllers unparalleled coverage of orbiting satellites for the price of only two ground stations. I applauded the new technology, but at the same time, grieved that our beloved network of tracking stations would soon expire, the victim of terminal obsolescence. Problems with the development of the TDRSS's launch platform, the Space Shuttle, was the only thing that had kept many of the stations alive for the past few years.

Tracking station work, however, was the only technician life I was familiar with. If I didn't stay in the network, what would I do? With absolutely no concept of how my stateside brethren occupied their time, I began answering classified ads for technicians in Florida.

At the same time, I wrote to a number of Florida universities requesting college catalogs, class schedules, and admission forms. While I didn't know much about general technician work, I had been around long enough to have heard and understood the career limitations faced by upwardly mobile techs. Bendix used the titles "field engineer" and "senior field engineer" to reward and compensate the best technicians. But the "field" qualifier also served to identify these engineers as non-degreed, and the lack of positions above senior field engineer served ample notice that the non-degreed engineer would essentially be stuck in low earth orbit while degreed engineers cruised the galaxy.

Like every other technician I knew, I came to resent this division. "There's no substitute for experience!" we argued and backed up our argument with stories of engineers who didn't know which part of a screwdriver was the business end. I denounced the unfair treatment of tried and true technicians as loudly as anybody else, but I also knew that it would be fruitless, not to mention unprofitable, to try to buck the system. Whether college professors whispered the secrets of the universe during commencement exercises or simply slipped graduates the key to a more exclusive club, I resolved to join the ranks of the few…the proud…the degreed.

My resolve was never stronger the day I opened my mail from the first university to answer my request for information. Inside was a twelve-page schedule of classes for the fall semester, and a somewhat surprising error.

The banner headline, huge and emphasized in bold type-font on each page warned students that this schedule was merely "TENATIVE." I *tentatively* placed the school at the bottom of my list.

I was wallowing in the job-search doldrums when an unexpected telephone call from a friend abruptly changed our focus. Pam, a model-cute, athletic blond Texan who had shared three tracking station assignments with us, had found herself a job at the Johnson Space Center. As the control center for Space Shuttle operations, JSC was gearing up even faster than the tracking stations were winding down.

Pam's new company, Ford Aerospace, had won the operations contract and was scouring the countryside for people who knew something about communicating with spacecraft. In other words, they were looking for Gloria and me.

Pam gave us a quick overview of the kinds of positions Ford was looking to fill. There was more good news; the requisitions were all for field engineers, no degree required. Pam had already taken the liberty of mailing us a couple of applications and warned us that if we wanted to consider working in Houston, we had better get our paperwork in as quickly as possible.

For some reason, the thought of working at JSC had never crossed our minds, possibly for the same reason that nobody else thought much about working there; ever since the last Apollo landing, the US manned space program had been moving in fits and starts. There were a lot of astronauts itching to ride a rocket, but rockets were few and far between.

The congressional approval of the Shuttle program, however, had turned everything around. With early forecasts predicting an unbelievable fifty flights a year, it looked like JSC's star was on the rise. Gloria and I filled out our applications and I pored over the University of Houston catalog that Pam had thoughtfully included in the package.

Two weeks later, Pam called us again; her supervisor had asked her to tell us that our offers were in the mail. This was wonderful news, of course, but always the pessimist, I assumed that any job that could be obtained without benefit of an interview might not be the job of my dreams. Pam, however, had excitement enough to go around.

"Wow, Dan," she said breathlessly, "You and Gloria will be working with the guys in the Mission Control Center. You're in the big leagues now!"

The Mission Control Center? The room where flight director Gene Kranz was sitting when Tranquility Base made its first transmission? Well now, maybe this *was* the job of my dreams! But a gut-gripping fear quickly replaced my euphoria. After all, I was just a lowly technician. Compared to the team that had sent men to the moon, I was a real bush leaguer.

On the other hand, these very same team members were the ones who had just mailed us our offers. With that vote of confidence and the added enticement of working in what I had always referred to as "the Walter Cronkite room," I would be hard pressed to find a reason not to go.

Even the school situation was on my side. The University of Houston boasted a brand new branch campus that actually shared a border with the space center. Fittingly, the school catered to JSC employees, offering evening sessions of all the courses I needed. From Pam's description, home, work, and school were all within a three mile radius.

The big unknown was the money. Not only were we ignorant of the going price for field engineers back in the States, we didn't even know what portion of our Ascension salaries to enter on our applications. I did know enough to discount the sacks of gold we reaped with every weekend we worked, but I had heard that our vaunted overseas hardship allowance was nothing more than a twenty-five percent bonus on top of a twenty-five percent pay cut. At the time, we had no way of knowing if this was true, but the rumor turned out to be pretty accurate; the five-day portion of our paychecks was on a par with that of our Goddard brethren. Luckily, I had chosen to believe the rumor and had entered the inflated salary as our "base" pay.

Gloria and I spent a restless two weeks awaiting the arrival of the job offers. When they finally came, we sighed with relief. Ford had offered me a nine percent raise. Gloria's raise, based upon her lower salary, was an even more impressive twelve percent. I managed a phone call to Jules (Julie) Conditt, our new boss in Houston, to see if I could wheedle out a few more percentage points on top of my offer. No dice: Julie stood firm. As I didn't feel I had any real bargaining chips, I accepted.

After supper that evening, Gloria and I stopped at the tiny commissary to pick up one of the popular "Ascension Me Come From" T-shirts. Although the Saints were known to turn a quaint phrase or two, this particular example hadn't been a part of the Saints vernacular until the previous year, following some Caribbean island excursions by a few of the crew.

The pedigree of the slogan's background, however, was immaterial; I didn't buy the shirt for its sentimental value so much as for its advertising potential. I carefully altered the lettering to give our coworkers a clue of our next move. My new shirt read, "Ascension Me Go From."

As the day of our departure grew nearer, I began spending more and more time in the water. This was one aspect of Ascension life I was going to miss terribly. Returning to the States meant I would never again have the opportunity to take a short walk to a deserted beach, dive in clear, clean water, and visit with fish in such astonishing abundance. I suddenly regretted taking the ocean for granted; during my last year on the island, my snorkeling or scuba trips had tapered off until I was averaging only one dive every three days.

As soon as I realized our final days were at hand, I returned to the daily regimen I had enjoyed in our first year, hitting the water within minutes of getting off work. My partner on many of these dives was Ken Roloff, a fit and friendly tech whose aquatic prowess and marine biology savvy made me suspect his family tree must have contained both Johnny Weissmuller and Jacques Cousteau.

Ken had proved himself an excellent model for my underwater photography, always managing to catch a blowfish, a lobster, or a bouquet of sea urchins for the camera. Once, while I waited with my finger on the shutter, he wrestled with an octopus, trying to pull it out of a hole under the rocks. Ken used his elbows and knees to dig for traction in the loose sand, and I heard him grunting through his regulator. Eventually, he was lying fully extended, face down in the sand, his arms buried under rock.

As my dive buddy struggled, a huge moray eel swam up between Ken's legs and squeezed under his stomach, positioning itself so its head was right under Ken's chin. Michael B had told me that octopus was like chocolate to a moray eel and indeed, this eel looked like he was waiting for Ken to pull a treat out of the candy jar. Ken, of course, didn't see his visitor; the diving mask severely limits a diver's field of view.

I was floating a mere ten feet away, but I may as well have been sitting on the beach; there's no such thing as a quick response underwater, at least, not for humans. I swiveled to the prone position and started kicking toward Ken, although I didn't know what I would do when I reached him. Maybe I didn't need to do anything; the eel was obviously excited about the prospect of an octopus goodie and wasn't about to bite the hand that was going to feed it. It continued to lie in the sand right under Ken, patiently waiting for his treat.

Ken finally solved the predicament himself when he bobbed his head, touching the eel with his chin. The unfamiliar texture that caressed his skin caused him to look down.

I was wrong when I said there was no such thing as a quick response underwater. Ken moved as fast as any fish I'd ever seen, and the air bubbles from his involuntary yell probably accounted for a full third of his tank. The unexpected movement and commotion also intimidated the eel, which streaked back to its own den like black lightning.

Ken was with me on my last Ascension dive, too. We jumped off the low cliff behind Saint's Hut, the area where Mike and I had run into the herring smorgasbord, and followed the very same path we had taken on that exciting day. This time, however, there was no such action. Quite to the contrary, the place looked abandoned, with only a few of the smallest fish hovering near their protective rocks. Even the morays were gone. We saw only their diminutive cousins, the tan and white spotted Greek eels, peeking out from their holes.

What's more, it was close to sunset, and I'd never been excited about diving in the shade; the water robs too much of the spectrum from the ocean. Only an overhead sun could enhance Ascension's color-deprived underwater terrain, providing us with a wide scale of sparkling, sharply-detailed contrasts as the surface waves alternately focused and diffused the sun's rays. After about six o'clock, however, the water's surface reflected more rays than it refracted, leaving us in almost dismal surroundings.

It was a struggle, but Ken and I stayed in the water long enough to use up most of our air supply. After we climbed out of the water and stripped off our gear, we sat at the picnic table at Saint's Hut, drinking a beer and sharing what we knew would be our last conversation.

While we talked, Ken and I cast occasional glances at the setting sun, and, just as Gloria and I had done for three years, we stopped talking as the top of the sun neared the horizon. Neither the sky not the sun had gone through much of a color change, and to the tune of the beach-cleansing waves, we watched the yellow orb vanish below a calm sea. In the blink of an eye, a rim of bright green light replaced the yellow, glimmering for just a moment before it, too, disappeared.

I looked at Ken.

"Did you see that?" I asked hesitantly.

"Yeah," he said, still staring where the sun had been. "The green flash. I didn't think those things were real."

Chapter 15

Escape

Bendix surprised us with a couple of last minute transfer offers to the tracking station in Hawaii. That we declined this chance to live on Kauai, Hawaii's garden island, was an indication of just how important we thought it was to make a radical career change.

Of course, I was flattered that our company had made us this unsolicited offer. I hadn't forgotten that three years before, these were the same people who had strung us along for six months with no reassurance that they would send me to Ascension to join my wife. There was some logic behind their recent actions, though. Gloria had advanced from a teletype operator position to a technician, and the Bendix overseas manager told me during his last visit that he thought I was one of the best computer techs in the network. I looked over his shoulder at Barry, Walter, and Stick and thought, *high praise indeed!*

Still, I swelled with pride and found it hard not to feel some allegiance to Bendix. After all, they had started me on my career seven years before as a very green, very raw recruit. But our paths were diverging, with mine going to the land of milk and honey. If I stayed with Bendix, the closing of their vast tracking network meant my path was sure to end up in a bread line.

The network's eventual demise was a bitter pill to swallow; I had spent seven years on the range, seeing the world while working on the equipment that had relayed Neil Armstrong's voice from the moon. I had already seen the farewell messages a few of the stations had sent out to the rest of the network and I felt like I was reading the obituaries of old friends. As Gloria and I boarded the Starlifter for our last flight out of Ascension, I consoled myself with the knowledge that the people I had worked with throughout the network would tend to stay in the aerospace business, which meant we would still be traveling in the same circles. I might even see some familiar faces in Houston.

The Devil's Ashpit

We saw our first familiar face in Florida. Not quite ready to dive into a new job after such a long stretch on the Rock, Gloria and I were treating ourselves to a week of rest and relaxation in a Cocoa Beach condo when we heard someone knocking. I opened the door to find that someone sitting on the sidewalk, leaning against the railing in the classic vagrant's pose, slugging down the last drops of a bottle of wine. The sight of an indigent at the doorstep of our swanky apartment was strange enough, but there was also the matter of the brown paper bag he wore on his head, with holes ripped out for the eyes and mouth.

The stranger put down his wine bottle and for the first time I could make out the lettering on his T-shirt: "Boogie Till You Puke." Cramer.

Cramer was emulating a popular comedian whose act Gloria and I had just caught on TV. Throughout his monologue, the nameless comedian wore a paper bag on his head. I thought I'd show Cramer I was wise to him.

"Hey Gloria," I called over my shoulder, "Look who's here. It's the Unknown Comic."

"Uh-uh," Cramer said, waving his empty bottle, "It's the Unknown Wino. Got any spare change, mister?"

Island fever had caught up with Cramer the night we said goodbye in the Volcano Club. He had decided to follow in our footsteps and flee the tracking station business. Hoping to find a job in his adopted state of California, Cramer had given his notice and requested a seat on the next plane out of Ascension, but not before applying a liberal coating of paint to the Lizard as insurance against ever coming back.

We easily convinced Cramer to join us for our trip to Houston, where he could stay with us for a few days before continuing his trip. I was glad he did; I needed his moral support.

Somewhere, possibly in my dreams, I had gotten the idea that Houston was more of a laid-back resort town than a bustling metropolis. Perhaps I could blame my misconception on my experiences at the tracking station in Corpus Christi, 200 miles south of Houston. After a year of fun in Corpus, I had projected that sunny image on every Southern city that bordered the Gulf of Mexico. I was dead wrong.

That's not to say Houston's skies weren't sunny. They were very sunny indeed. The temperature broke a hundred degrees every day for the first two weeks we were there, and the dying grass and plants began to give the landscape a look very reminiscent of the bleak, colorless island we had just left. Houston's topography did nothing to improve the scenery. Ascension had the mountains to break the monotony, but Houston was flat, utterly flat, with the only change in elevation being the concrete overpasses.

Then there was the traffic. NASA Road One wasn't just the four-lane highway that took us to the front gate of the Johnson Space Center; it also served as the border between space center property and a huge assortment of office buildings, restaurants, and both large and small businesses. That is to say, the road was absolutely packed with commuters who had business on one side of the street or the other. This massive, daily traffic jam was especially unnerving to someone used to Ascension's empty roads. When we pulled into our friend Pam's apartment complex, we guessed that her parking lot alone probably held more cars than Ascension had ever seen.

At the end of my first day in the Houston rat race, I plopped down in Pam's easy chair. I was hot, tired, and disgusted with Houston. How could anybody live in that place? Additionally, I had seen nothing during my first day at work that would help allay my fear of working for a new company; I had a desk in a rather bland commercial office building that Ford rented across from the street from the space center and I hadn't even set foot inside the JSC front gate, let alone the Mission Control Center.

My foul mood didn't ruin Pam's cheerful personality. She bounded into the room with some news that couldn't wait.

"Dan! You'll never guess who I saw at work!"

Pam's job occasionally brought her in close contact with the astronauts, so I assumed from her excitement that she must have met John Young or Bob Crippen, selected to be the first crew of the as-yet untested Shuttle. I guessed wrong.

"Alvin!" she squealed, "Today was his first day at work, too!"

Alvin was not one of the people I had had in mind when I was hoping to eventually see some familiar faces. His arrogance put him high on the list of people who would have put Will Rogers' famous congeniality to the test. I settled into a sulk; I would have been happy if I had never heard of Alvin again and the way things were going now, I figured we'd probably end up sharing an office. Pam, oblivious to my mood, checked her mail, still rambling about her encounter with Alvin. Then she stopped and waved an envelope at me.

"Dan! You'll never guess who wrote me a letter!"

For a moment, I thought I was going to hear that she was pen pals with Barry, Walter, or Stick, but the letter was from Ken, the islander who shared my last dive with me. Pam began reading to herself, then gasped.

"Wow! He ran into a whale shark last week! That's pretty exciting, isn't it? What's a whale shark?"

I could have cried. If I had stayed on the island for another week, I would have been Ken's diving buddy for this once-in-a-lifetime sight, the giant, docile whale shark. Instead, our last dive had been boring and colorless. Was this another omen that leaving Ascension had been the wrong choice?

The Devil's Ashpit

Houston never did win a place in my heart as one of the top one thousand cities to live in, but things did get better. After Cramer left, eventually to get a job building Shuttles in Palmdale, California, Gloria and I bought our first house and actually enjoyed mowing the lawn, installing ceiling fans, painting, and steam-cleaning carpets. There were other aspects of our Houston residence that weren't so enjoyable, like the electric bill, which existed mainly for the air conditioning we used to make the brutal climate bearable. Then there was flood insurance and car insurance, the cost, of course, based upon the lowest elevation in Texas and the highest incidence of traffic accidents, respectively.

There were more important, day-to-day drawbacks, too. One of the results of our overpopulated area was that the congestion spawned so much inconvenience, which could be seen in such diverse forms as long lines at every checkout counter, and narrower lines in all the parking lots. The summation of so many of these types of irritants caused everyone to develop a competitive edge in their interactions with others. This edge was also known as rudeness.

The most disquieting aspect of our new life, however, was our sudden exposure to the specter of violent crime. While the worst thing we had to endure on Ascension had been the possibility of a donkey bite, Houston had taken the lead as the murder capital of the world. One of the local newspapers even ran a daily scorecard (in the sports section, no less), of the previous day's homicides, rapes, and burglaries, although the burglaries column always contained a "not available" asterisk. I assumed this was because there were too many of these crimes to be counted before the paper hit the streets. Of course, Ascension life had been fraught with problems too, but none that were truly life-threatening. The safety I had felt while living on the laid-back island was nothing but a cherished memory.

Our jobs at the space center, however, were wonderful. The drab office I had seen on my first day was just a place to sit between console duty, where we ran Shuttle ascent, on-orbit, and landing simulations. As "ground controllers," Gloria and I didn't sit in the fabled Mission Control Center, (MCC) but that historic room was just a few doors down the hall and the venerable, Apollo-era engineers who did sit there relied on our support.

These were the engineers we had seen on television, smoking cigars and waving US flags after every Apollo splashdown. These heroes had already celebrated their glory days, but the impending launch of the first Space Shuttle meant a return to manned space flight in a way the old rocket-launchers had never dreamed possible. For the first time, an untested vehicle was being assembled. The Shuttle's first flight with a crew aboard would be its first flight, period, and Gloria and I counted ourselves fortunate to be involved in this pioneering effort. A "must-do, can-do" attitude permeated every corner of our workplace, and the professionalism with which everyone performed their jobs was in stunning contrast to some of the half-hearted efforts I had observed at the tracking stations.

Another stunning contrast to our previous careers came in the form of the pay increases. For each of our seven years on the range, we had collected minimal raises, usually on the order of three or four percent. But after only six months in Houston, Gloria and I both received fifteen percent raises—and in six more months, we received another fifteen percent! I had to smile when I remembered my first phone call with my boss-to-be and his refusal to add a few more bucks to his offer. (Gloria eventually smiled even wider; though her starting salary had been below mine, she excelled in her position and ultimately got promoted to a pay grade above me.)

Space Shuttle *Columbia*'s first flight finally occurred in April 1981 and was properly hailed as a major accomplishment. After the celebrations died down, I applied and was accepted for a "flight controller" position called INST—short for INSTrumentation. I was no longer associated with the tracking stations, but with the actual electronics on the Space Shuttle itself. This really was the big leagues, as Pam had so appropriately called it.

The first indication of my promotion to the majors was my new on-site office. Building 4 housed all the flight controllers, and as I found out during my first trip to the vending machines and waited for John Young to make his selection, my new building housed all of the astronauts, as well. Of course, we had been seeing the astronauts on and off over the months, whether at meetings, in the hallways outside the MCC, or at the monthly beer parties at the recreation center. Their presence, especially in the casual settings, brought home the understanding that the Shuttle's most important cargo was flesh and blood; I, for one, was motivated to do everything in my power to ensure that they had a safe ride on the rocket.

My new position moved me to a console in a room adjoining the MCC where my new boss, call sign INCO (INstrumentation and Communication Officer), held the seat closest to the public affairs photographer's favorite location, evidently chosen because the view captured the entire team as well as the projection area on the front wall. That wall often displayed the shuttle's location on the world map, serving to emphasize the truly global aspect of the shuttle's mission.

Fellow INST Joe Fanelli, another Ford Aerospace employee, was my nominal supervisor, handing me my paychecks and all other company-related paperwork. During my interview, Joe had explained that NASA man Ed Fendell was the actual team leader, the person who assigned everyone's tasks. The day of my transfer, Joe welcomed me to the group and began to summarize the qualifications of each of my new coworkers. My spirits plummeted when Joe began reciting all of the degrees the INCO

The Devil's Ashpit

department boasted. Everyone held at least a bachelor's degree in engineering. Many held a master's degree. Two held engineering degrees *and law* degrees, and one of these had a doctorate in this field.

To my great surprise, I learned that the person with the least impressive formal education was Ed. He, like me, had only a two-year technical degree. Nevertheless, Ed was an MCC veteran of the Apollo project, where his deft manipulation of the lunar rover's camera caught the liftoff of Apollo 17's lunar module from the moon's surface. Thus, Ed's work had already been seen by millions, or more likely, billions.

Despite the faith Ed and Joe had shown in me, I felt like I was the dumbest guy in the room. Toss in a helping of the qualms one normally feels as "the new guy" and I was very self-conscious indeed.

My coworkers greeted me cordially, but as happens with new arrivals, I knew it would take a while before they would consider me a member of their team.

That "while" turned out to be just one day. I was reciting my tracking station history to my office-mate, Fred Hoke, when his eyebrows shot up.

"You were on the *Vanguard*?" he interrupted, "Hey, did you know Gloria? Umm...Gloria Tucker?"

I smiled. I should have been surprised at the question, but I had learned long ago that Gloria's first-girl-on-a-ship status had earned her some celebrity in the aerospace community.

"Know her?" I responded, "Fred, I *married* her."

And just like that, I was accepted, though in a way strangely reminiscent of my first days on Ascension, as every introduction that followed carried the suffix, "Gloria's husband."

When I related my experience to Gloria that evening, her face brightened. She rummaged through our boxes of mementos and triumphantly held up a greeting card from December, 1973. Gloria had been on the *Vanguard* at the time, steaming in circles off Mar del Plata, Argentina in support of Skylab's third manned mission.

Part of Gloria's job on the ship was essentially that of a switchboard operator. When a Skylab pass was imminent, Gloria configured the *Vanguard* communication links to ensure that the Skylab astronauts' voices would ultimately be patched through to the MCC. Gloria's counterpart in the MCC was none other than the person sitting at the INCO position.

The INCO on Gloria's shift had become quite enamored with this sweet voice from afar and sent her little gifts from time-to-time. The greeting card was one of them. I understood Gloria's excitement when she opened it because inside were the signatures of the entire MCC team who had "adopted" her. At the time, the names of the so-called "Crimson Crew" had been meaningless to her, but eight years had passed and so had the circumstances.

I scanned the card and was delighted to recognize a number of my fellow flight controllers. The first name that jumped out was Julie Conditt, the manager who had sent us our offers. Julie's call sign, aptly, was Network. The second person I noticed had appended the CAPCOM call sign to his signature. Gloria naturally hadn't recognized the name in 1973 because, although he had been in the astronaut corps for four years, this console jockey had yet to make a flight. His name was Bob Crippen.

Ironically, the INCO who was responsible for the card had moved on— he no longer worked at JSC. Yet his long-forgotten card, spawned from a long-distance infatuation with Gloria's voice, became one of our favorite keepsakes.

By April of 1982, we had three Shuttle flights behind us. Having taken the first opportunity to enroll at the local branch campus of the University of Houston, I was busier than ever, taking three classes at a clip while working on system requirements for the next launch. My office work, console duty, class schedule, and homework left me little time to read the paper or watch the evening news. Thus, when I heard that Argentina had precipitated a war with Great Britain by invading the Falkland Islands, I didn't devote much time to studying the belligerents' military strategies. It was only when a coworker who knew of my recent Ascension experience showed me two pictures in *Aviation Week* did I realize that the war was going to touch me after all.

Both pictures showed the Ascension airfield. A dozen military aircraft dominated the first photograph. Although I had never seen more than two Starlifters on Ascension's runway at a time, the sight of airplanes on an airfield didn't seem out of place.

The second picture was the shocker. A hundred trucks and jeeps surrounded a mountain of supply pallets. This sudden influx of materiel in quantities unheard of since the GIs had come ashore in World War II was evidence that Ascension was going to play a major part in the conflict.

How ironic that our little island hideaway, the place I had come to remember as a haven of peace and harmony, appeared to be gearing up for a war. And gear up it did, becoming the staging area for thousands of tons of supplies and a base for the thousands of soldiers preparing to invade the Falklands. Ascension also gained notoriety as having hosted the longest round trip bombing runs in the history of warfare, as British Vulcans stationed at Ascension flew a whopping 3,930 miles to drop their bombs on the Falklands runway before returning to their base.

With all this military activity on Ascension, nobody could overlook the possibility of retaliatory strikes, either. What had once been a tiny communications post had suddenly become an important chess piece in the game of war. The conflict served as one of those reminders that in our

The Devil's Ashpit

world, anything can happen; in retrospect, even Barry's prediction that Ascension would be a primary target during a nuclear war was not as ridiculous as it had first sounded.

Thankfully, the Argentineans never mounted a strike against Ascension, but the two-month war had brought some major modifications to the island. In a place where change had been as incremental as the grain-by-grain formation of its beaches, the overnight construction of a Royal Air Force base was astonishing. The base wasn't just built for the war, however; the Brits, determined to protect their far colony from another Argentine invasion, have kept the base and the airfield fully manned and supplied, ready to take off on another Falklands mission at a moment's notice.

Another change occurred in 1990, which, on a personal basis, was even more significant. NASA relieved the Ascension Island tracking station of all of its duties. The station didn't just close its doors, however. Our contract with the Brits stipulated that the area upon which the site had been built had to be returned to its original condition. That is, every structure, every sign that the site had ever existed had to be removed. At the last minute, the Brits thought they might find a use for the main building and amended the contract to allow that structure to remain. The few station-hands still on site set to work razing all of the other buildings, as well as the antennas and towers.

When the crew thought they were finished, the Brit inspector surprised them with the announcement that their work was only half done. "Original condition" meant just that; what did the Yanks intend to do with the garbage dump beside the station?

The Brits were referring to the original Devil's Ashpit, a huge ash and cinder-lined cleft in the site's plateau that dropped precipitously a thousand feet down the mountain's south face. This crevasse could have more appropriately been called the Devil's Trashpit, as over the twenty-five intervening years, the Yanks dumped tons of scrap (even an old fire truck!) over the deep slope. The inspector was adamant; the garbage lining the entire thousand-foot scar had to be pulled out and trucked to a Brit-approved disposal site. After a much more costly cleanup than was originally anticipated, the inspector was satisfied; only a gutted, abandoned building remained of the station where my wife and I had worked nearly every day for three years.

EPILOGUE

When Gloria and I left the island, it had been with the unspoken agreement that we would never go back again. If our plans worked out, my engineering degree would provide me with a wide range of lucrative jobs in the States. Maybe our savings account wouldn't be enjoying the same fat deposits we had been pumping into it while we'd been living rent-free, bill-free, and tax-free, but neither would we be sacrificing what most Americans would consider a normal life to earn what money we did manage to put away.

And we were right. After I graduated from the University of Houston, McDonnell Douglas rescued me from the brutal Houston environment and brought me back to Florida to work on shuttle payloads. These days, I sit in the Delta IV launch control center, working for United Launch Alliance at the Cape Canaveral Air Force Station—right up the beach from Patrick Air Force Base. When the timing's right, I can still look over the ocean and watch the Ascension flight come in, carrying another cargo of island-weary contractors.

The sight of the tired old plane triggers a strange sensation of homesickness. I can't imagine signing up for another tour of Rock duty, but neither can I grasp the concept of not being able to return to a place that was such an important part of our lives. The island's few attractions after all, were a direct result of its very remoteness and corresponding inaccessibility.

This deep-seated nostalgia probably explains a recurring dream I have, a dream that has me smiling in my sleep. I'm underwater, swimming through arches of twisted lava, marveling at the neon-bright colors reflected from the scales of living clouds of tropical fish. I surface to see I'm only a few yards from the beach at Saint's Hut, where Gloria, tending fish fillets on the grill, smiles and waves her spatula. As I step up on the beach, Snoopy comes bounding across the sand, welcoming me ashore with his joyful barks.

The dream remained the same for fifteen years, but then a new character began to appear. Now, both Snoopy and our daughter Shelley are playing in the sand. Seeing me, she shouts, "Daddy!" and she and her pet race to greet me with a chorus of squeals and barks.

I tell myself that my dream is just a dream, it's not going to happen. But then again, there might be something to it. Our last week on Ascension had been so hectic that we never did find the time to paint the Lizard. If there's any truth to the island tradition, we'll be making a return trip. Maybe that was our plan all along.

> *"From this moment I began to conclude in my mind that it was possible for me to be more happy in this forsaken, solitary condition that it was possible I should ever have been in any other particular state in the world; and with this thought I was going to give thanks to God for bringing me to this place."*
>
> — Daniel Defoe, *Robinson Crusoe*

ABOUT THE AUTHOR

Dan Kovalchik is no stranger to hardship assignments, having worked on a ship at sea, atop the Andes Mountains of Ecuador, amid the ash and cinders of Ascension Island, and among the urban cowboys of Houston, Texas before he returned to civilization in the form of the Kennedy Space Center, Florida.

Today, Kovalchik serves as a system administrator for United Launch Alliance at the Cape Canaveral Air Force Station, where he helps test and launch the Delta IV rocket.

When he's not writing, Kovalchik enjoys fishing, diving, and telling stories that begin with, "One time, on Ascension…"

Visit the author's web page at www.rangerat.com.

BIBLIOGRAPHY

Bendix Field Engineering Corporation. *The Ascension Island Story*. Columbia, Maryland, 1974

Bendix Field Engineering Corporation. *The Quito Story*. Columbia, Maryland, 1974

Chubb, William B. (Editor). *Skylab Reactivation Mission Report*. Washington, DC: National Aeronautics and Space Administration, 1980

Ezell, Linda Neuman. *NASA Historical Data Book, Programs and Projects 1969-1978*. Washington, DC: National Aeronautics and Space Administration, 1988

Hart-Davis, Duff. *Ascension: The story of a South Atlantic island*. London, England: Constable and Company Limited, 1972

Packer, J. E. *Ascension Handbook: A Concise Guide to Ascension Island, South Atlantic*. Georgetown, Ascension Island, 1974

Made in the USA
Coppell, TX
01 June 2021